"A young woman from India's compelling, joyful, stunningly articulate tale of leaving family dictates and stifling cultural restrictions to come to America and find—herself."

—ADAIR LARA. author of *Naked, Drunk, and Writing*, a practical guidebook to essay and memoir

"A riveting memoir of truth and beauty. Mytrae Meliana goes where few writers dare to tread. In *Brown Skin Girl* she crosses the boundaries of race and culture to shine light on ancient taboos and secrets festering inside a family, only to emerge strong and radiant.."

—SHONA PATEL, author of *Teatime for the Firefly* and *Flame Tree Road*

"*Brown Skin Girl* is an inspiring, lyrically-written memoir that will transport you from the traditional sights and sounds of India to the dreams of freedom in America. Mytrae Meliana repeatedly challenges beliefs that don't align with her heart and soul, and courageously frees herself from generations of unquestioned loyalty to the past to create a life of her own."

—PAMELA S. ALEXANDER, PHD, author of *Initiation of the Soul: Myths and Fairy Tales as a Path of Awakening to Freedom and Wholeness*

"Trauma and oppression break our inherent sense of safety, belonging and dignity. They make chaos out of what could be connection and ask for submission where there should be empowerment. Here, Meliana speaks to the sheer wastefulness of violence, the profundity of human resilience, and our capacity to heal. It reminds me why we stand up and make change."

—STACI K. HAINES, author of *The Politics of Trauma: Somatics, Healing and Social Justice* and *Healing Sex: A Mind-Body Approach to Healing Sexual Trauma*

brown skin girl

An Indian-American Woman's

Magical Journey

From Broken to Beautiful

Mytrae Meliana

blue
leopard
media

san francisco

Brown Skin Girl
Copyright © 2020 by Mytrae Meliana

All rights reserved. No part of this book may be reproduced in any form by any means, including reprints, excerpts, photocopying, recordings, or by any information storage and retrieval system—other than for 'fair use' as brief quotations in articles and reviews—without written permissions. For inquiries, licenses, and permissions contact the author at her website www.mytraemeliana.com.

"Vocation" by Rosemary Aubert. Reprinted here by kind permission of the author.

ISBN (print): 978-0-9914606-2-5
ISBN (ebook): 978-0-9914606-3-2

Cover design: Kathleen Lynch/Black Kat Design
Text design and layout: Domini Dragoone, DominiDragoone.com
Cover art: "Woman in Garden" © Carole Hénaff

Published by
Blue Leopard Media
San Francisco, CA

disclaimer

This book is a true story. It depicts the author's truthful recollection of her life experiences. Most names, places, and identifying characteristics of people have been changed to protect their privacy. A handful of events have been compressed to give the reader a better reading experience. The author's purpose is to raise awareness about the issues in this book, offer hope and possibility to women with similar experiences, and create change.

contents

prologue 1

Part 1

1. childrening 19
2. oceans of crossing 53
3. Evan 85
4. wings 109
5. netted 125

Part 2

6. the first two months 147
7. a month, a swami 167
8. my scarlet sin 183
9. marriage liaisons 191
10. stepping stones 209
11. freedom 231
12. a good Indian wife 247
13. handfuls of truth 257

Part 3

14 finding my forgotten face 287
15 cinnamon and ivory 297
16 love, again 321
17 forgiveness 333
18 a circle of love 345

acknowledgments 369
about the author 373

For women, everywhere.

Speak your truth. Even though your voice shakes.

prologue

1985

I *will* return to what I love. To music. To Evan. To my life in graduate school at Chapel Hill. To Beethoven's Opus 110, Brahms' Variations and Fugue on a Theme by Haydn, and Mozart's Concerto in C Major. To my graduate recital and concerto competition next year. To my cozy attic apartment on Tenney Circle. I will return. Soon. I just need to hold on for three months.

I've been chanting this mantra since yesterday.

Since everything shattered like a crystal bowl.

I *must* talk with him one last time.

"I have to go to the bathroom," I tell Amma, my mother, after we check in at Delta Airlines at JFK airport in New York. I walk purposefully to a pay phone some distance away where, hopefully, she can't see me.

I check the flight monitors. Only an hour before we board. JFK's as crowded as a farmer's market and I weave my body, brushing a shoulder here and there, through the rush of travelers to get to the bank of phones. Announcements of departing and arriving flights, snippets of conversations in New York, Southern, and California accents, German, Hindi, and Chinese swirl around me.

My hands tremble as I pick up the receiver. I imagine him waiting anxiously in his Chapel Hill apartment, his lean face and lithe body strung out as he paces tight as a wire in his two rooms. From the corner of my left eye I see Amma, in black polyester pants and a maroon baggy sweater, watching me like a hungry cat. She won't give me a minute alone. I twist away so I don't see her. My eyes sweep over crowds of other Indian travelers reminding me, with irritation, that I'm one of them.

My fingers press the cold steel numbered buttons. My tongue, dry with worry and determination, tastes metallic and sticks to the roof of my mouth.

Evan answers after one ring.

"Hi, Evan," I say in a rush.

"Hi, love." His honey-like tenor is taut. The sound of him is home. "I'm so worried about you. Are you really going?"

"It's only three months. We can do it. You *know* we can." I imagine his brown eyes, his arms around me. I need to hold on to this moment, to his voice, to *us*.

"Of course. But don't you see? They won't let you come back."

"They will. They can't take me away from my education!" Our family's god is education. Amma always made sure I went to the best schools. Though she loves a beautiful home, my parents did without much furniture when we immigrated six years ago so they could pay for my college tuition.

"I don't trust them. Don't leave, Mytrae! Can't you go to the bathroom and flush your passport down the toilet? Or throw it in the trash?"

"Amma has it with her. There's no way she'll give it to me."

"Walk away, then. Don't get on that plane, whatever you do, love. Do something, *anything*."

His frantic voice makes me doubt myself. But this is the only way I know. Do what I don't want to ultimately get what I *do* want. They said if I stay in India for three months and still want to be with him, they'll let us be together. Just like they made me minor in Computer Science, when I wanted to major in music. I sigh, winding and unwinding the metallic phone cord around my fingers.

He's not Indian. He doesn't understand how we need our parents' permission for everything.

My shoulders tighten with decision. "I'm doing this *for* us. I'll call and write to you while I'm there. They're announcing our flight. I have to go. I love you, Evan."

"Always remember, I love you," he says slowly, deliberately, like he wants me to really know it. And hold on to it. "Goodbye, my love."

"Bye, Evan." I hang up, lean my forehead against the pay phone. Three months will be unbearable.

I walk back to Amma, feeling the thick rope between us and beyond us. It ties us to Daadi, my grandmother, then spools century upon century through my female ancestors to the very beginning of time. It wraps and knots around my waist, and hangs heavy, like lengths and lengths of six-foot saris. It binds us. It defines us. However different we all are, because of it we are the same.

I stop two feet from Amma. Her body relaxes with relief, but her mouth turns down with disappointment and disgust.

Guilt and shame twist me.

I'm here, my eyes tell her. I'm ready. I hate you, but I'm ready.

We turn, without a word to each other, and walk towards security.

I lift my head groggily from the tray table. The screen shows our jet crossing Afghanistan into Pakistan toward India.

"I can't bear to face Daadi with this news." Amma breaks our strained silence. She glances at me then turns away. I got only a couple of hours sleep the night before so I've slept most of the thirty-some hours from New York to Hyderabad, waking only for water and orange juice. I haven't been hungry since they found out about Evan. I can hardly feel. Let alone speak or eat.

My mother looks haggard, the ever-present dark circles under her black eyes even darker. Shaking her blue-gray asthma inhalant, she puts it to her thin lips, inhales sharply, then rests her head back against the seat and closes her eyes. The gray roots in her short black hair look more pronounced from that angle.

It's not that bad, I think. People fall in love all the time. Is it so shameful? I turn my head away from her, burrowing into the navy blue pillow. Her asthma always trumps every situation, and I feel the familiar tugs of guilt, pity, and resentment I did as a girl when she wheezed or had an attack. I don't want to hear her feelings—I'm too overwhelmed by mine. Why should my life be interrupted to convince her and Naina, my father, of my love for Evan? I'm furious about their power over me. And even more furious at myself for bowing to it. I want my own life. I want to make my own choices. I look around at the mostly Indian passengers. I don't want to be like them. Married with babies and boring careers. The last thing I want to be is a dutiful daughter.

A dutiful Indian daughter.

Two years ago, the summer after I graduated from Wake Forest, I stayed in India with Daadi and Thatha, my grandparents.

They were so proud of me then. Will Daadi shun me now? I avoid the thought. Surely, Thatha won't make much of it at all, Westernized and broad-minded as he is. After all, he studied at Cambridge and education is everything to him. They love me, and Thatha's proud that I'm studying music. They won't treat me the way *she* is. Thank goodness Roshan Uncle and Leela Aunty, who live next door to my grandparents, are broad-minded. They'll brush it off like a fly. And I *will* return to what I love. To my music. To Evan. And my life.

Soon.

Late and jet-lagged we arrive at Hyderabad airport, the dust, heat, and maelstrom that is India greeting us. Amma and I barely look at each other as we pass through customs, collect our bags, and are driven to Daadi's and Thatha's home, weaving through bustling, honking thoroughfares crowded with cars, rickshaws, auto-rickshaws, bicycles, and cattle-drawn carts. We are in India, the land of my birth, the city of my childhood, winding through timeless byways of my ancestors.

We lift the latch on the white picket gate to Daadi and Thatha's four-room cottage on Road No. 46 in Jubilee Hills, an affluent Hyderabad neighborhood. We enter the compound surrounded by a ten-foot-high stone wall. Daadi opens the teak door, grave with anxiety, Thatha shuffling close behind her. In his seventies, Thatha is balding, his remaining strands of hair white as dove feathers. Utterly gentle, his round wrinkled face has a big squat nose and giant ears, one plugged with a hearing aid which he frequently and anxiously taps. He peers at me with his one good eye, the other made of glass, having lost his real one at a Cambridge cricket match in his twenties. Loose white cotton pajamas billow about his frail body. Deep pockets hold an enormous white handkerchief into which he often and vigorously blows his nose; black, blue, and red pens; a note pad; and a hearing-aid modulator.

Daadi is all of five feet, her rounded form wrapped tight in a cotton sari block-printed with sky blue and teal vegetable dyes, which rises above her slender ankles. Her scant gray hair is pulled tightly back into a bun the size of an apricot; her intelligent, piercing eyes dart between Amma and me, and she sniffles through her knobby nose. Wobbling toward me, she draws me tight to her soft torso. I feel her large single breast and the flatness of where the other was before her mastectomy. She smells of coriander, garlic, and baby powder.

"Come in, child," she says to me in a quavering voice, tears welling in her eyes. "Come, Kamala," she says to Amma.

Her voice and tears flood me with guilt and love. I've worried them. Let them down in their old age when they should be proud of me. I hang my head as we enter the cluttered and over-decorated living-dining room.

"Stay here," Amma spits.

She leads them into their bedroom and closes the door. I hear their muffled voices. I wait, looking at framed pictures of my lineage. Daadi's father, a proud, distant lawyer in spectacles. Amma's freshness and pride at her college graduation. My parents' youthful innocence at their wedding. Amma holds Raghu, my brother three years older than me, like a prize infant. Group pictures of Daadi's and Thatha's three smiling children, two husbands and wife, and six grandchildren. I'm seven, sitting cross-legged on the grass in a pink and purple silk *lehenga,* long skirt. Me at eighteen, two years after we immigrated, by the fence of our first home in Winston-Salem, North Carolina. I'm wearing a black jacket over a cream cotton dress that billows around my legs, my lips pursed in a kiss as I pet our neighbor's golden retriever.

Daadi flings open the door and rushes out. She shrills with panic, "Are you clean?" She waddles close on her unsteady legs, and peers angrily at me like a lioness defending her pride, six inches from my face, her breath like vinegar.

"Yes, I am," I reply, my voice lower than low. I bow my head, feel like I'm eight. My body fills with shame that we're talking about sex. My sex. No one in our family, no Indian ever speaks, mentions, even hints about it. No one with any dignity or self-respect does. I wish the earth could open and swallow me up. A sparrow twitters in their garden as though marking my lie.

"If you dare tell them you slept with Evan, I'll kill you," Amma had threatened.

Like I needed to be told. Daadi can't know. It would kill her. Kill them all. With them, the lie is my only saving grace.

"Are you clean?" Thatha asks, anxiously shuffling up in his thick black rubber slippers.

"Yes, Thatha, I am clean," I mutter, looking at my lap, my hands folded one inside the other. Of everyone, I cannot bear to have fallen in his eyes.

"Can I have an airmail stamp?" I ask Amma the next morning. I sit on my bed wearing a green and white *salwar-kameez* I left here before. I want to write to Evan to tell him I've arrived.

"You're never going back!" Her voice slices me like a scythe.

I stare at her, aghast. Did she just say that? I frown in disbelief. She towers over my bed wrapped in a stiffly starched leaf-green cotton sari. Her face is like the night rain, her thick eyebrows furrowed, lips gripped in a thin line, her eyes a thunderstorm.

"What do you *mean*?"

"I mean just that. You're never going back."

My heart thuds wildly. My hands clutch the mattress. "I can't *not* go back! What about my music? My education? You can't do this to me! I'm in the middle of school!"

"Your music? It's all nonsense. We told you not to do it." Her tone could cut glass.

"It's my *life*!" I gasp. My body is wet with sweat. I can't believe it. This was a trap! I got on the plane believing they'd never take my education away from me. Our family doesn't go to temples, do pujas, go on pilgrimages, or have a guru. In fact, we barely pray. But Thatha was passionate about educating his children to the highest degree, and Amma has the same fervor.

I imagine Evan's beautiful, lean face, his warm brown eyes, expressive hands gesturing when he talks, our passionate nights and days in his two rooms. Beethoven's sonata Op. 110 in A flat, which takes me to the moon every time I play it. The practice rooms with baby grand pianos that smell of felt and wooden hammers. Swirling sounds of musicians practicing their violins, cellos, clarinets, and tubas. Singers belting German lieder and warbling Italian arias. My roommate Mary's smile brightening the day like a yellow poppy.

Amma's mouth curls with scorn. "What were you going to do with it anyway? It's absolutely useless. You'll never make a living with it. How much we told you not to do it. We've given you too much freedom. Do you know what you've done? I don't know how I'm going to face everybody." Her voice cracks with shame.

I don't care about them. I've spent the last two years plotting my escape. "But you said three months! And that I could call and write to Evan!" I feel like a caged wildcat, frenzied with panic. I want to hurl myself at something, out the door, back on the plane, back into my life. I clutch the mattress with its crimson and taupe Kalamkari bedspread block-printed with parading elephants and half-clothed voluptuous damsels. "I'm going back," I say.

"No you're not. Give me your wallet." She stretches out her hand.

There's no going against her. I've never been able to get through. Who can help me? The family won't. Everyone thinks parents know best. My college friends are in the U.S. or Europe. *Why* doesn't India have 9-1-1? I can't just run out the front door. They'd follow me. And call the police. Vikram Uncle is Hyderabad's police commissioner. I can't believe she trapped me like this. I can't think. Can't feel. My heart sinks into something bottomless. In slow motion, I rummage in my purse and give it to her, my hand limp with disbelief.

"Your address book."

Even if I hide it, she'll find it.

I hand it over numbly. I feel like I just gave my life away. But there's nothing I can do. Why ever did I get on that damn plane? She'll lock these and my passport in her lockbox inside her steel *almirah*, and hook the keys on a steel key-ring that she hangs from her sari waistband during the day and under her pillow at night. I have nothing now.

"I can't tell people why you're here," she wails. "Our family's reputation will be completely shattered. You'll never be able to get married. If word gets out, you're ruined. We'll all be ruined. We're telling people we had to bring you back because you used drugs and were in a cult."

"Used drugs and in a cult?" I echo angrily. My mind struggles to make sense of her wild story. How in the world did she come up with that? Now on top of everything else I have to pretend something's *wrong* with me?

"It's the only way to keep people from nosing around."

"But isn't it worse if they think me a drug addict!" I'm horrified. What will people think of me? That I'm sick. Depraved. I'll have to fend off nosy family's stares and smirks and digs? Nothing excites them more than juicy gossip.

She pays as much heed to me as to the fly that buzzes against the window mesh. She has it all figured out. "Only Roshan, Leela, and my cousins know about that boy. Only Roopa Aunty and Vasupinni know you *slept* with him." She hisses the word at me, like I may as well be a prostitute. "And no one else ever will. You're going to stay here. You're not going anywhere, leave the house, or do anything. I can't trust you. You can go to Roshan's house next door, but that's all." She glares at me.

I never thought Amma and I would talk about sex. But this is more brutal than I ever imagined. Turning on her heel, she strides out of the room, her slippers slapping the soles of her feet. He's not a boy, he's a man, I want to call after her. And, how can something so beautiful be so bad? But I don't dare. What's most beautiful and ecstatic to me is most depraved and immoral to her.

This can't be happening. It's not real. It's a dream from which I will awake.

My stomach burns with rage as I look around the fourteen-square-foot room. Its cream walls, high cupboards, and cluttered furniture close in. Its granite tiles are the color of monsoon clouds. Faded lima green curtains with emerald print tiredly dangle. Never go back? Stay here? I must get out somehow. I look out the windows desperately. One looks over Roshan Uncle and Leela Aunty's manicured lawn flanked by wide peepal and tall white-bark eucalyptus trees. The other window gives view to a few feet of shrubbery. Beyond it, a ten-foot-high compound wall of roughly hewn granite and cement looms, more like thirty feet, with five-foot-high loops of barbed wire entwined with bougainvillea. The sharp points of amber, green, and white broken glass bottles, stuck in its cement surface to slice intruders' soles should they try to jump over, glint in the blazing morning light. Like accusing eyes.

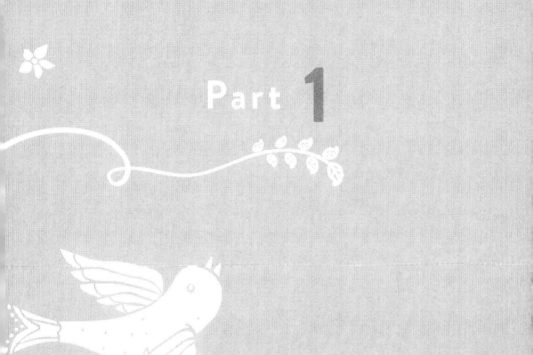
Part 1

"Go!" Seetha urges, her round breasts heaving behind her bodice, "go now, quickly, before the deer runs away."

Rama is still torn, loath to leave her, but he glances at her breasts and remembers their pleasures from last night. A spasm of guilt goes through him. She's come so far with him. Given up so much. Endured even more. She, who should be dressed as queen of his land, Ayodhya, bedecked with golden ornaments from head to toe, on a throne dressed and waited on by attendants, is in deer skins, bark cloths, wears jasmine in her hair, her hands rough from cooking and washing.

"Alright," he agrees, picking up his bow and quiver, "I will go and bring it to you. But Lakshmana, my brother, stay here and protect her. Don't leave Seetha, no matter what."

"Yes, Rama," Lakshmana says, standing a respectful distance away.

Rama takes one last look into her black doe-eyes, oceans in which he loses himself again and again, hoists his quiver higher on his shoulder, turns, and sprints into the forest.

Seetha walks into their hut, sits on the mud floor in a corner, and begins cutting bottle gourd and brinjal for their lunch.

Lakshmana goes to the wood pile a stone's throw from the hut and picks up his axe to chop wood. Seetha's thoughts swirl with the golden deer that appeared like a vision, making her heart leap, that morning on her way back from the river. How graceful and beautiful it was. Magical. Like a heavenly being.

Suddenly Rama's desperate cry, "Lakshmanaaa! Lakshmanaaa! Help!" pierces the air.

She drops her knife and bowl with a clatter and screams, "Lakshmana! Come, come quick!"

Lakshmana rushes into the hut, axe in hand.

"Quick, Lakshmana, you must go to Rama. He needs your help!"

"But he asked me to stay with you and not leave you alone."

Seetha draws her five-foot-four body up tall with rage. She lifts her chin and her voice is cold. "How dare you not go? He's dying, otherwise he wouldn't have called."

"But I mustn't."

"Tchih, tchih! Is it because you want me for yourself?"

Lakshmana's eyelids drop. He cannot face her wrath. He picks up his bow and quiver and walks outside. "Don't," he says, drawing a line in the mud around the hut, "cross this line. Whatever you do, don't. It will protect you when I am gone."

"GO!" she screams, pointing towards where the cry came from.

And Lakshmana rushes into the thick jungle.

Seetha paces up and down in front of the hut, within the line. Every minute seems like hours.

From the corner of her eye, out of the bushes, an old *rishi*, sage, bare-chested and wearing a white loin cloth appears. He approaches her, his palms cupped for alms. "Daughter, do you have any food for me today?"

"Of course, Swami," she says with a worried smile, and goes into the hut. She emerges with a bowl of upma, coconut chutney, and slices of mango from their breakfast, to see him sitting under a peepal tree some distance away.

"Come, Swami," she says, holding out the bowl, her toes at the edge of the line. "I have your food here."

"Bring it here to me, child, my legs are weary."

"But I have been forbidden from crossing this line."

"How dare you? How disrespectful you are! How dare you not serve me?" His voice is like a razor.

Her body stiffens. Hesitates. The last thing she wants now is to incur a sage's wrath. They are so quick to curse. Who knows what he'll say. He's old, she thinks, just a harmless sage. Surely, no harm will come.

She crosses the line.

Instantly, the sage springs up, turns into Ravana, a ten-headed demon, and grabs her by her arm. "Rama! Rama!" she screams. The jasmine falls from her hair, the bark cloth covering her shoulders and breasts drops to the earth. A flying chariot appears. Ravana picks her up in his arms. She bangs her fists against his chest and kicks with all her might against his legs, but she is a lamb against a lion. He pushes her into his chariot, gets in, flicks the reins with one hand, the other around her waist, and in a trice, the chariot is airborne, flying, flying, up and away towards his kingdom, Lanka.

1
childrening

1969

I am a child of the sun.

Before the golden god's pink and orange fingers wipe night away, I awake. *The fairies!*

I slide out of bed. Slowly turn the brass bedroom door handle so Raghu, my brother, doesn't wake. Wiggle the iron latch to the verandah door down to our garden so Amma and Naina don't hear. Dawn is sweet white jasmine and pink Queen Elizabeth roses. In my thin cotton nightie, I run on the crooked stones' path, down the stone steps, past the pond where frogs stare and tadpoles wiggle, past orange and fuchsia bougainvillea, past hibiscus with their open ruby mouths, to the bottom of our green, green lawn, so wet I curl my toes. Hills and valleys away, Hyderabad wears its gray misty *burkha*. The city hasn't woken yet. But the cool earth stirs and stretches her brown-skinned arms blistered with gray rocks and boulders up to the pink sky.

Here in the far corner of our lawn is where the fairies live, where they tell me to come to them. *There* they are! There's one sitting on a leaf, hands around her folded knees. A gnome with a pointed cap and a big broad belt on the rock by the plant beds peers and nods his head at me. And there's an elf in green. He's the fastest and busiest of them all. He's been up for hours, he says, making sure all the leaves get their drops of dew. Another fairy brushes by my nose and flutters in front of my face. She smiles at me and flies up around my face in circles so I feel like fizzy lime-juice bubbles. I jump and laugh at her. She jumps and twirls, and I do too. She kisses my nose and laughs like the tiniest of bells, smaller than my tinkling *gajjalu*, anklets.

I want to be just like her.

I fly with the fairies into the silvery blue eucalyptus trees that look like tall ladies draped in elegant saris. "See, I have wings too!" I flap my arms as they swirl around me. I lift my nightie to my knees and twirl with them in a circle on the wet, green grass. The circle makes magic. The circle is magic. *I* am magic.

The *world* is magic!

And my body sings, filled with morning and the koyal's song as she *koo-oo-ey koo-oo-ey's* her heart out to the hills.

Long before I know much of anything, I know these two things.

I'm different.

And.

I will never have an arranged marriage.

These two things are as plain to me as my brown skin. As being a girl. As loud as the boulders in Banjara Hills that Thatha said the earth threw up in a small volcano some centuries ago. They've cooled now, these boulders and rocks, otherwise we couldn't live here, you see. It would be red-hot and inhabitable. I learned that in Geography.

I love to spread my arms and press my body against these great, rough giants in the afternoons when Daadi tells me not to go out because I'll get dark, but I don't care. I listen to their gentle big, slow hum as my body warms and bakes like Amma's cakes. I ask them what their life was like in the stomach of the dark earth before they exploded red-hot, streaming from a mouth in the ground and landed higgledy-piggledy like pebbles scattered by a giant hand. They don't speak but my stomach feels them smile at my asking, and hear that they love me. I listen and listen to their deep slow *mmmmmmmm* as I warm to burning hot and must peel myself away.

As I do to the trees, each with a wide lap into which I can nestle I climb up to lie on tamarind tree branches, their bark long, rough strokes against my bare legs as I nibble their slender stalks and listen to air rustling through their small sour pinnate leaves. Their high, thin croon, *eeeeeeee*, soft and sweet like a mermaid might sound.

Or the ashoka tree at Vidyaranya school with long oval leaves we snap to see oozing drops of white sap. Big black ants wind long trails along its bark. It sings *aa-eee-aa-eee* of olden days, village tales, and is happy to see me with my friends when we eat our lunch below before climbing into its cool arbor to tell our stories and chew on mango-rind pickle.

Or the banyan tree by the school playground, its long branch roots dangling like Amma's hair after she washes it. I hang and swing on them with my friends back and forth, back and forth, then drop *thud* to the ground. It drones old and big and slow, *huuuuuuuum*, like Thatha's sister, almost ninety, sighs when she sinks her weight from her swollen feet onto a reclining chair.

Or when Caesar, my dog, is sad and lonely because he's chained up to the railing by the stairs down to the servants' rooms. I go to him, stroke and put my arm around him and my face against his lovely doggy-smell so he knows I'm there and tell him I love him, like no one else does. He licks my face and wags his tail, and whines *khoon-khooo-ooon* when I stop stroking his fur.

Or the high-pitched *ipee ipee* pain-shrieks of dragonflies Raghu catches. He knots a thread around their thin, long bodies, flying them like kites till their bodies break in two as I run around him, tugging at his arm, crying, "Stop. Stop. You're hurting them. Let them go free!" My whole body hurts all over. But he just pushes me away and laughs.

Raghu and the adults don't hear the boulders and trees. And they don't see fairies or feel their magic either. They talk about which trees and flowers to plant and know all their names, but don't know how they speak or feel.

Amma says, "You have a wild imagination. It's from all the fairy tales you read. This will change when you grow up."

So I don't tell them anymore. But I don't want to grow up if I can't hear them or see them.

They don't know magic.

Years ago she found the land, she said, miles outside Hyderabad, when she and Naina wanted to build a home.

"It's no-man's land," an uncle said. "No one lives there."

"You're *pichchi*, crazy," Daadi said. "Such a deserted place! No one civilized lives there! Only wild dogs and pigs. And people tending herds of buffalo."

"It's too far from everyone and everything," another uncle told her. "You're being foolish. You'll be alone with the children when your husband goes to the village."

"*Tch-tch*, it's bad luck to look at a graveyard from home. You'll even see the pyres burning," Amma's great-aunt said.

But Amma takes me when she surveys the plot, winding up a dusty red road in our white standard Herald. We get out of the car and the *loo*, oven-hot, dry summer wind from the North, burns my face. We pick our way through rocks and boulders, as I jump onto them, slithering down from their rough gray mounds like the backs of elephants.

A petite five foot two, Amma's long black hair that reaches down to her hips is pulled into a bun almost as large as her face, the color of hot chocolate. She has a beautiful smile and when she laughs you can see her small, pearly teeth. She stands on the hilltop, her maroon cotton sari block-printed with black paisley flapping in the wind, arms firmly akimbo on her waist, hips thrust out like Ben-Hur on his chariot, against the wide pale blue sky. Her *palloo* flies like a flag over her left shoulder. The wind hollows her sari into a canal between her legs.

I scramble to her side and we look out together. To the right, the horizon dips down to a valley through which a lake flows and ends between its brown and green thighs. Opposite the lake, as the land rises to the next hill, is a graveyard scattered with gray chiseled, curved headstones. Chills go down my back. To the left, Hyderabad is a colony of white, beige, pink, and mint julep–green ants. Its honks are faraway. Goats *meh-eh-eh-eh* a stone's throw from us.

A cool, sweet gust swishes my hair back from my face. The sweat on my neck dries. I look up at her. She exhales with a smile.

She can breathe. Here, I know she can enter into the wild power of her. Here, she can be queen—beautiful, powerful. Fiercely at home. Have a garden. Rule.

I drop to the red-brown earth. Squat and scratch the paisley design of her handloom sari with my finger in the dust. A tawny-gold chameleon inches out from the crevice of a dark rock, and darts back in when I startle. Its eyeballs, globes of unblinking amber beauty, stare at me from the shadows.

"*Laughing Waters*," Amma says to me as we stand in front of our new house looking at the bronze plates just put up on our eight-foot-high compound wall. Black letters etched in slanting cursive on gleaming yellow gold, proud against fragmented stones cemented together. Stones cut from the boulders cleared from the land to build our house on Road No. 7 in Banjara Hills. "From Longfellow's *Hiawatha*," she says. "It's a beautiful poem I learned in school. A long one. You can learn it when you're older."

And she recites, like music,

There the ancient Arrow-maker
Made his arrow-heads of sandstone,
Arrow-heads of chalcedony,
Arrow-heads of flint and jasper,
Smoothed and sharpened at the edges,
Hard and polished, keen and costly.
With him dwelt his dark-eyed daughter,
Wayward as the Minnehaha,
With her moods of shade and sunshine,

Eyes that smiled and frowned alternate,
Feet as rapid as the river,
Tresses flowing like the water,
And as musical a laughter,
And he named her from the river,
From the water-fall he named her,
Minnehaha, Laughing Water.

Her voice swings like a vine around the compound wall with *this is ours, this is our beautiful home, unlike any other.* And I want to skip and sway, but I know not to. I want to be beautiful Minnehaha. As beautiful as the river. Certainly as beautiful as the lilting poem.

She steps back to look at both signs, and I do it with her. *Laughing Waters* on the right side of our white wooden gate. *R.M. Reddy*, Naina's name, on the left. The house is painted white, and features a sloping red roof, arched doorways, roses all up the driveway, a terrace with a swan-necked railing that leans out over the valley to the lake. Completely different from other Indian homes with flat roofs with names like *Santiniketan, Pushpa Nivas,* or *Amritha Bhavan*. I decide then and there that we live in the most beautiful home with the most beautiful name. And glow that Amma might be the only mother in Hyderabad who recites such lovely English poetry to her daughter.

Naina, my father, is there, but not really. He's unreachable as a tall, broad, quiet mountain. Remote. His face, the color of wheat, has wide cheekbones, a flat nose, and flaring nostrils. A black puff curves on his head. When he laughs, it gurgles up from his stomach, his full lips widen to reveal perfect white teeth, and his eyes crinkle into little slits.

He owns a harvesting equipment factory with his friend and works late on weekdays. Weekends, he relaxes with the newspaper and a bottle of Kingfisher beer on our back lawn, legs propped on the iron railing.

On Diwali, the festival of lights, he comes alive with the rest of India. Naina takes Raghu and me to buy fireworks from rows of stalls piled high with razzle-dazzle. He always knows which ones to buy, just like when he sniffs out the ripest and sweetest fruits. We buy two baskets full. At home, we excitedly sun them on old newspapers for the brightest blaze and bang.

Then begin the weeklong festivities. We bang *patakas*, fireworks, against concrete ledges that hold Amma's precious potted roses. Whirl sparklers around and around. Light little black tablets that smoke into long, squiggly black-ashen snakes. My favorites are the *chakras*, dizzyingly bright whirling orbs, and we squeal as they spin between our feet on the red terracotta floor behind our kitchen.

Nights, I marvel as Naina lights the biggest, brightest, loudest, and most dangerous fireworks. Rockets that spiral into the sky. Fountains of light showers. Deafening strings of red firecrackers. Bombs that make me plug my fingers with my ears, yet spellbound at how he bravely lights them and darts away like a street urchin before they explode into thunder and lightning.

"Can I learn ballet?" I ask Amma as we drive home from my school one day. I've been wanting to ask her for many days, and I do so now because we're in the car together and she smiled at me when she picked me up.

Some evenings, when Naina plays his Western classical music records, I hold the square cover of *Swan Lake* on my lap to look at the ballet dancer balanced on one tiptoe, her left leg stretched out behind her, in her pink dress. She looks like the fairies in our garden. And sometimes in Amma's American magazines—*Time, Life, Newsweek*, and *National Geographic*—I trace the shape of a dancer with my finger. In pictures in my storybooks, ballerinas dance like white dandelion seeds adrift on a breeze from the page. I want to float like them. Wear a taffeta skirt.

It's the closest thing to being a fairy.

Our car approaches a circle where a policeman in starched khaki clothes directs traffic. Amma hangs her arm out her window, twirls her wrist to go right, and makes a face at the policeman. His eyebrows shoot up in surprise. He grins wide with white teeth at her after he gets over his shock that she made a face at him. She waves at him as we drive away.

She's one of the few mothers who drive. All the other mothers have a driver or take their children home by bus or auto-rickshaw, but she's Ben-Hur. She drives through anything and anyone, even the narrow lanes in Secunderabad market lined with stalls crammed tight and high with fruits and vegetables, jute sacks of rice and wheat and lentils, and tins of oils. She weaves through bustling crowds and erratic traffic, rapidly changes gears, and constantly brakes. "*Lanjakodukka!*", whore's son, she shouts at a bicyclist dashing in front of us. "*Nee Amma!*", your mother! when an auto-rickshaw brakes a foot away. "*Aikkadaa pothunnao-oo?*" Where are you going? She shakes her right hand as a question mark and puffs her cheeks as a man darts across the street. She's not afraid of anyone. Or anything. She's not like any of my friends' mothers that way. She's a lion on the roads.

"You're too fat." Her voice is like iron. She changes gears. "You have to be thin for ballet."

I scrunch in my stomach. She always tells me I'm fat, to pull my Mary, my belly, in when we go out. My thighs are big but not as big as Swathi's or Payal's. But I'm not delicate like Vasantha or willowy like Renuka. A hole balloons inside me and I curve into the car seat, turn to stare out the window at the bicycles, auto-rickshaws, and the man beating the bony horse pulling his cart because it won't go any faster. I blink back my tears.

"Why don't you play the piano?" she asks, after we pass Panjagutta, Lakdikapool, and Masab Tank, and climb the hill where the traffic lightens and the air cools, towards our home.

The piano? Like Kavitha Aunty? I perk up and look at her. Kavitha Aunty is one of Amma's best friends. She has a piano piled with music books with a round wooden stool that swivels. I like to turn round and round on it when we visit for long lunches. Kavitha Aunty's home is simple and free. She doesn't fuss like Amma does about having everything spick and span and in its place. Her family is traditional Tamilian, Brahmin, and vegetarian, not like ours. Her parents do pujas and go to temple. We're Telugu and Andhra, two levels below her on the caste system, devout meat-lovers, untraditional because we're Westernized, and don't do any pujas or go to temple. Kavitha Aunty's always kind to me, calls me "My-three-ahh" and loves that I love food. When she invites us for lunch she makes *bise bele bath*, sambar rice that she piles high on my plate. She drizzles spoonfuls of warm ghee over my brown-orange mound speckled with carrots and beans and fried cashew bits. I watch its goldenness ooze over my little hillock and make holes in it with my fingers so it mushes in.

The next time we visit her, Kavitha Aunty plays for us as she reads from dots on lines in her book. Her fingers flit across the black and white keys like butterflies. She is elegant, her arms bare and bold in her sleeveless blouse. No other Hindu women wear blouses like that, only Anglo-Indians. But, like us, she's more Western. Above her piano hangs a picture of two young girls in long dresses, their hair tied back in bows at a piano with brass candlesticks. The girl with golden hair and a white dress reads from a music book as she plays, the other, with chestnut hair, bends over her, listening. I want to be beautiful and graceful like them.

"So pretty," Amma says.

Yes, so pretty. Her music is colored confetti and rainbows. I want to learn to play like her, and the girls in the picture, and wear sleeveless blouses.

When she finishes, Kavitha Aunty asks me, "Do you want to learn, My-three-ahh?"

I smile at her and look up at Amma eagerly.

Amma asks, "Do you want to learn, Mytrae? I learned as a girl. Roopa Aunty did too. Thatha had us take piano lessons and we had a piano at home for some years."

"Why did you stop?" I ask.

"Because we did so many things," Amma says. "Tennis, swimming, sports. My thing was tennis. We couldn't do it all. Yes, why don't you learn piano? With dance you'll have to stop after a certain age. So many girls learn Bharatanatyam but stop after they get married. But music, you can always have music."

My head bobs up and down with delight. "Yes, Amma. I want to learn."

"Where can she learn, Kavitha?" Amma asks.

I look at Kavitha Aunty and hope she'll teach me.

But Kavitha Aunty says, "She can take lessons at St. Teresa's. I'll introduce you to Sister Carmel."

Every time Thatha and Daadi visit, Thatha asks, "Will you play for me?"

"Yes Thatha," I say, and feel special as I take his hand and lead him down the stairs to Raghu's and my bedroom. It has green mosaic tiles, two twin beds, a book case, a built-in desk by a window, a carpet printed with three racing cars that Amma bought for Raghu. And the upright piano Amma rented for me.

He sits on my bed in his khaki, mud-brown or forest-green shirt with four big pockets, white pants, and big black shoes. His hearing aid is in his upper left pocket, and his earpiece is in his right ear. In between pieces I turn around to look at him but he looks down at the green floor tile. He can't hear me. He's ninety percent deaf in his right ear and seventy-five percent deaf in his left, which he tells us all many times. But I play anyway, one piece, then another, and another for him, because he's listening to me and only to me, and I want to keep him here as long as I can. No one else asks me to play. When I finish, I look at him. Somehow, he always knows when I'm done because he looks up.

"Finished?" he asks.

"Yes, Thatha."

"Very good. Very good. Keep it up. Keep practicing. Keep it up." Then he comes to my bench and kisses me, once on the left cheek, then on the right, and again on the left, inhaling deeply with each kiss.

These are the times I love him most of all and know he loves me, because he comes and sits and is happy to listen to me play, when he can't hear much. Even if it's only because he can't hear anyone when they talk upstairs.

One morning, I sight-read from a new piano book and sing when the pieces have words. Suddenly, Amma walks into the room, grabs my shoulder, swivels me around, and sweeps me off the piano bench.

Her face is contorted with rage. She beats my face, my arms, my back.

I curl into a ball, trying to protect myself. "What did I *do*?" I howl.

Her palms thud into me. Her fingernails tear my soft child flesh.

"Owww! Owww!"

But she's deaf to my cries, a storm raging through her. She beats me again. And again. And again.

I cannot think. The blows thunder into me like they'll never end. Sobbing and helpless, I hold my arms up over my face until she finally stops. I lie on the floor, a blubbering shivering mass, my face a pool of tears and snot. Suddenly, she lets go of my arm and walks away. Goes into her room and shuts her door. What did I do? Was it because I was singing? Did I disturb her? I'm bad. I am bad. I don't know what, but I must have done something terrible for her to beat me like this.

Quietly, I slip out the back door to where Caesar lies. Wrap my arms around him, huddle close to his warm, furry body, listen to his pants, his belly moving quicker than mine. And I stop crying.

Later that afternoon Amma calls me into her room. I enter, frightened. She lies on her bed, arm bent over her eyes. "I'm sorry I beat you. I don't know what came over me."

Confused, my head hanging, I search for meaning in the black, gray, and white dots on the pink mosaic tiles, but they offer none.

For the next few days, I proudly and defiantly display the marks and scars on my neck and arms that turn red, violet, then black to my school friends. "See! See what she did to me!"

They are silent. Look away.

She thrashes me when I do something wrong. She thrashes Raghu too. Naina punishes him too, but he doesn't thrash me. But this time she didn't even tell me what I did. Must be because I was singing. I must have disturbed her rest. I was too loud. Maybe my voice is terrible. I won't sing again.

Never ever.

And I don't. I sing in my head when I play after that. Lilt the lovely words in my mind. Like the magic and make-believe I never talk about.

"We're not like other families," Daadi says, leaning over to look at the pink and yellow flower I'm sewing on a cream cloth from a design thin and translucent as onion-skin. I wrinkle my nose at the vinegary smell she always has except after her bath, when she smells like lavender talcum powder. She's been teaching me to cross-stitch and sew buttons the last few times I've stayed over. "Every woman must know how to sew," she says, and I know by now that when Daadi says to do something, I better do it. My flower is higgledy-piggledy untidy, with fat, loose stitches, some not even in the right holes, not like the beautiful purple and blue bouquet she's neatly stitched on her embroidery hoop. "It's satin-stitch," she tells me when I ask. "You can learn it when you're older." I don't like to sew a quarter as much as I like to read, but maybe when I grow up I'll have a hoop like hers and embroider beautiful cushion covers in satin- and feather-stitch for my home.

We sit on her divan, leaning against ruby- and emerald-colored silk cushions in her living room. Their flat is on Road No. 12, about a mile from us, so Raghu and I come here often after school or stay overnight when Amma and Naina are out at a party. Daadi and Thatha's cozy flat hugs me like it has arms. But Daadi thinks it's too small so she says "flat" like she's spitting it out. They moved from Bangalore two years ago because they're getting old, because my Roshan Uncle, and Amma live here. Roopa Aunty, their third daughter, lives in America and she visits every few years. We used to go every summer to Daadi and Thatha's Bangalore house, which had enormous rooms upstairs and downstairs, a huge library lined floor-to-ceiling with Thatha's books, a garden with ponds and flower beds and fruit trees, and beehives Thatha kept for honey. They had lots of servants then, like we do now. Daadi tells everyone who visits her, "Such a small flat, we had such a big house, but what to do, this is our life now. Who thought we'd ever live in a flat, but times are changing. This is all we can have." Daadi grumbles a lot but she loves us too.

"It's coming along," she says, peering at my cross-stich. "You'll improve." She looks up as the maid enters.

"I'm going, *memsahib*," the maid says.

Daadi looks around the room. "Have you cleaned everything well? Finished everything for the day? Did you clean the brass water *binda* with tamarind and put it out in the sun?" she scolds.

"Yes, *memsahib*," the maid says, her eyes big, afraid of Daadi like I am.

"Okay, then, go. Come on time tomorrow."

The maid nods and leaves.

My grandmother looks at me. "You have to stay on top of them, otherwise they'll sit on your head. It's so hard to find good servants these days. Always slip-shod. Everything's going to the dogs." She puts her hoop down in her lap and looks up at the three-foot-high oval photograph on the wall. The man in the black and white picture is mostly bald, wears glasses, looks serious and distinguished. I'd be a little afraid of him if he were alive.

"Tell me about your father, Daadi," I ask. I like when she tells stories about our family.

"My father was a fine man. Brilliant. He was the best lawyer in Vijayawada. So distinguished. So much integrity. People would come to see him from far away. Those days it was all about integrity. Not like now, where people are chasing money and jewelry. It was all about hard work and dignity, not showing off everything you have and dressing like Christmas trees."

"What about your mother, Daadi?"

"My mother, poor thing. Those days women weren't educated much. She must have done a few classes, then got married at sixteen. Like me. She was quiet, and looked after the house." She looks at me. "Do you remember her? You used to call her *Akka* when you were small."

Akka is sister in Telugu. "I don't, Daadi."

Her eyes water as she looks at her father's picture. "That's what makes our family different. We come from a long line of people who didn't live just for money but cared about people and did good. They were *zamindars*, landowners, educationists, and reformists, some were even in politics. They did public works. They were good to the farmers who rented land from them. They set up schools, libraries, and hospitals. My uncle, Sir C.R. Reddy, was a speaker and famous educationist. He started Andhra University. My father loved your Thatha because he went to Cambridge. Because he has strong beliefs and thinks for himself. Because he's a self-made man."

"What's self-made, Daadi?"

"That means he came up on his own. He didn't have an inheritance or business or company handed to him. His father didn't give him a *pai*. We were so poor those early years, in Ooty. He earned only 100 rupees a month. What will 100 rupees bring you nowadays? Nothing. After paying the rent he'd bring the rest home and give it to me. I had to run a whole house on it. Ten rupees for the cook, seven for the gardener, ten for the driver, five for the maids, but everything was so cheap in those days, not like now. Every few months I could buy a new sari. Every now and then get a piece of jewelry made. But we were haaaaappy, haaaaappppy, haaaaappy. We played tennis at the club and had lunch with our friends."

"You played tennis, Daadi?"

"Yes, and I was quite good," she laughs. "Those days we played in saris."

"How could you run in them?"

"We just lifted them up. Your Thatha was City Commissioner then. He cared about everything and everyone. Everyone loved him. Everyone wanted to know his opinion, if it was a dam at the Moyar river, the price of rice, schools, hospitals, or planting trees beside the roads. That's what makes your Thatha your Thatha. Generous to a fault and won't tell a lie. He did so much good for so many people. Even now, you know how people come and thank him."

I nod. People always do come to see him. And he loves to help them and give them advice.

I glow with pride every time she talks about our family. And I'm swept back in time, through generations, feeling their hands from centuries ago rest on my shoulders. My family is who I come from. My family is who I am. Like a petal in a chrysanthemum, I am part of them and they a part of me. Our dignity, education, and integrity is our most precious possession. When I grow up, I too will add to our family's pride, respect, and name.

"Your Thatha wants the best for everyone," she continues. "Like sending your Amma and Roshan Uncle to the best schools. Roopa Aunty too. When we lived in Madras, he interviewed all the principals. Everyone sent their children to one of two big schools, but he chose another smaller, less-known school because it was run by the British. He had a tennis wall built for your mother, hired Ramanathan Krishnan, the best tennis coach in India to teach her. He even had cricket nets set up for Roshan Uncle. No one else in Madras had that. Then he sent them to the best boarding schools. When you and your brother were born, he insisted your mother reserve seats for you in boarding school. You'll go when your Amma thinks you're ready. No stone unturned," she says, nodding and circling her head with pride as she does when she agrees with herself. "That's your Thatha."

That instant I know who I want to marry. A self-made man.

Someone not like everyone else.

Someone who cares about his work and doesn't just make money for money's sake.

Someone who thinks for himself and doesn't live like everyone else.

Someone different.

I don't remember when worry first curled into me, like smoke from the blacksmith's pounding hot anvil seeping into my dress, my hair, the bare skin of my arms. Maybe it's the nights I startle awake.

Something's wrong. I feel it before I know it. My eyes spring wide open. Hear the slow click of Amma opening her bedroom door to the verandah between her and Naina's bedroom and mine and Raghu's. Quietly closing it. Wheezing. Long, heaving gasps for air. Desperate. It's happening again. I wish it would stop. I wish I could make it stop. She's been waking up more and more often. Raghu doesn't stir in his bed two feet from mine.

I turn to lie on my back. Taut. My ears strain to listen. *Haaaaaaahhhh… … huuuuuuuhhhh,* My stomach curdles. She's in the beginning of her attack. How bad will it be this time? Will her next breath be easier? What if this breath is her last? This one? I wait for the gasp. Or this one? Another gasp.

Doesn't Naina hear? *Why* doesn't he come out to be with her? *Do* something?

I swing my legs off my bed and walk barefoot on the cool tiles. The night is ink and silver, rustling with eucalyptus breeze through leaves and our iron mesh windows. I clutch our door handle. Should I go to her? She doesn't like me seeing her like this. She prefers to be alone, like a wounded tomcat. She won't want me with her. But I must do something. Can't leave her like this.

Very, very quietly, holding my breath, I push the cold brass handle. It's slippery in my sweaty palms. There. It didn't click this time. I inch the door open to her heaving gasps, to the smell of terror and panic.

In the verandah, the light of the crook-necked lamp on the telephone table streams on her. She's wearing her pink-and-white-flowered dressing gown that Roopa Aunty brought from America. She's hunched over the wicker sofa with maroon cushions, arms impaled on the armrests, palms gripping them as each frantic breath caves her back into a C. She's drowning, just not in water. Every breath could be her last. Her inhales like flapping fish on the fisherman's hook that I can't bear, can't do anything about. She hasn't heard me. What can I do to ease her torture? Something, anything to make it stop, make her be well, make her breathe again.

I listen some more, then whisper-walk towards her, sideways, to not startle her. Her eyes are squeezed shut, fingers gripping her blue-gray Ventolin inhaler. She lifts her head back and gasps four more deep, long puffs. Keeps her head up so the medicine goes into her lungs. Clears her throat. Waits. Lifts the Benadryl bottle and takes a long swig. We wait. Usually the Ventolin eases her lungs. Sometimes it doesn't.

I take another step. She still doesn't know I'm here. Another. Gently cup my hand on her shoulder to say I'm here. What do you need? Anything at all.

"Go back to bed, Mytrae," she pants, without turning to look at me.

"Can I get you something?"

She shakes her head. The next round of wheezing begins. Hot tears roll down my cheeks and I stiffen my trembling belly.

"Shall I wake Naina?"

She shakes her head. "He can't do anything."

"Do you want to go to the hospital?"

She shakes her head. "This will pass. It just takes a few minutes for the medicine to kick in. Go!"

I can't move. Don't want to add to her pain, but I can't leave her like this.

"Go! Go!"

I walk backwards slowly, eyes wide open. Better I stay in my room. Mustn't disturb her, agitate her.

I leave my heart with her in the verandah. Shut the bedroom door, my back to it. Slide trembling to the cold, hard floor. Squeeze my arms tight around my knees. I'll wait till it's over. Till she breathes easy again. Till she goes back to bed. Every second feels like an hour as I listen to her *haaaaaaahhhh huuuuuuuhhhh* in the soft eucalyptus night, to the croaking bullfrogs. I don't know it but I'm breathing with her, long breaths in my throat, squeezing tight for the next wave.

The next morning my first thought is She's better now. She'll wake up late. I bathe, dress myself, pack my school bag, and go upstairs to Caesar tied with his iron-link leash to the servants' staircase behind the kitchen. He licks my face as I stroke him in long caresses from his head to the tip of his tail. Scratch him behind his ears. Give him his milk and bread breakfast. Kiss his wet snout. "She'll be okay," I tell him. "She'll be okay today."

Nair, our cook, calls me for breakfast. When Amma has an attack, the house drips heavy like our maid's sopping-wet rag she sloshes from her orange mopping bucket onto the mosaic floors. Naina and Raghu, silent and morose, are in the pale pink pantry at the white linoleum table on white spindle chairs with rounded high backs. Nair serves us porridge, toast, and fried eggs. We eat without words, without looking at each other. When we're almost done, Amma swings open the pantry door in her purple and white caftan, white crumpled handkerchief and Ventolin inhaler in her hand, and sits. We look at her. The storm's passed. She's emerging. Her face is lighter, her breath regular. Nair appears with her tall mug of steaming tea in her favorite mug with purple and yellow flowers.

"Coffee today, Nair," she says. He goes back into the kitchen.

"How are you feeling?" Naina asks, his voice from the bottom of the sea.

"I'm okay." She nods, but her eyebrows furrow with a look that says I'm-not-but-that's-okay-don't-worry. A small smile. She's putting up a front.

She's *not* okay. She's like the mangled rat, shredded to the bone, Caesar once dragged inside.

"Did you wake up in the night?" Naina asks.

Doesn't he even know? Can't he tell? He sleeps next to her. How can he not know?

She nods, yes, like *don't worry about me, I'm okay.*

"Was it an attack?" he asks.

She nods.

"Hmhhh. Another one. Do you want to see the doctor?"

"I'm okay, kiss," she says. She calls him kiss sometimes.

Naina's quiet. He just needs to hear she's okay. Then he's okay. Then we're all okay. We know not to disturb her, not make her talk, so she can conserve her strength. Raghu looks down at his plate and shovels eggs in. He's pretending he's not there. Like if he doesn't think about it, it's not real. As though there's nothing else but his plate of eggs and toast and the world doesn't exist. He gets that way when he's worried. Or scolded. He doesn't know what to say.

I don't know what to say, either. My stomach hurts. I just want her to feel better. I want her asthma to stop. Not just this morning, not just tomorrow, but forever. I wish I could take it away like when Caesar whines or is restless and I stroke his thick black and white and gold fur and shush him quiet and peaceful with my love. But Amma doesn't like to be loved. Not like that. The only way to love her is not to bother her. So she can do what she wants. Only then she sometimes smiles at me.

After she has two mugs of coffee, she'll call Daadi. Coffee helps me, she says. It opens my lungs. After Raghu and I are in school and Naina at his factory, she'll telephone Daadi and tell about her night in a way she can't tell us. She doesn't want to worry us, you see, and we all try to make it seem like we're not worried so she doesn't worry. But she can talk with Daadi, who'll ask her about which treatment she's trying now and which doctor to try next. They'll worry together and that is how they love each other.

I can tell you what she's trying now. Grass. She's growing thin blades of special grass six inches tall in a big round clay pot on the ledge outside Raghu's and my bedroom window. Someone in Madras told her to try it. In the mornings, after her coffee, she cuts fistfuls of young grass, stuffs a handful in her mouth, and chews it for five minutes as she strolls on the lawn outside our bedroom looking at the valley below, swallows the juice then spits out small balls of green cud. Like what sometimes hangs out of water buffaloes' mouths, with long, gooey dribbles of spit on both sides of their thick black lips.

But her balls are small, tidy, dry, compact.

"How does it taste?" I asked her once.

"Like grass. Not bad. Just like grass."

She's brave like that. She keeps trying this and that. Goes to doctor after doctor. Homeopathy didn't work. She got worse. Really bad worse. Like when she tried Ayurveda. That made her even more sick for weeks. Every time she tries something new she feels like morning. And we all feel like that. New. Fresh. Like anything can happen. We all wait. Hoping. Waiting and hoping this will cure her. That maybe the sun will come out this time.

On Saturday and Sunday mornings I pretend I'm not watching her when I see her cut and stuff handfuls of delicate green strands in her mouth. I hope they save her.

She looks at me from across the white Formica pantry table now.

I know what she's going to say even before she says it. I nod and push my chair back before she says, "Go, it's time for school."

I know what I need to do. I don't want her to worry even one thought about me. Just let her take care of herself. Just let her have the day to look after herself. Call Daadi. Eat grass. Eat dry toast later. Lie down and rest.

Breathe again.

Bored during my Hindi tuition in Raghu's study, I open his desk drawer and find a card from one of my close friends who lives in the U.K., crumpled, its stamp ripped out. He stole my letter! Without letting me read it, or simply asking for the stamp. All because he collects stamps. But I do too!

"How dare you!" I sob and storm after my tuition, attacking him like a wildcat, wildly beating and scratching. "She's *my* friend. You have no right to take the stamp and no right to steal my letter."

"Stop it, Mytrae," Amma angrily intervenes.

"But he stole my letter and stamp and didn't even show it to me. I found it just by accident. Who knows how many other things he's taken."

"I'll kill you if you say another word," she threatens.

Every cell in my little being fills with hate and anger. "Kill me," I say, my eyes defiant, my fists clenched.

She doesn't say another word. We blaze at each other. For a very long minute. The air steams. Our cook pauses his kitchen clatter.

Raghu, standing behind her, peers out at me and smirks. I know, then, I'll never win against him. She'll always take his side. Always. She loves him more. Because he's a boy. I search long and deep for specks of love behind her rage in her eyes, but can't find any.

Naina's eating breakfast in the adjoining pantry. But he just sits there, listening. He never corrects or questions her. My wishing won't make that happen. Clutching my crumpled letter, I walk past Amma, push the pantry screen door into the verandah where Caesar lies, and collapse beside him. Blubber into his neck. He's where I always go when life and adults are unfair and hurtful. He knows when I'm sad or hurt. Nestling against me, he whines softly, nuzzles my cheeks with his wet, cold snout, and licks my tears with his rough tongue.

I know her anger. But her fury shakes me to my bones. She'll kill me if I harm her son.

And the truth I desperately don't want to know rises like a welt in my heart.

Never let her know how you long for her love.

My bum roasts on my wooden chair at my desk. I try to read on my bed but my mattress is an oven. Even the trees droop, wilting, these burning dry May afternoons. The birds and squirrels are silent. Too hot to sing or twitter. Sweltering, Amma says. She's napping. Good. I can chat with Narayana, our gardener. I pad barefoot to the verandah door and go into the garden. The heat hits me like a bonfire.

Narayana squats on his haunches, weeding blood-colored coleus beds in the shade by the coral and shocking-pink bougainvillea, crooning his strange, out-of-tune Telugu songs. He smiles from ear to ear when he sees me. I sit cross-legged a few feet from him in a damp flower bed, so my bum and bare legs cool. No wonder this is one of Caesar's favorite spots.

"Tell me a story," I ask, cupping my chin and resting my elbow on my thigh. "Tell me a story about when you were a little boy. What did you like to play?"

"In my village," he says, "I used to play in the river with my brothers. We swung from banyan-tree branches and jumped in. We laughed and shouted and swam in the afternoons. But in the mornings we had to work. We woke up an hour before dawn to draw water from the well. I carried a big clay pot back and forth eight times to the hut for my mother's cooking and washing. When I grew older, we worked for the farmers in paddy and sugarcane fields. We planted the seedlings and cut the harvested rice."

"What was your hut like?"

"It had two doors, one for people, the other for our goats."

"How did you all fit in it?"

"In the summer we slept outside on a dhurrie on the ground in the cool moonlight. My father slept on a *charpoy*, a cot made of jute rope, and after he left my mother slept on it."

He told me once about his father, who drank all the family's earnings and beat him and his mother and brothers. So he ran away at twelve to a neighboring town and found work.

I would have loved to grow up like him, so free, without school.

But I feel sorry for him, how hard he had to work. How lonely and scared he must have been when he ran away. How spoiled and lucky I am because we're rich and I don't have to work, as poor children do. We have so much. I wish we could give some of what we have to the poor.

"Mytrae! Come in! Come here!" Amma calls out angrily.

She must have heard our voices in the garden. I jump up and go find her. She's in my room arranging my clothes in the cupboard.

"Don't talk to him anymore," she says, leaning into the cupboard neatly piling my blouses and dresses. I can never do that. I don't put them back neatly like she tells me to.

"Why?"

She looks at me, her eyes steel knives. Her bushy eyebrows furrow. Her jaw contorts with anger. She grabs a wooden hanger from the cupboard and beats me all over my body.

Thwack. Thwack. Thwack.

I try to wriggle away, but she clutches my arm.

"I said *don't* talk to him, and that's *that. Stop* with all your silly questions. Just *do* as I say," she shrieks. *Thwack. Thwack.*

The wooden hanger thrashes into my soft, stunned flesh, but she's a hurricane. A hurricane who'll never stop until she gets all her hate of me out. I scream. I howl. I cover my head with my arms but she pulls them away. She's not stopping. She wants me to die. *Thwack. Thwack.* Time blurs. Everything blurs. Can't think. The hanger burns red-hot fire all over my body. It seems like it will never, ever end.

Finally, after twenty minutes or so, she flings down the hanger. Strides out of my room. I lay huddled on the floor, trembling, whimpering, crying softly so she won't hear, my arms wrapped around my head and shoulders. My body hurts all over. What's wrong with talking to him? whirrs round and round in my mind, like the fan's *whoosh-whoosh*.

I don't know how long I lie there. Mastaan Bee, our round-faced, cockeyed maid tiptoes in panting, sits cross-legged beside me, and gathers me into her lap. "I heard you screaming," she whispers fierce and fearful. Her body quivers. She pulls me into the pillow of her large breasts. I burrow into her soft warmth, inhale charcoal and grime in her sari folds, my arms tight around her, squeeze my eyes as though if I do I can forget what just happened. "I was washing clothes at the bottom of the hill. I threw them down and ran up when I heard you screaming. I wanted to stop her but I didn't. I waited until she left."

We're both afraid. She has a drunkard husband and ten children. I don't want Amma to throw her out, and she will if she sees her holding me. I love her. I bury my face in the soft pillow of her chest. Drink her protection and love like a big green coconut. My tears come like Narayana's village river. No one holds me like this. So much love here. Does she hold her children like this? How lucky they are. I imagine I'm one of them she holds in the evening as she cooks rice for them. Slowly, my shudders subside.

"Why shouldn't I talk to him?" I sniffle into her sari.

"I don't know, baby, I don't know what *memsahib* thinks is wrong. But maybe you shouldn't anymore, okay?" She gently strokes my hair and lightly touches the angry red streaks on my arms and neck where welts are rising, as though her fingers can wipe them away. Her touch is waterfall love. Amma doesn't like me touching her. Pushes me away.

I love how Mastaan Bee smiles from ear to ear when she sees me. Sometimes I make her sit on the rattan chair in our verandah to rest awhile from her work even though servants are not allowed to sit on our furniture. She does, giggling, nervous in case Amma or Naina see her. But I keep watch and snap pictures of her with Amma's old camera.

I don't know why talking with Narayana or so many things I like are bad and make adults angry.

Maybe I'm adopted. Maybe someone dropped me off on my parents' doorstep. Maybe I was switched at birth. I think about the story Amma proudly tells her friends about me: "Her eyes were blue when she was born. The Irish nurse in the hospital took one look at her and squealed, 'What mischief have you been up to, Kamah-la?'"

Of course! I must have had an Indian mother and an English father who weren't allowed to marry. They had to give me away and took Amma's baby instead. I'm part Western, I must be! Who are my real parents?

"I must be adopted," I tell Daadi.

"Don't be silly!" she says and laughs. "What nonsense! Must be some throwback from generations ago. Some gene from an invasion centuries ago."

I'm a little sad I don't have an English father. "So our family isn't completely pure, then?"

"We're pure. But you never know how these things creep in. We're such an old country and so many foreigners have invaded us. That's why people in the North have brown, even blue or green eyes. But we're in the South. It's very rare."

Rare. I like that.

At two, my eyes turned amber. Still, they're unusual for an Indian. My friends peer at them sometimes and tell me they speckle green in the sun, and I feel shy and special.

As I lie in Mastaan Bee's arms, I think, *I'm different, I'm different.* One day I'll grow up and meet my real family and they won't beat me but they'll love me and hold me like Mastaan Bee, warm and soft and safe, and tell me stories in the night.

After that beating I still talk to Narayana and ask him to tell me stories, but secretly, when Amma and Naina are out, and when Raghu's busy so he won't tell.

"Let's ask the child," Daadi pats the space beside her on Amma's and Naina's bed so wide I could roll six times over from one end to the other. "Come," she nods kindly.

Amma, Roopa Aunty, and Leela Aunty smile at me. Amma's jewelry is spread all over the bed. Diamond earring studs and a necklace. Ruby and emerald flower studs with matching necklaces. Pearl necklaces. A gold brocade necklace with ruby and pearl pendants. A gold amulet and belt. Velvet boxes soft and crimson as the ladybugs I peer at on my finger before they fly away. Every few months the same ritual, as with their saris. Why do they love their boring jewelry so much?

"Look," Daadi points. "Your Amma's brought two diamond-and-emerald necklaces and matching bangles from Kishan Das for you. Which one do you like?"

Kishan Das, the velvet box reads on top. Our family jeweler. I stroke the indigo velvet. I like the emeralds' green, like grass. But I don't like sparkly diamonds. They're too showy. Hard. My favorite stones in Kishan Das' store when we visit are sapphires, their blues like star-night, but Amma says they're too expensive.

I wrinkle my nose. "They're so shiny. When will I wear them?"

"When you grow up!" Leela Aunty says. "You'll dress up and look beautiful."

"Not now," Amma says in her don't-you-know-that-silly? tone. "These are for your trousseau."

"My trousseau!" I imagine a treasure chest, the kind that pirates steal, piled high with jewels and crowns and necklaces hanging down its sides. Dread shivers through me. I don't want to grow up or get married. Growing up is as distant as the Thar Desert, and I like it that way. I don't want to be like them.

"When you go to weddings and *pujas*," Daadi says. "You'll have jewelry to match all your silk saris."

"And parties with your husband!" says Leela Aunty excitedly.

"Everyone will say wow, how beautiful you look!" Roopa Aunty says with a big smile. I smile back at her. I like that she says wow like an American. But I don't feel wow.

"You have to have jewelry for when you get married," Amma says. "And jewelry is expensive so we'll make you a few pieces whenever we can."

"What if I don't want a trousseau?"

"Don't be silly! Every woman has one. You're a tomboy now but you'll change," Amma says. "Daadi and Thatha gave me mine." She strokes a thick bracelet with uncut diamonds, rubies, and emeralds that she loves.

"But that's dowry! I thought our family doesn't give dowries."

"We don't. Your Thatha wouldn't do that. You know him. He'd never pay a man to marry his daughters or granddaughters," Daadi says firmly.

"My trousseau is *mine*," Amma says. "Naina and his family can't touch it. We're not like other families that way. I can do whatever I want with it."

"It's something you'll have your whole life, no matter what," Daadi says.

"God forbid anything should happen." Leela Aunty's voice cuts the air like the axe Narayana uses to chop branches.

Everyone purses their lips and falls silent.

"What could happen to me?" I ask though I know the answer.

"No one knows." Daadi's voice is a thin wisp of smoke. "Anything can happen. Anything at all."

She won't say it out loud so bad luck doesn't have a ghost of a chance.

I say it anyway. "Like if my husband dies?"

"Yes," Daadi says. "Or who knows what else? A life is a long time. We never know what fate has in store."

I think of Amma's friend, Amala Aunty, who's unhappy in her marriage. I've been overhearing Amma's phone conversations with her. Amma even said the "D" word out loud, which no one ever says. Ever. No one in our hundreds of relatives is D'd. It's scandalous. Even I know that. Raghu says Amma's encouraging Amala Aunty to leave. Why would she, we wonder, shocked. If she does D, Amala Aunty will vanish from society. No one will talk to her, only stare with eyes that accuse, "*Tchih!* Shame on you, you've lost your dignity. You have no place with us now." And they'll gossip with each other, "No self-respecting woman leaves her husband." She won't be invited to weddings, functions, or pujas because she'll bring bad luck. Contaminate people and their happiness. She'll live a secluded life, like a widow. And only a few people will care when she dies. Her father was well off, so is Amala Aunty glad she has a dowry or trousseau so she can live comfortably?

My knees quiver. I don't want to be like her. D's worse than being a widow because it's your fault. I look again at the jewels. I better like something. I clasp a gold woven *kada*, bangle, around my wrist, its ends two lion heads with ruby eyes in open-jawed roars. My arm lowers with its cool weight. Which of these will I wear when I grow up? Who will I be? Who will I marry? I can't see that far ahead. I don't think about marriage like some of my giggling school friends do. I stroke a double strand of pearls. They're soft, gentle, with pools of light in their bellies. They spirit me to the sea, to oysters in deep blue-green waters. They must have hurt when sand got in their shell and rubbed against their skinless flesh. I roll one between my fingers.

Do the women feel sparkly when they wear these? Like when I played with the fairies? Do they feel like they wear a thousand stars, like I would if I could wear chiffons and nylons splattered with sequins that I point to in fabric stores and tell Amma I want? Cotton-candy pink. Grass green. Deep, dark blue like just-before-night. But Amma says "*Thoo thoo*! Only Muslim girls wear those." And picks out flower-printed cottons and voiles. So I hang out our car window and stare at Muslim girls, and think how lucky they are to wear sparkly dresses.

I won't have an arranged marriage like them. I know it at every wedding we attend. I just do. I feel it when the couple is buried under heavy silks and garlands, with *pujaris* chanting Sanskrit prayers for hours in loud reedy voices like *shehnais,* and the musicians bang their *tavils* and blow their *nadaswarams.* And I rise, along with Daadi, Amma, and hundreds of family and friends wearing our finest silks and glittering jewelry, to throw saffron- and turmeric-stained rice blessings at them. But I don't tell them. They'd be shocked.

They'd say, don't be a stupid, of course you will, how else will you marry?

2

oceans of crossing

1979

"Come, sit, Mytrae, we want to talk to you," Naina says as I enter the living room. His forehead ridges like tree bark, his eyes and voice are like someone's died.

My heart catches. I join him and Amma on the peacock blue and green sofas, a brass and glass center table between us. Our upstairs with its dining room, study, and window-nook looks through large windows at the valley below and red-brown craggy hills beyond. The lake shimmers, tranquil. Emerald paddy fields softly wave. The spicy headiness of chicken curry says morning is becoming noon.

Amma's solemn too, her eyes dark with worry. Her lower lip pushes up into her upper one, as she does when life throws her a challenge or when nothing more can be done.

"Mytrae, we're going to immigrate to America." Naina's voice is an apology. His eyes soft with concern look into mine.

"America?" I gasp. My body screws shut. Leave everything? Go to the other end of the world? My mind struggles to absorb the news then, slowly, the dots connect. Something *has* been simmering for months. I didn't know what, but I *felt* it. The air ripe with worry. Long phone calls. More visitors than usual. Amma and Naina talking late into the nights with a visiting American friend.

"Yes, Mytrae," Naina says. "You know Surya hasn't been doing well for some time now.

I nod.

"It's too ahead of its time. India's farmers simply aren't ready for this technology."

Surya Engines, the avant-garde harvesting equipment company he started with his friend Mukesh a few years after they returned from university in Illinois, has been writhing a slow and tortured death. For years I've grown accustomed to his coming home late, his face and eyes increasingly lined, not even unwinding on Sundays with family and Kingfisher beer as he used to. Worry oozes gray-heavy around legs of tables and backs of chairs and the space between everything so I don't bother him. Speak only when he asks me a question or two, his mind still in his factory with large, clanking machines, a desk piled high with thick files, and the dank smell of engine oil.

"Also, Amma's been very sick, as you know. Many people tell us her asthma will clear with the air quality there." He stretches his neck out to the right as he does when he's worried.

Amma *is* ill. And worsening. Her once-occasional attacks are now frequent. She was hospitalized twice, both times her heaving body bent double carried from our downstairs bedrooms up the stairs by emergency medics.

"Can't you get another job here?"

"I tried in Bombay, even Nigeria, but nothing worked out. Things are changing here. But the main thing is Amma's health.

That's why we think America's best. And your education. You can go to college there. Raghu will come with us for a month then he'll return to Manipal for medical school. After he finishes, he'll come to the U.S. I'll get a job." His eyes sparkle, like when he lights fireworks and darts away like a delighted street urchin. He had lived and worked in Illinois for a year after college. "But I don't know if they'll accept my experience from here. Something will work out. It'll all work out."

I look at Amma with a question mark. She presses her hanky to her nose. "What to do? I don't want to go but I'm not keeping well here. Not at all. You've seen me, no?"

I nod. How can I think of myself when she's sick? "When?" I ask.

"In about three months," Naina says. That'll give us time to rent the house, close Surya, and wind everything down.

I stare at him, my stomach writhing like a fish on a hook. But wait, I want to say. Why so far? Why go to a strange new land where everyone's so different? I don't want to go. Not to a strange new land where I don't know anyone. Leave my friends. I'm fifteen, not yet ready for the world. How can home be anywhere else but here? I look at our spacious home, its big windows opening to the sun. The last thing I want to do is leave.

My beautiful brown country.

In half an hour and a few sentences, life has become precarious as a bubble on an afternoon pond.

"You're throwing that sweet child to the wolves," Daadi warns Amma.

"She'll be okay." Amma's tone is flippant and strong, so Daadi won't worry. "We'll be with her."

"I don't know. You have to be careful. All those boys. That age…" Daadi trails off and looks at me worriedly. "She's so young and innocent. So unspoiled."

"I'll be fine, Daadi," I say. "Don't worry."

"Remember who we are, our family, and where we come from. Don't ever forget that."

"How can I, Daadi?"

"You'll have to be careful with her," counsels an aunt. "It's a difficult age."

"She's ripe for the plucking," another aunt says.

"We bring up our girls so carefully. Their culture's so different… so many boys, dating… be careful with her, so many influences and attractions. They can go bad so easily," my grand-aunt, cautions.

"She'll be fine," Amma shrugs off their fears. "She'll live at home with us while she goes to college."

I shrug off these fears too. I don't think about men. I'm only fifteen, not even close to a marriageable age. Besides, dating's for Americans. And I'm old enough to know what's what. Look away when men stare. Be a cold cucumber out in the world. Stand beside women at bus stops. Ignore catcalls. Stick out my elbows in crowded buses to escape gropes and squeezes. When they do grope my waist, breasts, or bum, I say *ooofff!* loudly, stare angrily, and elbow them, but hate that my protests only make them smile. Of course I'm old enough to know.

I'm worried what college will be like. Will I make any friends?

"Why don't you want to go?" ask my astonished friends. "It'll be so exciting. You'll have so many things to do, so many wonderful things to buy. The shops there are beautiful, big shopping malls, and you'll wear such nice clothes! You're so *lucky*, Mytrae!"

"I *don't* want to do or buy those things. I *have* enough and like things just as they are. And I don't want to leave *you*!" I look into their puzzled eyes, my heart already aching for their sweetness and fun. We navigate every detail of our lives together. Talk about our classes and teachers, study and prepare for exams together, eat hot samosas and *chaat* from street carts, jostle in buses from hanging straps, visit each others' homes on weekends, and wonder what we're going to do with our lives. Will I ever make friends there as sweet and dear as Arati, Sangeeta, Eliza, and Nina? How will I manage college all on my own?

"You'll have an American boyfriend," they tease. "Don't forget to write and tell us all about him, okay?"

I can't imagine *that*.

"Promise we'll be friends forever."

"Of course we will. I'll write to you often and tell you everything."

"I'll miss our bike rides," I tell my friend Nina. "And you!" From ten to sixteen, we have lived a five-minute bike ride from each other, shared a love of food and dogs, and rebelled against our parents' stringent rules.

"I'll miss you too!" She says, as we hug each other.

We cling to each other with long hugs, crying, vowing letters and lifelong friendship.

Every moment before we leave seems precious. One arm hanging out our Ambassador car window, my heart calls good-bye to the hustle and bustle of Hyderabad. To Vidyaranya, my old school, where everything was play. To *rickshahwallahs* pulling children to school. To the fruit vendors with *seethaphals*, guavas, papayas, grapes, and sweet limes piled high. To the policeman I waved to as a child going to school because I loved his black lacquered mustache that curled four inches on either side of his face, and his khaki shorts starched knife-stiff, fanning out six inches from his chocolate thighs.

Amma empties *Laughing Waters*, room by room, into others' homes and lives. Friends and strangers buy her precious furniture and knick-knacks. She gives each thing away like it's a part of her, telling each new owner the story of where and when she bought it. Naina's so busy declaring bankruptcy he doesn't have time to think about missing India. He's just moving forward, meeting with lawyers, accountants, immersed in stacks of files.

One by one, I bid good-bye to each garden alcove, rock, servant, and room in *Laughing Waters*. To my favorite trees and boulders along bike trails in Banjara Hills, making sure to furrow my memory with them. To trails on which Nina and I ride so much we've come to believe they're ours. To trails by the Nizam's summer palace, fortressed by a wall high enough to keep out the world, only we befriended the security guard who grins and waves cheerily as we sail in, wind in our hair, over acres and acres of rambling, unkempt gardens forgotten by time. To trails on open stretches of land upon which granite crags and boulders lie as though strewn by a giant wrist. This is the land I want to brand into my memory as the land from which I come.

This is the land I never want to forget.

I've jogged here before the sun bloomed. Rode my bike up and down hillocks on simmering afternoons. Watched herds of ambling water buffalo return from their evening waterings at the lake. And sat on my haunches on the copper earth to watch chameleons transform from burnished red-gold to ashen gray as dusk smolders with the smell of wet, steamy fresh cow dung. "I'll never forget you," I whisper, nestling in a favorite rock hollow, stroking its rough, sparkling granite, then pressing my ear to hear its *huuu-huuuummmmm*.

"I'll never forget you," I murmur as I embrace the trunks of sprawling tamarind, ashoka, and peepal trees, their bark rasping against my cheek. They sing, *eeeeee, aaaiieeee* and *we love you, child*. Wrap my arms around silvery gray bark of eucalyptus trees, regal kings and queens who whisper to the sky, *Go with love*. Especially the one beneath which we buried Caesar. The neem tree in our garden from which I stripped a twig like the servants do, chewing it till my mouth fills with bitter sap then brushed my teeth with its fibers. *Hiiii-hiiiiih*. The vast banyans with hanging branch-roots from which I swung as a girl.

"I'm leaving, but you're all in me."

I go to the bottom of the garden, where I played with the fairies as a girl. I can't see them now, but I know they're there. "Goodbye," I whisper. "Take care of *Laughing Waters*."

Goodbye, goodbye, goodbye. To you, to everything, to everyone I know. To my ending childhood.

To my sweet, warm, dusky land.

America hits me like a brick when we land in Roanoke, Virginia. *We're different!* How brown we are. How much our little family stands out with our black hair and Indian features. Suddenly, I want to cover up my brown skin, as centuries of British rule rises up in my throat. The way Indians bow and scrape before foreigners, my culture's fever for fair skin, British and "foreign" accents, education and things. In this sea of white, my brownness brands me inferior. Second class. I can never be their equal. I look to Amma and Naina for direction. But Naina's shoulders are hunched, his head bent with eyes looking upwards servilely. Amma, who's never thrown, stares at our new land unable to speak.

We stay with my aunt Roopa Aunty, Madhav Uncle, and their two sons till Naina finds work. My aunt and uncle introduce us to sanitized grocery stores, immaculate but empty streets, and Kentucky Fried Chicken. We watch *Charlie's Angels*, *Laverne and Shirley*, and *M.A.S.H.* Devour popcorn shrimp, hot dogs, and ice cream sandwiches. We buy Levi's and T-shirts on sale, trinkets at dollar stores, and Amma sews me skirts from Butterick patterns. In small return for my aunt and uncle's kindness and generosity, Amma cooks; I vacuum, help in the kitchen, wash dishes, do laundry, and type Naina's letters. And mow their acre yard in my new flamingo-pink shorts that make my cheeks flush and want to hide. I want to wear what American girls wear but stopped wearing shorts in India after I menstruated, like other girls my age.

One month after our arrival, Raghu crams his suitcase with jeans and checkered shirts and returns to India for four years of medical school in Manipal. He'll be back after he graduates. Three months later, Naina gets a mechanical engineering job in Winston-Salem, North Carolina. I roll the city's hyphenated name on my tongue. Two names. Doubly glamorous. He's overjoyed. "It has two of the largest tobacco companies in the country and is much bigger than Lexington," he raves. He looks at me. "Even a university for you." We're relieved we don't have to depend on my uncle and aunt any longer. Naina buys a used beige Chevrolet for three thousand dollars that sails like a large ship upon the roads. Sitting in its backseat, watching him proudly shift its automatic gears, it seems we might be arriving somewhere after all.

My parents buy a house in Lewisville, a stolid suburb of Winston-Salem. Reading the neighborhood names as we drive there—Salem, Pfafftown, Bermuda Creek, and Reynolda—I feel like I've landed in a book of faraway lands I read about as a girl. I wonder, how we, with names of Rama Mohan, Kamala, and Mytrae, and family name of Reddy, will fit into a town called Winston-Salem.

Our new house has two bedrooms and a huge backyard. We quickly buy the essentials: mattresses, a used card table and folding chairs for a dining table, a sofa, and TV. Amma's happy to finally have a place of her own and clucks about, setting it up, decorating it with knick-knacks from India. She stocks up on dals, rice, and spices at the only Indian store in town. "We'll furnish the house a room at a time," she explains more to herself than me. "We've just come and it'll take some months for us to afford the rest." She combs furniture stores, a cloud of wistfulness hanging around her as she strokes the back of an expensive sofa and sighs at an exquisite lamp. She spends afternoons watching *I Love Lucy*, *As the World Turns*, and Alfred Hitchcock movies. Nights, she curls up in a kaftan on our new tan and beige checkered couch, sips Mountain Dew, and watches Masterpiece Theatre.

Naina's excited with his new job. "Fairchild Industries is a large airplane-parts manufacturer," he tells us. "The job's below my experience level, but it's a start with a good, solid company." He's happy and relieved, but a shadow of indignity flashes across his face. Good. Solid. Words he often uses. Words I associate with him. It pains me that he has to be servile here to provide for us, and that this is the way we all need to behave in this new land.

Weekends he tirelessly mows the yard, sweat pouring down his bare chest in the 80-degree summer heat, pausing to hobnob with the Tuttles and the Joneses on either side of our chain-link fence to learn about dogwood, maples, the best gardening supplies stores, and barbecue tips for our Saturday tandoori chicken. Though he didn't touch a hoe in India, he's most at peace and in a quiet gentleness when he labors, communing with soil and loam in the tame wilderness of his yard.

"You'll live with us, of course," Amma says. "It's a new culture and you won't understand many things. They have different values. We come from a different culture and must keep ours. You're a girl. You're young and impressionable. We don't want you getting spoiled."

I'm glad I'm going to live at home too. America's too daunting. Even though we speak English fluently with our Indo-British accent, everything else is a foreign language.

"We'll have to get a loan." Naina says.

"A loan!" I feel embarrassed. I never worried about money in India.

"It's a private school and it costs money. But we want you to have a good education rather than going to the state colleges. They have something called work-study where you'll work a few hours every week and this helps us get a loan. I'll ask for you to work in the library."

I haven't worked before. But a library sounds nice. Anything with books.

We're relieved the University accepted my Indian high school certificates and didn't murmur about my age. I just turned sixteen. Indian high school has ten grades after which we attend college, of which I'd attended a year. I passed my SATs after immigrating.

Naina takes me to Wake Forest University to sign up and I walk in awe through its green expansive campus with stately brick buildings. An American university seems like a wonder of the world compared to Kasturba Gandhi Women's College's small, ancient, rundown buildings. The Quad lined with dorms has an exquisite chapel with pillars like Greek buildings. So noble. So dignified. A temple of learning. I can't believe every subject has its own building. I could happily get lost in the massive library for months. Working there would be heaven. I feel so very lucky.

"My-?" The woman beside me in Western philosophy class doesn't finish my name. She *can't* finish my name. She stares at me, her face a question mark, lips and cheeks rounded as if filled with pins. I may as well have sneezed and asked her to repeat the sound. She's afraid to offend me, but can't say "thray-yee". Like everyone else, she stops dead in her tracks. Thr, the Sanskrit syllable, is impossible for Americans. No one can say it, not properly that is.

"-tray-yee," I offer, lopping off the 'h.' After three months in the U.S., the Southern "Maaah" ("My") is endearing.

"-tray-yee," she echoes with an embarrassed smile. Grateful. "Maaah-try-yee?" She says it slowly, cautiously, like she's trying to locate a grain of sand in a mouthful of food.

"Yes, that's right!" I smile encouragingly.

She nods, mouthing the syllables to herself. Looks at me and smiles, then turns to the woman on her right.

Another conversation dead-ended because of my name.

If my brown skin screams that I'm different, my name is a red light that screeches conversations to a halt. Everyone looks away. It's too much work. Like I'm just as unpronounceable, unreachable.

Some try "My-tree?" which makes my skin crawl. To my horror, one or two even helpfully offer, "Myrtle?" Any way and every way they try, no one can say My-thray-yee. Their tongues just don't work that way. But I don't want to be a language lesson every time I meet someone. I must come up with something which they can't massacre. So. "My-tray." That's it.

"My-tray, like my tray of food," I tell them. I cringe to dilute it so, and feel guilty to amputate my Indianness, (what would Daadi say!?), but it's the closest and most bearable pronunciation. So, with their Southern drawls, I become "Maah-traaiiy," which makes me wince and smile at the same time.

It'll do.

Freshman year at Wake Forest University is bewildering. I'm completely at sea with Baptists, Demon Deacons, American football, baseball, sororities, fraternities, preppies, panty raids, and add-a-beads. I have no idea how to fit in or make friends with the almost all-white, mostly North Carolinian, students in preppy clothes. I go to freshman orientations and International Student get-togethers, but after short introductions and polite smiles, the Germans, French, and Argentinians look past me and talk to each other. I wish I could disappear into the ground.

I'm thrilled when I spot two Indian women who look like sisters one day. As I walk up to them, I hear their American accents. "Hi," I say with an excited smile. They stare at me like icicles then turn their backs and continue talking to each other. My smile fades and my heart sinks. If *they* don't want to talk to me, who will?

I expected a warm, inviting embrace as happens in India, where we reach out to newcomers and invite them into our fold. Here, there's a social language of cool I have no idea how to speak, and it's every man and woman for themselves.

I want to be cool. But everything about me screams *not*. My skin. My hair. My clothes. How can I fit in or be accepted in unfashionable Sears and J.C. Penney clothes, or ones Amma sews from patterns? We can't afford Belk's or Dillard's. To make things worse, my thick, straight, unstyled hair falls to my waist because Amma won't let me cut it. So I wear my one pair of Levi's, or plaid skirts with knee-high argyle socks.

"It's my clothes," I wail to Amma. "Everyone wears such expensive clothes. They look like they've stepped out of a Belk's catalog."

"It's a private university, Mytrae. They've been living here all their lives, come from rich families, and have built up their wardrobes over the years. We've just come. In time, you'll have clothes like theirs," she says.

I feel guilty for wanting more when Naina works hard. I don't complain again. Yet even as I long to fit in, I'm conflicted about the preppy girls' fashions with add-a-bead chains, papadillos, and mostly beige, gray, and black clothes. I think their color choice dull, and miss the vibrant fuchsia pinks, tangerine oranges, lime greens, and turquoises of my homeland. How can only a few colors be fashionable when nature adorns herself in a multitude of shades?

Also, I wonder why American girls chase men like they're all that matter. Why, with so much education at their fingertips, would marriage be their main goal? My Indian friends and I assume our families will choose our husbands. Though I envy American women's flirtations and dating lives, I also feel sorry for them.

Homesick, I yearn for my Indian girlfriends, all giggles and shyness, yet bold in ways I'm accustomed to. I write them letter after letter describing my strange new life, but no number of sheets can convey my lostness.

"You're in a country where you can do anything. Meet anyone. Go anywhere. You've arrived!" they reply, delighted for me.

But I have no sense of arriving anywhere.

After months of failed attempts, I slowly grow another skin over my brown one—disbelief. Why would any white person ever want to be my friend? When anyone does talk to me, I'm painfully shy. In between classes, I sit alone in the Student Union, studying, and eat my bologna, lettuce, and tomato sandwich, and Lay's potato chips. When I pass groups of students, I hug my pile of books closer to my chest. When tears of loneliness well, I walk through library stacks that tower like wise banyans to feel the lofty presence of books, marvel at the different subjects, and read Keats or Shelley at a secluded desk. And when I emerge into the sunlight, my heart is a little quieter and somewhat soothed.

"What do you think, Ms. Reddy?" Dr. David Smiley calls on me in Western History. "What do you think about Claudius' strategy in the Roman conquest of Britain in 43 A.D.?"

I freeze. My skin burns, conscious of twenty pairs of eyes on me. What can I say? Do I have anything intelligent to say? A few scattered thoughts flash through my brain. Nothing of consequence. I can't say *those*. I'd sound stupid.

Ms. Reddy. Dr. Smiley addresses his students as Mr. or Ms. I've never been called that before. Never been treated with such respect before, like I'm an adult, an actual person. Certainly not by a man in his sixties. But he waits, rotund and bespectacled in his navy blue bowtie with parrot green polka dots.

My head feels like it might float away. I piece together a couple of stray thoughts and squeak them out. I can't imagine they're important. Were they even related to his question or did I just babble incoherently? But he listens, tilting his head, as though his ears are open flowers. His soft brown eyes look at me like my words matter, like *I* matter. He smiles at me. Kindly, not irritated or scornful. What I said is okay. He's not going to laugh. He nods approvingly, looks at me a little longer, then expands on what I just said. I exhale. He didn't say I was stupid. I can learn to think for myself. *I* can have opinions too.

I think back to my Indian teachers who treated us like we were children. Scold and shame us, "*Tchah*! Don't you know anything?" in front of the class when we fumbled. To do well was to memorize and repeat word for word from our textbooks. But here in Dr. Smiley's class, in English Literature, Romantic Literature, Music Theory, Music History, Anthropology, and almost all my classes, I'm asked what *I* think about something.

And something small and green begins to grow inside me, sprouting one shoot after another, eager and hungry for more.

Then there's the whole other issue of men to contend with. Sitting next to handsome men in class, their rugged Western features, lean, muscular physiques, and self-assuredness stirs my libido in ways it didn't with Indian men. But when a man speaks to me, I feel shy enough to shimmer into the walls. Besides, the unspoken cultural wall around dating looms tall and forbidding.

Peggy, our friendly neighbor, asks, "How do you like school, Mytrae?"

"Oh, the men are so good looking!" I grin. "I can't stop looking at them."

She laughs. "Well, it won't be long before you're dating!"

"No, she's never going to date," Amma retorts sharply.

My shoulders droop with the weight of her sentence. I wish she'd be more open when I feel ready to date, but my arranged marriage feels like a future I cannot escape. Like Amma and almost every other woman in my family and in India, I'll be introduced to two or three appropriate men my family carefully selects, and I'll need to decide after a couple of meetings. It's a fate I haven't thought too much about and seems distant. I *am* curious about dating but feel completely naive about it.

Walking on the quad one day, a tall, broad, black male student approaches me. "Hi," he smiles.

"Hi." An unnameable unease sweeps through my body.

"I'm Tyrone."

"I'm Mytrae."

"I've seen you around," he says. "Where are you from?"

"India."

"I play on the football team. Do you like football?"

"No, I don't understand the game."

He pauses. "Your hair's so beautiful. Would you like to have coffee with me?"

"Coffee?" I repeat like I've never heard of it before, unnerved by his compliment and attention.

"Yeah, coffee," he smiles, looking me up and down.

"No, I have to go to class." I shift my weight to my left foot, uncomfortably.

"How about another time?"

"I have to go." I nervously hurry away.

"See you later," he calls cheerily.

See me later he does. Sizzling with sensuality, he approaches me a few more times, persistent yet respectful. Each time, that unnamable unease arises in me. I don't want to be attractive, not to any man. I don't want to *be* attracted to anyone. I've grown up fending off men and their gazes on Indian streets. I've grown up knowing it's dangerous to flirt with or encourage men. Now, even talking to a man I haven't been introduced to in a proper setting makes me feel like I'm loose in people's eyes.

"I have to go to class," I say abruptly each time.

I learn to quickly cross to the other side of the quad when I see him. To my relief, he stops after some months.

"Why don't you bring in the pieces you last played?" Dr. Goldstein suggests when we first meet. He's tall and lanky, delicate even, in his thirties. He has a slender, sensitive face and soft brown eyes that slant downwards. His shoulders stoop slightly in a camel corduroy jacket with suede elbow patches. His large sun-filled office has two baby grand pianos, a music system, a wall of shelves stacked with music books, modern art and music posters from concerts on his walls. It's inviting, unlike the stark convent rooms in Hyderabad with a solitary bleeding Jesus on the wall and one worn upright piano. The nuns who taught me, Sister Carmel and Sister Philomena, counted "1-a-and-ah, 2-a-and-ah…" beating time with a thin, long stick. Sister Philomena beat students' hands when they made a mistake. I'm shy to learn from a man, but Dr. Goldstein's soft voice eases my nervousness. I feel oddly safe with him. He's like the depths of a tranquil lake.

I take my Trinity College of Music books for my first lesson. He picks out a Beethoven Rondo and plays a few bars. "How do you like it?" he asks, his thin lips slanting in a smile.

Neither Sister Carmel nor Sister Philomena ever asked me such a question. "I like it."

"Perhaps you can also learn a couple of Bach inventions and Chopin preludes. Buy the Verlag edition."

And so we begin. Lessons from him are unusual. He's gentle, respectful, and always interested in my thoughts and feelings about each piece. Each week, after I play for him, he leans over the piano to mark dynamics, interpretations, and musicalities with colored pencils in my book. As the pieces develop over the semester, so does my fascination with them. It's as though each one takes root inside me. Each week, I bring in new shoots, buds, leaves, which he always recognizes. When I play a phrase in my own way, he notices it immediately, "This is wonderful," he says in his gentle, resonant voice. "Not just for this piece but for what it means about your musicianship." He teaches me that to know a piece is to enter into its playfulness and its profundity. To let it sing through me. I learn to wait, to listen to the notes and phrases until they reveal the composer's intention, clear as ink streaming from pen onto manuscript paper, then find my own.

I delight in my lessons, never having been taught this way. All week I wait, excitedly, for the next. What will he hear in my next lesson? No one's ever given me this kind of attention before. Apart from my music, I feel like my soul and I are sprouting shoots and flowers.

Every two weeks, Dr. Goldstein holds a studio evening for his students to perform. My first time, I play the Bach Inventions No. 8 and 13, as do two other students. Dr. Goldstein asks everyone to compare our interpretations.

A senior says, "Mytrae's interpretation isn't Bach-like."

I cringe.

Dr. Goldstein says, "But the line, phrasing, and musicality are completely unique. How she plays speaks and that's what interpretation is: how can each one of you make each piece your own expression?"

More than what he says, I brim over with gratitude that he speaks up for me. Nobody's done that for me before.

In the solitary practice rooms, just large enough for an upright piano, music seeps into me. It finds its way to the song of my cells, the song of my body. As I play Beethoven's Sonata Opus 2, No. 3, Chopin Nocturnes, and Bach's Partita No. 4, something happens. Their melodies and harmonies touch some melancholy depths in me, from before memory and beyond. From where do such feelings arise? From where such loss and longing?

And something happens as I encounter this great beauty. My soul stirs, awakes, and reaches towards music, like a sunflower lifts its face to the sun. And in that beauty I see myself, my own reflection. This, this great beauty, humanity, and sacredness is who I am. It is my home and I am home in it.

I weep with sorrow for my long separation from it, and joy to find this beauty which knows me more deeply and profoundly than any human being.

Our eyes catch in the crowded cafe, its air greasy with onion rings and French fries. Olive skin. Dark brown ringlets tumbling to her waist. An upturned nose, chiseled cheekbones on her heart-shaped face. She's more beautiful than goddess sculptures with her perfect features. And she's not white, like me! A rocket of hope streaks up my chest. Our eyes don't let each other go across students eating burgers and grilled cheese sandwiches and playing Pac-Man.

Should I approach her? She gestures with the slender long cigarette in her hands to the chair opposite her. I smile, and slosh a little tea from my Styrofoam cup on the sticky carpet as I hurry towards her. We smile as I sit down. There are two empty cups of coffee to her right. She's on her third.

"Farahnaz," she purrs, her voice like thick honey.

"Mytrae."

"Where are you from?"

"India. And you?"

"My family immigrated from Iran this summer. The Shah, you know," she gestures.

I nod. Scores of people fled Iran after the revolution last year. "When did you come?"

"This summer."

"How do you like it so far?"

"It's still new. They don't know much about other cultures, do they?"

I laugh. And so we begin to get to know each other. She's a day student and lives at home with her parents, too. Her English is impeccable, her accent sultry. Her regal confidence and exquisite clothes reveal her family's wealth, and very, very upper class-ness.

"My father was an ambassador. We had to leave. We didn't want to but things became intolerable. We practically had to leave overnight." A shadow falls on her flawless face.

In that instant, seeing her ache for her homeland, I know I've made my first friend at Wake Forest. She's two years older than me and several years more self-assured. She lights cigarette after cigarette, tosses her tousled curls like a woman of the world, and talks passionately about world affairs and politics.

"They're like children, no?" she says about Americans, waving her hands with rings on almost every finger. "The men still have to grow up. They're boys, not yet men. And they think they know it all. The man I marry will be very different. My father will want me to marry an Iranian. I will have to meet him, of course, and like him, but when I choose he will be Someone."

I drink her in. I wonder why the male students don't swarm around her and ask her out, for, to me, she's beautiful as Cleopatra. But apart from her skin color, she emits an air of superiority.

Like me, her face and body are expressive, unlike Americans. Our sentences rise and fall like the coo of doves. Our eyebrows furrow and lift as we speak. Our hands gesticulate like conductors. Our emotions play on our faces. Like me, she doesn't fully understand Americans or fit in here, and they don't fully understand her or her world. Though I'm so different from her shy, naive, not at all sure of myself, and think American men are men compared with Indians—we're grateful for each other. We befriend each other in the greasy, smoky cafe to drink endless cups of coffee and tea, stroll around campus, visit each other at home, and lie under wide maples and magnolias to talk and study.

And so we create our brown oasis of two.

I work on Schumann's *Papillons* Op.2 for a competition. Like its title, it's a composition more delectable and delicate than any I've played. In my lessons, Dr. Goldstein reads stories and letters from Schumann's life aloud to me so the piece unfurls like a filigreed fairy tale in my fantasy.

The evening of the competition, Farahnaz asks, "Are you nervous?"

"I feel like a performing dog at a circus," I reply. "I'm so excited, I can't wait to get on stage. I don't get nervous."

People stream into the magnificent Wait Chapel where a Steinway grand awaits on stage. The rows fill up with music friends, faculty, my parents, and other students' families. One by one, we perform. At the end of four hours, the judges huddle then ask another student and me to replay the last five minutes of our pieces. After a second huddle, they announce her the winner.

Some of the faculty protest at the replay. Dr. Goldstein glowers. "I don't like that they did that. It wasn't fair. You played beautifully."

I glow at his protectiveness and care. I didn't expect to win as a sophomore, for the juniors and seniors play so much better than me. And I'm so filled with making music, bringing to life the fantasy of my collage and the deliciousness of that beautiful evening, that winning doesn't seem important.

The next day I receive a letter marked "Special delivery" from

Dr. Goldstein. My heart leaps to see his handwriting and I tear open the envelope.

Dear Mytrae,

Last night I felt that I did not adequately express to you the pleasure I experienced in your performance of Papillons. *I did not intend to speak simply as a teacher congratulating his student for satisfactory work. What I meant to convey was the genuine delight of a musician who had the opportunity to hear a beautifully conceived and executed performance of a sensitive and delicate composition. The success with which you capture the charm and spirit of* Papillons *is exceptional. Furthermore, it is something which cannot merely be taught: the student must have her own ingrained musicality with which to learn it. Quite aside from the very good progress you have made over the last three semesters, last night's performance was outstanding.*

Very sincerely,
Louis Goldstein

I read it over and over in my room. How beautiful I felt playing last night. I became the music, as I always do. Became each exquisite filigreed moment in *Papillons.*

Later, I show it to my parents while they're watching Dan Rather on the CBS Evening News. I hope they'll be proud of me, that maybe with the letter they'll understand a little more why I want to play music. That I'm actually good enough to do it.

"Why did he write to you?" Amma's tone is suspicious.

Why shouldn't he?

"It was nice of him to write," Naina says begrudgingly, looking at me curiously.

Their words cut me. I shift from one foot to another. An awkward hush falls between us. I wish I hadn't shown it to them. They make what's so beautiful, dirty. They don't understand. Know such beauty. What music means to me. And what it's like to enter into such beauty with a wonderful teacher like Dr. Goldstein. My music teachers and friends do, but they never will. There's no point to speak of such things. It's like when I was a child and they didn't understand magic and the fairies.

I take the letter from Naina as they stare at me, then resume watching the news. I retreat to my room. I read it again. He thought it important enough to send a letter by Special Delivery. What he has to say can't wait till our lesson next week. He wanted me to know right away. In writing. That he liked my playing.

I feel special in a way I never have before.

I drive home from campus feeling like a comet streaking through the sky, my fingers still playing Beethoven's *Waldstein* on the steering wheel. I've been practicing it for three hours, and my heart is a blazing sun aglow with its music, harmonies, and passion. If I am to do anything at all in life, anything worthwhile, it is this.

And this alone.

Music.

"I *must*," I say out loud, for I'm about to burst. "I must follow my heart. It's the only thing worthwhile. To not do it is to not live."

Music has sung its way into my heart as nothing else has. I must follow it wherever the path will lead. Everything else is gray, vapid, nothing. Certainly not medicine, engineering, or law like my parents want. I don't care how much I have to fight them.

"I want to major in music," I ask-tell them for the nth time at dinner.

"Don't be stupid. You're not going to major in it." Amma's thick eyebrows knit angrily.

"I'm going to. I love it."

"What will you do with music?" Naina scorns. "You can't make a living with it. Nobody does it. There aren't any jobs."

"Yes, there are. There are plenty of jobs and I want to go to graduate school."

"You're not good enough. Do you know how good you have to be to have a career in it?" Amma waves a spatula wildly.

"Dr. Goldstein said I can do it."

"Yes, but down the road when life gets tough you won't be able to do it. You're too young to know anything about life."

I stare at them, silent and stubborn. I refuse to have a life like theirs, without beauty. I am very relieved and happy for Amma that her asthma is much better since we immigrated two years ago, but I chafe at how much my parents cling to staying Indian. Amma watches *General Hospital, As The World Turns,* TNT's *Love in the Afternoon* movies, and plays tennis, but mixes mostly with Indians. She socializes with the small Indian community, talks with Roopa Aunty and other relatives, pines for India and her life there, and is always saying how superior Indian culture is to American. Though Naina grows peonies and petunias, barbecues chicken, guffaws at Benny Hill and *The Beverly Hillbillies*, and steals glances at gorgeous blondes, his roots dig deep in his love of tandoori chicken and lamb *biryani*, his fierce loyalty to his extended family, and my mother.

"We thought you could do medicine, but you don't want it. You don't want engineering either, even though you could. Why can't you do something professional like everyone else? Be practical. Music is fine for your enjoyment and it's good you're learning it, but it's not a career," Naina says.

"I'm not good in biology or math. I got a D in biology. And I'm struggling in calculus."

"You just came and are still getting used to college here. If you work harder, you can."

"I can't. Besides I don't want to. There are so many other subjects that people major in here. Why should I do only those three?"

"We won't allow you to do music. We're telling you for your own good. Nobody does music. Look at Seema and Deepika. They've done medicine and are doing very well. Or Indrani, Latha, and Uma. They're engineers. They have good jobs and make good money. Why can't you be like them?"

That is the issue. Why can't I be like everyone else?

We've been feverishly arguing about it for most of my sophomore year, as I have to declare my major. Every day I feel more and more adamant about music.

"The only way we'll allow you to major in it is if you minor in computer science," they finally concede.

Computer science? Only people without imagination or sensitivity do that.

"It's just a backup in case music doesn't work out for you," Naina wheedles. "So many people are doing it. So-and-so and so-and-so."

"Yes, but *I* don't want to. I hate calculus! How well can I do in computer science?"

"We don't care. The only way you can major in music is if you minor in computer science," is Amma's granite ultimatum.

So with a disturbing sense of self-betrayal, I write "major in music and minor in computer science" on the form in the registrar's office. Okay, I'll blunder through a few horrible courses. As long as I can have my precious Beethoven and Bach.

One evening I wait by the door of the music building for Naina to pick me up. Ward, a pianist in my cohort, waves to me from the other end of the corridor, and lopes towards me. We sit beside each other in Music Theory and Music History and talk music sometimes. Or about a performance and pianistic style at Rep Hour or a recital. We like and respect each other as musicians.

"Waiting for your dad?" he asks, leaning a languid shoulder on the wall opposite me.

"Yes." I'm suddenly shy to be with him, alone in the corridor.

He's tall and good-looking. Perfectly proportioned. Of all the men in my classes, I'm most attracted to him and his effortless, panther-like sensuality. His long, wavy auburn hair hangs about his ears like Keats or Shelley and shouts artist. At Rep Hour or recitals, he listens, one leg crossed over the other, head tilted away from the performer, fingers against a cheek, like he's listening to the stars. I like him because he's unique, has a fragile, unworldly sensitivity like me, and doesn't at all want be like anyone else.

"I really liked your performance of *Papillons*." His expressive hands move the air like silk butterflies. "You played with a beautiful vulnerability." His soft brown eyes look into mine. He means it. He really heard me, my music. My body stirs with his nearness.

"Thanks. It's such a beautiful piece. I love playing it."

We talk about recent performances, technique, how good Dr. LeSiege, our Music Theory professor is, and slowly our conversation turns to where he's from, and where I'm from. I grow warmer. It's hard not to stare at his full lips. Hard to stay with the exactness of words and thoughts while the space between us swells, dense and steamy. My brain and legs feel woozy and my body feels like it's evaporating with desire. I lean against the wall.

Naina drives up in his white Honda to the front of the building.

"I have to go," I say quickly, flustered that Naina might see me with him.

"It's nice talking with you," Ward smiles. As the door swings shut behind me and I hurry to the car, I feel his eyes on my back, watching me.

"Who was that?" Naina asks.

"Oh, just a student in my Music Theory class."

In the following weeks, an open question pulses, expectant and sweet, when Ward talks with me. But I keep our conversations short and about music, hoping he won't take them in a different direction. I wouldn't know what to say if he did. I can't encourage him. More isn't possible, however curious and attracted I am.

My friend Nina from Hyderabad visits for a week before starting college in Berea, Kentucky. She's ecstatic to be away from her strict parents. She's going to study business as her parents want her to.

"I can't believe I'm here in the U.S.! Did you ever imagine we'd be here together, Myt?" she asks.

"I'm so excited for you. You're lucky you'll live in the dorms without your parents on your back."

Her visit makes me bold. Chafe at my parents' rules. So one day, while we window-shop at a mall, I tell her, "I want to cut my hair!"

"Why do you want to cut it? It's so beautiful."

"It's almost to my hips! Amma won't let me cut it. I just want a trim."

"What will Auntie say?" she asks worriedly. Her mother is as strict as mine.

"Oh, she won't be able to tell. Just two inches." We walk into Supercuts and she watches anxiously while they trim my hair.

"Can you tell?" I ask her after it's done.

"Yes, I can. Just a little. But what are you going to tell Auntie? She'll kill you!"

"When I'm with her, I'll just walk and sit holding my head up so it looks longer in the back."

"Silly, how long can you do that for? She'll definitely notice."

Amma didn't notice. A few days after Nina left for Berea, after I washed my hair, Amma said, "Let me comb your hair, Mytrae."

I'm nervous. We don't, as some mothers and daughters do, pretty ourselves together. But I don't want to raise any suspicion by refusing. So I sit on my bed and hand her my comb. She stands behind me and begins to comb it. I look upwards a few inches so it will seem like my hair falls to my hips. I'm a little scared but pretend to be calm.

"Your hair looks shorter." She sounds surprised. "Did you cut it?"

"No, I didn't."

"But it's much shorter. You must have done something. Did you cut it?"

"I didn't. How could I have cut it?"

"You must have. It looks so much shorter."

She knows. There's no way out. My shoulders sag. "I got it trimmed when Nina was here."

She clutches my hair in a bunch and digs the comb into my scalp. "You *what*? How *dare* you? Your beauty is your hair. You know that. You're an Indian girl. You're not going to become like these white girls and cut your hair. Who do you think you are? You *have* to listen to us and maintain our culture. Wait till I tell Naina." She flings the comb on the bed and goes to the kitchen.

I don't say a word. She seethes the rest of the afternoon and I closet myself in my room, buried in biology and music history. When Naina comes home after work, I hear her angry voice in the kitchen. Here it comes. He's going to yell at me. It was just two inches. Why are they so angry? I have to cut it *some* time. I haven't cut it in the two years I've been here. Two years! How long is it supposed to grow before they let me cut it? Below my bum? To my knees?

Soon he comes into my room, his face dark and grim. "Amma told me you cut your hair."

I'm on my bed, my music history text open on my lap. My eyes widen, afraid at the stern clench of his jaw. He closes the door walks towards me, his eyes narrow, lips pursed with rage. "How dare you?" he barks. I shrink, grip my book tight against my chest. "We're Indians. And you're an *Indian girl*. Do you understand? And how *dare* you lie!" he yells. Lifts his arm above his head and begins to beat me.

"Don't, don't!" I scream. Twist away from him. My arms go up around my head.

He thrashes me with all his strength on my shoulders, my arms, my face again and again. "How *dare* you disobey us. *Bad* girl. You're getting spoiled here. Don't you *ever* lie to us again. Have you no shame? You're *not* going to become like these American girls!"

I fall on my bed, sobbing. He continues to pound my shoulders and back. I can't think. His sweat is rank as stale garlic. My face buries into my cream quilted bedcover printed with rose sprays. The mattress bounces and the polyester grazes rough against my cheek with each blow. I lose track of time.

"Don't *ever* do it again without telling us or you'll see what you get. We've been too soft and good with you. We'll send you back to India if you don't behave yourself." He pulls away, sweating, breathing hard. He storms out.

I lie there, trembling. After my sobs stop, I turn out the light and crawl under my bedcovers. I lie in the dark, listening to their low voices at dinner. A shiver goes through me every few minutes. He's never beaten me before. Never thought he would. I remember when I was a girl, how I peeked from the doorway while he chased Raghu around the twin beds in our bedroom, thrashing him when he could lay his hands on him. Amma was the one who beat me, and she hasn't since I was ten or eleven. I'm too big for her now.

I never expected him to do this.

I gently touch my tender shoulders and back. I don't know what's worse: my aching body, not being allowed to make simple choices like students my age, or that they don't understand what it's like to find my way in this new land. They can't send me back. I won't give them reason to. I'll just have to go along with what they say. I'll do what I always do. Pretend to go along, tell them only what they want to hear, and live a whole other life inside.

Like I always have.

How ironic they want me to go to college. It's carrying me far, far away from their choking ways and rules. Away from them I'm discovering my own mind. My own heart. In this country, I can choose and pursue what *I* love, not what *they* want me to do.

I toss and turn that night. Music, I promise myself fiercely, no matter how long or short my hair is, will be my path to freedom and beauty. In two years I'll go to graduate school. Then I'll be free. Free of them. Free of having to be Indian. Free to do what I want, what I love.

Cut my hair.

And listen to the song of my soul.

3

Evan

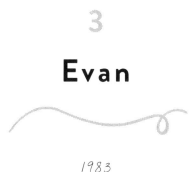

1983

Evan's hand rests on his heart, abdomen billowing, his long, lean legs planted wide apart. His rich tenor fills the fluorescent practice room with Schubert's *Der Erlkönig,* and sometimes quavers on its higher pitches. Between singing and instruction from his burly voice teacher, Evan smiles down at me on the piano seat as I accompany him. Tall, lithe, and broad shouldered, his sweatshirt and Levi's reveal his well-proportioned frame. His slender face has a broad forehead, precise nose, and sensitive cheekbones. Lush, brown hair falls to one side over dark brown searching eyes and intelligent-looking eyeglasses. I smile back from my bench at the Baldwin baby grand, making sure not to flirt.

"You play with so much passion," Evan says after his lesson, his eyes traveling down my waist-length black hair. "You really get the piece, don't you?"

"Thanks, I love it," I smile, gathering my books from the piano stand. "Schubert's simply gorgeous."

"The left hand's so difficult." He leans into the baby grand piano's curve.

"Yeah, it's a bear! But so dramatic! I love when the father's galloping wildly through the forest. We're with him on that stormy dark night, feeling his desperation to save his son. You bring that feeling out really well."

"You think so? I'm trying."

"Yeah, especially his anguish when he discovers his son's dead."

"Oh yes, I love that part. So dark and tragic." He pauses. "How's your application process going for graduate school?"

I tell him about my upcoming auditions.

"I'm sure you'll get into a great school."

"Thanks! See you next week!"

I'm shyly flushed and pleased by his attention. But I don't want to lead him on. When friends ask me about my non-existent love life I joke, "There's no way! My parents would ship me back to India!"

I'm determined to let nothing get in the way of my dream to go to graduate school in music.

Besides, Evan's a biology major so doesn't fit into my music life, I reason, as I prepare for my senior recital and graduate school auditions. Nor my fantasy of concert tours with a musician lover someday.

I lean against the wall in the corridor by the practice rooms, massaging my hands as I take a break.

Evan walks by. "Hey. You've been practicing for hours, haven't you? Let me show you something. Come, sit."

I can't let him do that! What if someone sees us?

"It'll help you," he offers again.

'No' is on my lips but something in his tone and eyes makes me hesitate. Trust. He cares, he isn't coming on to me. "What is it?"

He gestures for me to sit. We sit on the wide steps of the carpeted staircase which curves like the interior of a giant cream seashell between floors of the Scales Fine Arts Center.

"Here, give me your hand." He takes my hand and begins to press and squeeze points on my right palm intently.

I'm shy to have a man touch me. And touch me *this* way. I hope no one I know walks by. My throbbing hand goes limp. "Ohhh, it feels so good."

"It's acupressure," he says. "You can press here, or here, or here. It's a really good way to take care of yourself. The amount you practice, your hands must ache."

My brown cupped palm rests slack and trusting in his square white hands, dark hair on their backs. I watch his sure, long, elegant fingers ease the tension in mine, which have never been so tended. Focused and unhurried, his head bent with intent, it seems he can continue for hours. He doesn't seem to mind, I wonder with surprise. That, more than his tender, sure touch, makes me relax. Every cell in me oozes into softness. I sigh. Lean my head against the cream wall. Delicious minutes trickle by. Woozy, the air around me speckles.

The stairway door suddenly clangs opens. My head jerks up. My stomach lurches. Some of my music friends are walking down the stairs. Oh God! What will they think? Do they think I'm encouraging him? They pass, looking down at us, then turn back to smile at me, intrigued. The last thing I want is to be seen with a man. Word could get back to Amma and Naina.

I snatch my hand back.

He looks up in surprise.

"Thank you! That felt wonderful!" I stand up hurriedly, pick up my books, try to regain my clarity and composure, remember who I am, and that I can't do such things. I don't know whether I'm more flustered by how good his touch felt or that my friends saw us. "I have to go."

He says with genuine pleasure, "Remember you can do it too, just press those points."

"Thanks again." I hurry up the stairs, feeling his eyes on me. I must keep my distance. Not encourage him. If anyone tells my parents, it'll all be over.

Later, my friend Ellen teases, "He likes you!"

"He was just being nice," I retort flippantly, my heart thudding with fear.

I pace backstage at Brendle Recital Hall, Bach's *Italian Concerto* flowing through my mind and heart, my fingers rippling it against my thighs. For months I've rehearsed it, along with Mozart's Sonata in B-flat K.333, Schumann's Fantasie in C, and selections from Morris Pert's "Voyage in Space." Now, I simply want my senior recital to be over.

Dr. Goldstein finds me there. "You're trembling." He rests his hand on my shoulder.

"I can't believe tonight's finally here."

"You've done the work. Now just enjoy it." He hugs me. My cheek against the warm russet corduroy of his jacket, I breathe in his affection and a faint scent of licorice. I tremble with love and sadness. I'll miss him, his gentle, vast, beautiful being. Over four years, like a call and response chant, he's called out to my soul, which has awakened and responded with my own music. He's opened worlds of beauty to me. Portals to loveliness and passion. Led me to musical vistas I never imagined. The gardener of my musicality that has grown and bloomed with his teaching. And, he's wound into my heart and secret desires. We're close and warm as teacher and student, but we mostly speak about, and love, music together. He's in his mid-thirties, married, with two daughters and another on the way. I'm a twenty-year-old student. My recital marks the end of our duet and I don't want to leave the shelter of him and his teaching. All year I've looked forward to and dreaded this evening of my recital. Bittersweet, it's our grand finale.

"Thanks so much. I'll see you after."

Backstage, I sway to Schumann playing through me, my skirt swirling about my hips and legs. Amma tailored an ankle-length iridescent skirt for me from one of her precious silk saris. It shimmers around me and I feel like the ocean's center.

Sensual. Silky. Flowing.

Evan searches me out and hands me an exquisite violet iris and a card. "I wanted to give this to you in private without your friends around. You look gorgeous. You'll be fabulous tonight. Good luck!"

He gives me a long, warm hug. I'm touched that he came and surprised by his gift, and *very* glad he came backstage—my parents are in the audience.

When I walk onstage, the hall is almost full. I didn't expect so many people to come. I play, pouring myself into the music, into inner realms of sound, light, passion, rainbows of feelings, and exquisite presence. For the Pert, I asked the light technician to play with colors to match the music. The piece, a space voyage, rockets the listener from Earth and whizzes them past Saturn's rings, pulsars, quasars, galaxies, asteroids, and black holes. As I play, the stage streaks, sparkles, and swirls with blue, green, pink, purple, and orange. And I feel the audience travel, transported across the cosmos with me. A together voyage.

At the end, I feel like a comet flying across the universe, radiant and high after sharing my deepest realms. I'm hugely relieved it's over, pleased with the parts that went well, and wincing over those that didn't.

Faculty and friends gather around, congratulating and hugging me.

"You played beautifully. I loved the Schumann."

"What a fascinating piece the Pert is!"

"You look ravishing!"

"You were great! Absolutely grand!"

I float, high on ambrosial support and love from my friends and the community I've made in four years.

My parents watch me, Amma in a beautiful silk sari and Naina in a navy blue suit. They hang back from the small crowd, but I can tell they're reassured to see faculty congratulating me. I look for Evan, but he isn't there. I'm disappointed but not surprised. He usually doesn't approach me when I'm with my music friends.

After the crowd thins, my parents come and hug me. "You played well, Mytrae," Naina says.

"The Schumann was beautiful," Amma says. "Naina forgot his camera at home,"

"I'm sorry, Mytrae," Naina says.

"Oh, that's okay."

I hadn't thought to take pictures. I'm just pleased they came. Maybe they won't think music is such a terrible choice after all.

After our graduation ceremony, Evan and I run into each other in the Student Union. "Congratulations!" He hugs me.

"Thanks. Congratulations to you, too!"

"What's next?"

"I'm going to UNC-Chapel Hill for graduate school in the fall." Amma and Naina finally gave in to my pursuing music. "What about you?"

Evan says, "My dad gave me some money as a graduation gift. I want to travel. I'm going to Israel and Europe for six months."

"Wow! That sounds great!"

"Wanna go?" he asks with a quizzical smile and twinkling eyes. His head tilts to one side, an eyebrow cocks with flirty invitation.

I stare at him in disbelief, marveling at his spontaneous, adventurous overture. Do you think I'd drop my plans to travel with you? I hardly know you! Even if I did... travel alone with a man? My parents would freak out. We're struggling for money. Besides, I'm off to graduate school.

"I can't, Evan. It sounds wonderful, though. I wish I could!" His free-spiritedness makes me feel wistful. "Have a great trip!"

"I'll write you," he promises.

He's just saying that. We're not friends, not really.

We hug and wave goodbye.

On a late North Carolina summer day, when sugar maples are a verdant green, the air sweet and moist with hickory, birch, and sweet gum, and a warm breeze blows, my parents drive me to

Chapel Hill. I'm going to get my master's in music with a specialization in piano performance. At the vast, unpretentious campus I see students of all nationalities and statuses, which makes me feel hugely relieved and at home. I won't stand out here like a brown berry among a field of wealthy snowdrops like I did at Wake Forest.

I have a teaching assistantship that pays my tuition. I'm delighted I won't be dependent on my parents anymore. Finally, at twenty, I'll be free of their stranglehold and live in a dorm like everyone else. I can barely restrain my delight.

We find my suite with four dorm rooms and a shared bathroom. Each room has two twin beds, worn carpeting, two desks, closets, and a window. No sign of a roommate yet. Either way, it'll be heaven.

"There's a sign on the bulletin board for a small second-hand fridge for fifteen dollars," Naina offers. "Shall I buy it for you?"

"That'll be nice. Thank you." He leaves to buy it and I start unpacking. Amma goes out to explore. They return soon.

"There's quite a large kitchen, but it's dirty." Amma wrinkles her nose, holding a Kleenex to it.

I sigh, yearning to be free of her ever-present criticism.

"That's OK, Kamala," Naina counters, setting the fridge down. "They're students. They'll manage."

"There are students from other countries but I don't see any Indians. The woman from Africa in your suite seems nice."

I nod, trying not to show my irritation. I don't want her intruding into my world, which she often does. I want to make my own friends without her judgments.

"I'm sure there are some. She'll meet them in time," Naina's tone mollifies. He plugs in the fridge.

"Oh, it's a good one!" I exclaim. "It even has a freezer."

"Yes, and it was so cheap too."

I can't wait for them to leave. I sit on my bed, legs fidgeting, trying to hide my excitement.

"So much dust!" Amma says. "You should scrub it down. The carpet's so dirty. Borrow a vacuum cleaner from someone."

"Eat well, Mytrae," Naina says.

"Yes, cook for yourself. You can make a few things now. They'll smell your spices and come running. And be careful. Don't stay out late. Come home before its dark. You're on your own now."

"And get a decent job. Try in the library or one of the offices."

"I will, Naina. I'll find something. Don't worry. I'll be fine."

Eventually, we lapse into silence.

"Shall we go, Kamala?" Naina asks.

Amma's shoulders sag. She nods. "Alright." Her tone is soft, her face wistful.

We amble down to the parking lot and pause, an awkward trio. They look anxious and scared. A tinge of guilt ripples through my belly. What will they do without me to fret about? Raghu will come to the U.S. in a year after medical school in India. I've dashed their hopes of being proud of my career with my passion for music. All they can look forward to, now, is my stellar match a few years down the road. I don't want to think about *that*. For me, graduate school is freedom. The doorway to the rest of my own life as *I* want to live it. But I can't tell them this, not yet. I have to find my way to it first. Then I'll let them down gently. Tell them I'm never going to live the life they want for me. Our eyes meet, then flicker away, the triangle of space between us churning with everything we don't talk about.

"Don't worry," I say. "I'll be fine."

"We should go," Naina looks at Amma. "Alright, Mytrae, take care of yourself. We'll call you tonight. Call us every weekend."

"Yes, yes, I'll call."

"Be careful at night," Amma warns. "Make sure you lock your door."

"Make sure you're in your room no later than 10," Naina shadows.

Amma hesitates, then her face grows grave. "Remember you're Indian. We have a rich heritage. Write to Daadi and Thatha once a month. They'll be happy to hear from you."

What she really means is: "Study well. Make us proud of you. Above all, don't lose connection with your culture. Especially your virginity." Letting a daughter attend graduate school in America is "letting her go to the wolves," as Daadi warned Amma before we immigrated.

I nod. "I will."

We hug, my body impatient in their embrace. They look at me for a while then climb into their white Honda Civic. I wave as they drive away, then eagerly bound up the stairs two at a time to my new life.

I get a job waitressing at Papagayo's, a Mexican restaurant on Franklin Street, Chapel Hill's main drag, to pay for my expenses.

"I've found a job as a waitress," I excitedly tell my parents.

"How can you think of doing *that*? It's menial work," Amma scolds.

"Why can't you find something in the library?" Naina's grouses.

"It's what I want to do!" I retort, grateful for miles of separating telephone wires.

How can anything to do with food be menial? I'm ushered into an exotic world of hearty burritos, chimichangas, crunchy tacos, quesadillas, warm yellow corn chips, piquant salsas, chili con queso, and silky garlicky guacamole. Robyn, the curly-haired manager, rules with a light touch and a large heart. The staff is warm and friendly. We gather for dinner on Fridays to share our lives before customers surge through the doors. After hours of solitary piano practice, the spicy food and their warm camaraderie wrap around me like a toasty blanket.

I get to know my suitemates: a bright, responsible Nigerian woman; a studious woman from Wisconsin obsessed with library science and Monty Python; an effervescent German woman studying English; and a couple of women from Virginia who seize life with passion, wildly sowing their oats.

I eagerly plunge into my music. My teacher, Barbara Rowan, is kind but exacting. Every morning, I wake early to practice five or six hours. Scales, arpeggios, and exercises. Chopin études and ballades, Beethoven sonatas, and Brahms' Theme and Variations. I share a teaching studio with Susan, a gentle blonde pianist, where I enjoy teaching undergraduate students. Kathy, a willowy cellist, and I become fast friends and musician soul-mates. We scour Chapel Hill and its environs in her beat-up Ford Falcon the color of green beans, sight-read Beethoven piano and cello sonatas, listen enrapt to LP recordings, cook ramen noodles and Kraft macaroni and cheese for dinner together, and giggle endlessly.

I lie on my bed trying to read my musicology text, but the huge fight I had with my parents yesterday keeps replaying in my mind. They don't want me to waitress or work late anymore. We've argued about it for months. "Decent Indian girls don't waitress," they kept shouting. "I'm an independent adult now," I yelled back. "You can't tell me what to do." And hung up. I tossed and turned all last night. I hate how they try to control me even from a distance. I thought graduate school would set me free. How can I break away from them even more?

My fingers play with the fringes of my robin-egg blue and turmeric paisley bedspread.

Suddenly, fragmented memories from when I was six flood through me. Like a film, images, feelings, and sensations course through me. Raghu's dusky face with big, bulging black eyes, rubbing his cheek and chin as he stares at me. His armpits smelling like dried fish. His clammy palms on my bum. His weight on top of me as I writhe, pushing him away, pushing him off of me…

Shame slowly swallows me whole into its black belly, like a snake engulfs a mouse. I feel nauseous, dizzy, as my memories erupt.

Nights. How I dread them. I dilly-dally as long as I can in our living room nibbling a guava, my nose in a storybook, ignoring Amma's and Naina's urgings.

"Go to bed, Mytrae!"

"Come on, go to sleep now!"

Their tone becomes strict, insistent. I reluctantly close my book. Trudge down, down the wooden stairs with one, two, three landings into the dark verandah, into the bedroom.

Our bedroom. Full with light and sparkle during the day but oh so dark at night. Where he lies. Raghu. Motionless in his bed like a giant black spider waiting in its clammy web. Is he asleep or awake tonight? I ease open the door and creep in, feeling his coal-black eyes on me as I make my way in the dark to the bathroom. I close the door. Switch on the light. I dawdle, peeing, brushing my teeth, listening to the bullfrogs croaking and leaves rustling, daydreaming fantasy upon fantasy, hoping he'll be asleep when I make it to my bed.

I open the door as silently as I can. Pad barefoot to my bed. Slide in. Draw the sheet over my ears so I don't hear. Turn away from him. Curl into a ball. Close my eyes and hope sleep will overcome me in a second. Long minutes later, Amma and Naina come downstairs and go into their bedroom. He's awake tonight. The air prickles with his alertness. I lie still, a petrified breath.

My twin bed is a foot and a half away from his. He leans over and shakes my shoulder. My body stiffens. I pretend I'm asleep. He squeezes my arm and shakes me harder.

"Mytrae! Mytrae!"

I whine.

He shakes me again. Harder.

"I'm tired. I'm sleepy," I whimper.

"Come on. Lie down here."

"Leave me alone. I don't want to." I whine.

"I'll tell Amma and Naina if you don't."

I hate it. Hate this. It makes me feel bad. Bad bad bad. But he'll tell them if I don't. Tell them about this. I'm part of it now so am bad for it. They'll scold me. Amma will beat me. I hate him for making me do this. I hate his power over me. But he's thirteen, three and a half years older than me and knows so much more—how to play cricket, throw a ball hard, do more difficult things in school. And he's bigger.

The green mosaic tiles are cold and hard against my bum when I lie down between our beds. I lift my thin cotton nightie up to my stomach and pull down my panties. Yes, I know exactly what to do. He lies on top of me. He's heavy. Stronger. His legs push mine apart roughly. Hate him. Hate this. My head turns away from his face. Press my cheek against the cool floor. My eyes squeeze shut. If I squeeze them tight enough, I won't see him. Won't see *it*.

He puts it into me. I push my back and bum hard against the floor. Hate him. Hate this. Push his shoulders back with my hands. Don't want it in me. Dry. Hard. Stiff. He moves it in and out. Jabbing. Poky. Painful. Can't feel. Can't think. My body goes limp. Still as a stick. Waiting. Waiting for him to finish heaving up and down. Finish thrusting. If I don't move, it isn't happening. If I don't feel, it won't be real. If I don't think, I won't remember. If I leave, I won't have to feel him, feel it.

And a part of me, wraith-like, floats out of my body keeping watch, hovering a few feet above my bed. Watching the door, the room, the windows, for anyone who might intrude. Keeping vigil. *No one must ever ever know.* No light from bulb, star, moon, or eye must rest upon this sight. My body swells with black, blacker than the night with every second, with every thrust. Blackness oozes into every limb, every organ, every cell, every pore with black repulsive, disgusting shame. I am bad, bad, bad. No one must ever know how bad.

When he's done, I pull up my panties and climb into bed. It's over. For tonight at least. Curl up on the far edge of my bed. Wish I could throw my insides out like when I vomit after eating bad food. I turn away. Stare out the windows at night's ink.

It's over. For now. Will he ever stop?

I close my eyes tight so I don't feel. Think. Or see the dark night and its bringings.

The memory fades. I look down at my hands. They're clenched so tight my nails dig into my palms, the blue and yellow strands of my bedspread interlacing my fingers. I unclench them. Exhale. I look around in a daze at my stark, fluorescent-lit dorm room. The brick walls close in.

I'm stunned to remember. It went on for four years, from when I was six to ten, stopping only when Raghu went to boarding school. I learned about sex from my school friends when I was twelve and wondered if I was pregnant. For two years, anxiously, I looked at my belly in the mirror, turning this way and that, for signs of growth, for signs of a child within. Even though I hadn't had my first period.

This explains everything. The disturbing undertows I sometimes feel. Stirrings I don't know what to do with. Slithering snakes inside me I sometimes touch when I practice an especially dark and mournful piece.

What am I to do with this erupting magma? These memories must never see the light of day. They're in the past. No one must know. Ever. Never ever.

I turn to face the window, through which spring sunshine streams, warming my cheeks. I *can't* remember. This is much too big. Dangerous.

I push it down into my psyche's caverns.

One morning, as I teach in my studio, there's a knock on the door. My jaw drops when I open it. It's Evan, leaning against my door frame, smiling at me. A different Evan. His shoulders and chest are broad with confidence and ease, his hair longer, and he has a sexy, well-traveled air.

"Evan! What are you doing here? How did you find me?"

"I'm visiting David, my friend in medical school here." He

peeks into my studio. My student's listening curiously. "When do you finish teaching?"

"In a couple of hours. Let's get together then?"

To my surprise, Evan had followed through on his promise and written me long letters on onion-skin paper from foreign lands. Each time I got a letter, I was surprised to see his slanting hand on the blue, red, and white envelopes as the stamps changed from French to Italian to German. As I read two, three, even four pages of his fascinating experiences, I marveled at his freedom and boldness to roam the world and was touched he thought to write to me. Not wanting to be rude, I replied with shorter, stiffer, and much less eventful letters about my graduate school life.

I never expected to see him again.

That afternoon we loll on lush grass under fragrant magnolia trees on campus, eating falafel wraps, while he regales me with stories from his travels. He backpacked for six months through Europe, then another six in Israel and Egypt. Nights he spent on the pyramids. Months at a kibbutz. A job harvesting and crushing grapes at a vineyard. His spiritual experiences. He tells stories like a lark sings to morning—true and wild and free. I listen wide-eyed and enrapt. Travel's been good for him. He's more manly and assured than the earnest tenor I knew. His voice, which once quavered on high notes in Schubert lieder, is now rich and sonorous. Like a tuning fork, I vibrate in response.

He says, "I wanted to visit David for a few days before going to my mother in Florida. I thought I'd look you up while I was here." Smile lines crease his cheeks. His eyes soften. As does his voice. "I've thought about you."

I'm surprised. It's been a year since we graduated and he's lived so much compared to me. When he casually alludes to a few women on his travels, I don't want to imagine any casual, passionate encounters. But he doesn't mention a girlfriend. The next couple of days we spend time together, talk effortlessly about music, travel, and the what-nexts of our lives. I allow myself to drink in the lean cut of his face, dark hair against his white forearms and legs, the sinewy length of his body and limbs, his shoulders wide and loose with confidence and freedom. My body tingles in response to his maleness, casual brushes of arm, deep looks, and smiles.

Away from him, I wonder, What would it be like to open the door to more? I'm so curious about sex and feel so inexperienced compared to some of my suite-mates, who tell me the one thing they most enjoy about college is "sowing their oats." And why not? After all, I'm an adult in graduate school and free of my parents.

One afternoon, when he drops me back at my dorm room, I invite him in. Sprawling on opposite ends of my twin bed, we continue talking, my body increasingly thrilling with his nearness. We pause and look at each other, the space between us breathless, magnetic. Leaning over, he kisses me on my lips, his tongue gently searching for mine. Surprised by its soft, wet sweetness, I kiss him back, deliciously falling into the kiss as if I've always known how. Our tongues drink each other, endless tunnels of succulence. When our mouths aren't enough, our bodies hungrily reach for and wrap around each other. I open into something that feels like home.

The next two days and nights, my body kindles and sizzles as Evan's lips, mouth, and hands touch, lick, and suck me in ways never imagined. Exuberantly, I put aside my six hour practice regimen for my initiation into sexuality. Gentle, attuned, and sure, he leads me into rivers of delight and pleasure. I respond to his desire and intensity like a thirsting fish—these are waters I instinctively know. Waters in which I'm unafraid. Bold. Waters into which no memory of childhood abuse drips.

"You're a natural," Evan exclaims. "I would never have known you haven't been with anyone before. Are you sure you haven't kissed before?"

"I haven't, Evan!" How can one not know what to do?

Yet, I'm terrified to lose my virginity, so we do everything except have intercourse. I can experiment, but I'm afraid my pierced hymen will be as obvious as a nose-ring. Losing her virginity before marriage is the worst fate for an unmarried Indian woman—she'll be shamed, gossiped about, and ostracized. She's better off dead. I can't yet put two and two together that I wasn't a virgin since I was six—those memories live in a different room.

"All a woman has is her virginity," my grandmother's words run through my mind as I writhe to Evan's fingers stroking deep in my vagina, as I arch with delight under him. "Otherwise she's lost. No one will marry her."

He looks questioningly at me when our mouths surface, panting, drenched with juices and sweat. "I can't, Evan," I say, aching to feel him in me, yet certain of the uncrossable line. "I'm too afraid."

"That's okay, I understand. But I really need to come!" he exclaims, and rushes to the bathroom for his release.

After three days of delicious experimentation and falling into each other's eyes, pausing only to sleep spooning, or eat yoghurt, fruit, bread and cheese, Evan prepares to leave for Florida.

His arms hold me tight as he nuzzles my ear. "It's been really great to see you."

"It's been great seeing you!" I'm suddenly shy. Is this it? I'll never see him again. I wish I could but how, when he's heading back home to Florida? I'm probably just one of the women he's been with on his travels. I wish American relationships weren't so fleeting. My fingers entwine in his hair, my palm cups the nape of his neck, and I press my body against him as I inhale the earthiness of his skin below his ear one last time. "Good luck with everything."

How can he possibly fit into my life? I'm partly relieved, for I've neglected my music and classes for a week. Because I know I can't for long withstand the tsunami of desire he's unleashed in me. Nor keep down that which lurks below the swirling waves.

My second year at UNC, I move to a house off campus with Mary, a psychology graduate student. She has big brown eyes, freckles, frizzy brown curls, and her wide smile lights up her face. We warm to each other and our new home on Tenney Circle, a second-floor attic converted into a two-bedroom unit. My freshly painted cream room with hardwood floors and sloping ceilings gazes out at lushly waving maples, elms, and ashes. A twin bed, built-in bookcases, and a large desk complete its perfection.

One night, I leave Papagayo's after my night shift to see Evan waiting at the entrance.

"What are you *doing* here?" I squeal. It's been three months since he visited.

"I'm moving here," he grins irresistibly. "There's something about you I just had to come back to."

I leap into his arms, almost knocking him over, as my legs wrap around him. "Really? You have a habit of just showing up, don't you?" I kiss him breathlessly.

He laughs. "I'm staying at David's until I find work and a place to live."

After two weeks we still haven't consummated our relationship, though my body's clamoring for it. We're talking about it. He doesn't push and tells me I need to decide, which makes me feel safe and trust him. I'm going back and forth about crossing the sexual line my family and culture have drawn in the sand.

I've grown up with the idea that my family decides matters about my sexuality. My responsibility is to make sure I'm a virgin when I marry. If anyone finds out that I'm not, I will bring shame upon them and be shunned for life.

I'm entering territory uncharted by any Indian woman I know. But, in Evan's arms and feeling the delicious turgid strength of his penis at the entrance of my throbbing vagina for the nth time, I can't bear it any longer. I want him *in* me. "I'm ready," I say. "Will it hurt?"

"I'll be gentle. I'll stop when you tell me to. I'm not going to hurt you or force myself on you. And let's make love here." We're at his friend David's apartment. "David's away. We don't have to worry that Mary might hear."

I'm afraid of what sex will unleash. Memories of my abuse occasionally surface, but I push them away. My fears melt into intoxicated tingling with his touch and kisses. Attuned and sensitive, with the protective care of a future physician, he listens to and feels my body's rhythms and elasticity. Each night, we go a little deeper, and in a few days I can finally take all of him into me. I'm intoxicated with so much pleasure I don't think to notice whether or not there is any blood. Once I explode into the ecstasy of orgasm, I'm insatiable. Each evening I wait impatiently for him to come home and hurl myself at him.

He laughs and gathers me into his arms.

Sex is a wonderland. I treasure it all.

Times we make love at night on a blanket in different places on campus. Nights full with moon softness. Nights black with sky and canopied with trees. Under lush maples. Under giant magnolias, their fragrance dripping into our skin.

Times he sits on the floor of my piano studio listening to me practice. When I stop, he kisses and caresses me and we make love by the piano, under the piano, on the piano, the keys clinking, my being and body intoxicated with music and love.

Times when memories of Raghu surface and I think Evan will hurt or force me to have sex. Shuddering and shivering, I cry, pushing him away. Folding me into his arms, he talks tenderly, rocking, and holding me until my tears subside. I tell him whatever I remember about my abuse, my pain, confusion, and fear. Making room for it all, he lets my memories spill—large wet tears of a terrified little girl. Soothed by his tenderness and protective arms, we hold each other close and sleep. Then reach for each other in the middle of the night or after sunlight streams through the blinds and begin all over again.

Times we go away for the weekend, making love in nature's wild innocence and raw freshness to the calls of wrens and hoots of owls. Our bodies and sexualities blossom full and sweet as nasturtiums.

Evan finds work as a line cook at Pyewacket, a vegetarian restaurant, and moves into a furnished in-law unit on a quiet street close to my home. His two-room home soon becomes our love nest. The living room has worn gray carpeting and a saggy twin bed draped with an olive-green bedspread for a couch. He proudly places his Bose music system and boxes of Joni Mitchell, Simon and Garfunkel, Carole King, and James Taylor cassettes on a rickety wooden chest. He spends hours poring through catalogs to buy the best convection toaster oven. "I want a good one, even if it's half my paycheck," he says, when I ask him why he just doesn't buy one at K-Mart.

From that tiny toaster-oven he cooks every few nights. Enchiladas smothered with salsa and guacamole. Grilled Gruyère sandwiches. Vegetarian lasagna. I lie on the sofa studying Romantic Piano Literature or Contemporary Chamber Music, and watch him in his "kitchen," really a refrigerator in a corner. Sitting cross-legged on the floor with a kitchen towel over his shoulder, he slices and dices with his cherished Wüsthof knives on a thick chopping block. Sips from a St. Pauli Girl bottle every few minutes. "You gotta have good knives," he says, slicing an onion like lightning into translucent leaves. "A kitchen just isn't a kitchen without good knives." On the aluminum roasting plan, he places two pieces of salmon in the center, making sure they're an inch apart and don't touch the sides of the pan, drizzles them with olive oil, and the toaster oven temperature's exactly right. He tidies up, washing the dishes in the tiny sink singing and humming "I Feel the Earth Move" or "You've got a Friend." Every five minutes he crouches on the floor to peer into the toaster oven window. "It's gotten in my head and won't leave," he says, exasperated, as he sings the songs over and over. I love him singing like a lark in the morning. Songs burst from his chest, free and wild and open as Copland's *Appalachian Spring*. He pulls out the tray, pokes the fish to check if it's done, then carefully slides them on two plates. He wrings a lemon over them, meticulously places a sprig of dill, and spoons broccoli he steamed on his hot plate. He comes over, sets the plates on the low table beside the couch.

"Dinner's ready, love. Come and get it when it's hot."

"It's a masterpiece, Evan!"

He smiles at me. Inserts a tape into his cassette player. The sweet melody and harmonies of "Scarborough Fair" fill the room.

And we sit, smiling at each other, to feast.

4
wings

1984

I feel like a woman now, no longer an adolescent. I have my wings. And I want to fly even further from being Indian and under my parents' control.

When I tell her what I want, Becca the hairdresser says, "I want to take before-and-after pictures of you. I like to do that when clients want something completely different."

She pulls out a Polaroid camera and clicks.

"Turn around," she says, "so I can see what it looks like down your back." My hair's at my waist.

We watch the blurry square print become clear.

"This is going to be so much fun!" she says excitedly.

I sit in the chair, with the design book on my lap, open to the cut I want. The model has a pixie cut, short on the back and sides, slightly longer on top, with sleek long bangs that frame her face.

Becca's scissors snip deftly around my ears. Chunks of weight fall away. I look down from the corners of my eyes. Tufts of hair, seven to eight inches long, tumble on the floor. With each clip I am lighter. Freer.

With each clack of Becca's scissors I feel like I'm shearing away my family rules and expectations. Snipping away their rigidity and strictness.

Emerging into freedom, independence, and adulthood.

When Becca finishes, she takes my hand and leads me to a tall mirror. She stands behind me with a large hand mirror and a big smile. My brown eyes grow wide with delight. I look like an Indian version of the model. My hair wisps like feathers around the sides of my face and back of my head. My bangs are side-swept to the right. "I love it!" I squeal. I turn my head this way and that in the mirror, admiring my haircut, feeling light as a dandelion flower. "I love it! All that weight's gone! It's darling, Becca. You're amazing!"

"It came out great," Becca says. "It really brings out your face, which was hidden behind all that hair. You look so cute. Adorable, really. Here, let me take another picture."

She takes a few.

I can't stop beaming. I've really done it! I'm free! Free to do what I want. Free to be me.

I can't stop touching my hair.

As I look at my reflection, for the first time in my life I think I'm pretty. Sexy, even.

Sexual, I blossom like a magnolia in spring. Wide, receptive, open. My eyes sparkle and glow. My skin feels like petals. My hair like silk. I glide, not walk, and my movements feel deliciously sensual.

I arch, stretch and roll each morning in yoga, supple and playful as a cheetah.

As though my sexual awakening isn't enough, I also have a spiritual awakening.

Evan and I go to a meditation group. I wasn't keen at first, but there's something soothing and magnetic about it that makes me return each week. The candlelit room fragrant with incense. The altar decorated with flowers. The hypnotic chant of Sanskrit mantras *Om* and *Om namah Shivaya*, "I bow to my true inner self." The swell and sigh of people's breathing. The large photograph of a gorgeous, powerful, young Indian woman teacher in ochre robes on the altar.

Meditation and chanting make my body tingle and thrill with pleasurable energy that runs up and down my body. I learn to tune into, follow, and surrender to it. Let the ebb and flow of the mantra reverberate through my cells so I sink like a stone into myself. As with music, my body softens and opens like a lily.

My eyes frequently stray to the photograph of the beautiful young woman. She's regal, magnetic, and powerful as a lioness. And knows it. I've never seen such a powerful Indian woman. I'm in awe, curious. Evan told me Nityananda and Muktananda were gurus in the the centuries-old Siddha Yoga lineage. Muktananda passed the tradition down to a brother and sister. Her devotees call her Gurumayi.

In a few weeks, I start getting *kriyas*, energy movements where I shiver and tremble sometimes for as long as ten minutes. I spontaneously do *yogasanas*, yoga poses, even complex ones I didn't learn as a girl in school. I go into trance during the meditations and when I come to, my arms and legs are twisted into a pretzel. I'm unnerved by what's happening but George, the man who leads our group, explains, "When *shakti*, energy, moves through you, people have all kinds of experiences. *Kriyas* are one way the *kundalini*, Divine Feminine energy, awakens and expresses herself. *Shakti* has the intelligence and wisdom to know what you need. It heals emotional wounds, clears blocks, and opens your *chakras*, energy centers. It's very auspicious because it's Gurumayi's grace and a sign of your spiritual progress. Your body will integrate it in time."

Pat, his wife, says to me, "Don't worry. The only thing that's important is that it's happening. The energy's wiser than our minds. It knows what you need and it'll find its path through you. All you have to do is allow it. Trust its wisdom."

I'm frightened and unnerved to lose control of my body. And I'm skeptical. How is it I'm Indian but haven't heard about such things? What they say doesn't seem scientific. How can an energy be intelligent? Can I believe them? It seems so far out. I wish I could ask my family if they know about *kundalini* and *kriyas*, but they'd only freak out and tell me to stop going.

Despite my doubts, what I can't deny is how familiar and comforting the *kriyas* feel. As though my body gets to express my innate truth. And that I'm simply remembering an ancient language I've always known.

The *kriyas* come while Evan and I have sex too. Energy ripples up and down my spine as my body pulses and floods with ecstasy. *Kriyas* and sex have unplugged a whole new reality for me. Opened a doorway to energies and realms out of this world. Images flash through my mind's eye and I instinctively know they are my past lives: a high priestess, an Egyptian queen, soldier, wanderer, musician, scribe, slave, dancer. Always with themes of love, murder, war, violence, power, and betrayal.

Evan's fascinated and wants to know every detail with his scientist-like objectivity and precision. "What are you seeing? Who are you? Where are you? Who is there with you? What year is it?" Jealous, even. "I wish I could see my past lives."

When I return to normal consciousness I can hardly believe the images. It's all so fantastical. And I'm really scared. I can't control any of it. Why is this happening to me? Am I going crazy? Still, the images are beautiful as a movie, and just as real as Evan, his chocolate-brown sheets, banged-up yellow bureau, and my music.

Sometimes, during sex, I regress into child-states. I am in my childhood home being molested by Raghu and talk in a child's voice. Evan, of course, immediately stops what we're doing, and tells Raghu to leave. Which he does. Evan protects me. Tells me I'm safe.

When I return to my normal adult self, I don't believe him. So he audiotapes my voice. I'm shocked to hear myself—my twenty-one-year-old body with a six-year-old's voice and speech patterns.

But I cannot deny how relieved I feel that he knows my secret and enters the dark caverns of my past with me. Each time after I emerge from an episode, I trust him more, as I've never trusted anyone before.

Still, I feel like I'm becoming unhinged. It's disorienting for me to pull myself together for school or work and leave the safety of his home. I have one life in his apartment and another when I step out his door. What do I do with this? Yet I still can't bring myself to tell anyone about it. Who would I tell? And would they think I'm crazy?

Evan consults with David, who's studying to become a psychiatrist.

"David says you have PTSD from the incest," Evan tells me. "Some of what's happening is you're remembering and feeling emotions that were intolerable for you to process at that age. Because you feel safe with me, you can enter into and process those feelings. David said, 'For her to feel you there, protecting her at a time when no one protected her, is a huge healing. It's great you're doing this, man, but she really should be in therapy. There's going to be much more here than you can handle.'" Evan looks at me, concerned. "I love being here for you, but I think you need professional help."

"Therapy? I don't need therapy," I say abruptly. I don't know much about therapy. India doesn't have it. All I know about therapy is that it's for crazy people. I don't want to be labeled crazy.

"Think about it, Nitro." His eyes and forehead crease with worry. He calls me Nitro, which I don't like but can't tell him.

I brush him off. Confused and scared though I am by what opens up during sex, the last thing I want to be is out of my mind.

Evan and I go to the Siddha Yoga Ashram in South Fallsburg, New York, to learn more about *kundalini* and what's happening to me. We enter a *darshan* hall the size of a football stadium. A recording of *Om namah Shivaya* plays and we settle down to watch the hundreds of mostly American devotees with a sprinkling of Indians filing in. The brother-and-sister teachers enter with a large retinue of American women in Indian attire. After meditation and a brief talk, we join the hundreds lining up for darshan—to bow and *namaste* to the teachers, and have the tops of our heads brushed by Gurumayi's peacock feather fan.

I'm stunned by her beauty. With short black hair, high cheekbones, and glistening skin, Gurumayi is gorgeous in person, with luminous coal-black eyes. Queenly, magnificent, the pomp and circumstance fit her. I fold my hands in *namaste* and am about to move on but she rests the peacock feather fan on my head. I look up, surprised.

"What's your name?" she asks, lifting the fan from my head.

"Mytrae."

"Where have you come from?"

"Chapel Hill, North Carolina."

"What do you want to know?"

"I came because I'm getting *kriyas* and I have some questions."

"Come and meet me tomorrow at 6 p.m."

"But my flight leaves tonight!" I sputter.

"Don't worry. We'll make the arrangements to change it so you can leave tomorrow. We'll drop you at the airport. Give this woman your ticket and she'll change it for you." She signals to a curly blonde among her retinue in sequined Indian *lehengas*, ankle-length skirts.

"I will," the woman answers.

"*NOW!*" Gurumayi roars.

The woman leaps to her feet to wait in the aisle. I go with her to change my ticket.

When I see Evan, he's just as surprised. "What does she want to talk to you about? It's so wild she talked to you, out of so many people. And boy! How she commanded that woman to go with you!"

The next evening I meet Gurumayi who sits, queenly and stunning, on a lavish purple davenport with embroidered cushions in a gigantic hall. She exudes a strength, power, light, and intensity I've never seen in a woman. Her body glows and crackles with electricity. Her skin warm and golden as honey. Dark with watchfulness, two black Dobermans lie before her and raise their heads menacingly when I enter. A dashing Middle Eastern bodyguard looms behind her. No semblance of spiritual gentleness here, I think, approaching her to sit cross-legged at her feet.

"Hello," she smiles kindly at me.

Her relaxed smile puts me at ease. She's not as daunting or commanding as she was in the darshan hall. She feels like an older sister.

"Hello," I smile back.

"What are you studying?"

"Classical music. Piano."

"Where?"

"Chapel Hill. University of North Carolina."

"How old are you?"

"Twenty-one."

Questions and answers, in true Indian style, ricochet back and forth. Fact. Question about fact. Fact. Inquiry about fact. Expansion upon fact. More inquiry. Exposition about fact. Next question about another fact. She asks about my parents, Evan, and what I want from life. I tell her about my *kriyas*.

"*Kundalini* is *shakti*, an energy," she says in a husky voice, "that moves through the body to transform, purify, and awaken it. Some signs of *kundalini* are trembling, shaking, sounds, intense energy and heat, waves of emotions, visions, and past life experiences. It can seem chaotic, bewildering, and overwhelming, but it's a completely accepted and valid path of spiritual evolution. *Shakti* focuses on certain places or *chakras* where healing is needed, and you can know where she's working if you have pain or sensation there. She changes the location when the work is completed. Integration of the work can take days or years.

"Your getting *kriyas* means the energy is moving through you. What's happening is perfectly normal. There's nothing wrong or bad. The *shakti* knows what you need, which blocks are to be cleared, places to be healed, and purifies your body. All you have to do is get out of the way by surrendering to her."

Her words calm and reassure me. Thank goodness I'm not going crazy. I warm to her, and her power that fills the whole room. I've never met such a powerful, sensual, radiant Indian woman before, and I'm completely fascinated.

"Thank you. That's really good to know. But, why did you want to see me?"

"I just wanted to talk with you. Do you have any more questions?"

I shake my head. Drink in her sweetness and regality.

She looks at me for several moments. "After you leave, feel free to write to me if you have any questions." She holds out a bowl of exquisitely wrapped chocolates as *prasad*.

I take one, thank her, and leave.

When Evan and I tell the meditation group about our experience, they're stunned.

"I've been there four, five times, and I've never seen her single someone out to talk to them. Everyone's dying to get a word from her. But a private darshan that she initiates? I've never heard of that happening," George says.

"You're so blessed," Patty says.

I don't think much of it.

She probably just wanted to talk to me because I'm Indian.

My feet skid to a halt at the doorway to my room. My mouth opens in shock. Amma's sitting on my bed. Naina's on the chair at my desk. My room's scoured and spruced.

They stare at me, stunned.

"What are you *doing* here? When did you come?" I gasp.

"What have you done to your *hair*?" Amma exclaims, horrified.

"I cut it." I step inside my room. "When did you come? Why didn't you tell me?"

"We came this morning," Amma says. "Your hair's all gone! Look at you! It looks terrible!"

"You didn't even tell us," Naina says.

Like I would call and ask their permission.

Amma stares at me with disgust. "I can't even look at you."

I stare back at her. "It's my hair. I can do what I want with it."

Amma says, "It's so short. No one will marry you."

"Well, I like it. We're in America now. Lots of people have short hair."

"Not Indians," Amma says.

"You cut yours!" I'm angry now. "You cut it in India before we came here!" Throughout my childhood Amma's thick, long hair cascaded to her hips, which she put up in a big bun, pinning it in place with hairpins. She looked like a queen. But, when I was eleven or so, she came home one day, her hair skirting her shoulders, flipped out in a curled wave like Jackie Onassis in *Time* magazine. She looked younger and fashionable. I thought, proudly, how very bold she was to look Western. "It takes so long to dry," she'd said. "It's too heavy. It gives me headaches." She curled her hair with curlers Roopa Aunty brought from the U.S. and I'd watch her admiring herself in the mirror, turning left and right, pouffing her curls with her cupped hands.

"You know I did it because of my health," she says. "I wasn't well. Otherwise, I wouldn't have done it. It was too heavy for me. It gave me migraines."

I can never argue when she talks about her health. I'm silent.

"Your place is filthy. Don't you ever clean it?" Amma asks.

"I'm busy. And it's not filthy!" So what if it has a few dustballs because I'm practically living with Evan. She's obsessively clean and spends hours scouring her home. She's trained Naina to scrub her pans the way she likes, and he dutifully obeys. "You didn't have to clean my room! Why did you come? Why didn't you tell me you were coming? And who let you in?" Mary isn't home.

"We wanted to see you. Your landlord downstairs let us in."

They never just want to see me. Something's up. But they won't say what. They spend the next hour scolding me. And I keep asking them why they came.

Finally, they sigh and look at each other.

"Mytrae, we came because a proposal's come for you. It's a good one. A very, very good one," Amma says slowly and reverently, "Most families would just close their eyes, thank God, clutch it to their heart, and jump at it. But we're different. We said you're in graduate school, that we'd put it to you. See if you're ready."

"He's an excellent catch," Naina says. "A very successful businessman from a very good family."

"But with your short hair," Amma shakes her head, "Who'll even *look* at you? We can't even *think* of putting it to you. All your looks are gone."

"You look so un-Indian," Naina says mournfully.

A silent scream rips through me. "I'm not *ready* to get married!"

"Mytrae, proposals will come. You're of marriageable age. It's time you start thinking of your future," Naina says. "Music is fine and all, but it's time to think about settling down."

"Things are not going to wait till you finish your college," Amma says. "We're a well-known, sought after family. And we give our children the best. We've given you the best education. We'll put proposals to you as they come. After your hair grows out. No one will look at you now."

I can't breathe. I have to push things out. "I won't be ready to get married for years. I'm going to finish graduate school then get a doctorate." It's a vague plan I have but it's a way to buy some time. I don't have the courage yet to tell them I don't want an arranged marriage.

"It's not for you to say," Naina says.

"It's definitely for me to say. I want to finish school." My voice rises anxiously. "You can't tell me what to do with my school."

"Now, there's no need…" Naina explodes.

"Mohan, it's okay. Let her be," Amma says. "This one's gone. We'll just have to wait for the next one."

We sit in a glum silence for a while, and through lunch.

I'm hugely relieved when they drive away. Thank god they're gone. This was close. What if Evan was with me? I shudder to imagine. I must tell them I don't want an arranged marriage. I'll have to think of what to say. I feel fierce about it. And terrified. I'll tell them when it's time, at some point in the future. I wobble at the thought.

There's no way I'm marrying someone they pick for me.

I've just performed my recital in Brendle Recital Hall. On my program was Mozart's Sonata in C Major K330, Haydn's Sonata in C Major Hob. XVI/50, Skryabin's Prelude and Nocturne for the Left Hand, and Debussy's *L'isle joyeuse*. My friends surround me, warmly hugging and complimenting me.

"You play so beautifully!"

"I loved the Skryabin—I couldn't tell it was for one hand. It took me a while to realize you were using only your left hand."

"Your fingers are magic!"

"Good work, Mytrae. It was a great success! Well done!" my teacher Barbara Rowan says, clearly pleased.

I glow at her praise.

"You were wonderful! And beautiful!" Evan's arms are tight around me. His lips brush my cheek. Intoxicated by each other and the thrill of the forbidden, we giggle, and press our bodies close. I feel heady after my recital and, though I know I'm playing with fire because Amma and Naina are there, I don't care. I feel much bolder, more in charge of my life than when they visited with a proposal a few months ago. Besides, among so many people they're not going to suspect a thing. I linger in his arms.

Amma and Naina are in the back of the room at the reception table. Amma prepared *khalakhand*, an Indian sweet, cucumber mint sandwiches, and bought cookies for an after-recital reception. I hear her saying, "Don't scrape the silver paper off the *khalakhand*. It's not aluminum foil. In India, where we come from, eating a little silver is good for health. It's an Ayurvedic medicine." I smile, hearing her and seeing the Americans' puzzled faces. I'm transported back to Hyderabad markets where we watched workers hammer a tiny ball of silver into a flat sheet delicate as a butterfly's wings. Sandwiched in Evan's arms, I realize how much I love being part of both cultures and wish my parents could, too. And how bringing together who and what I love feels daunting and dangerous as climbing Mt. Everest.

I want my parents to meet my friends for lunch, and I'm glad when they agree. And I want Evan and Kathy to meet the parents I'm running from. I'm not yet ready to disclose my relationship with Evan to my parents, but want them to know I have male friends. It's how I can prepare them for the time I will tell them I'm not going to have an arranged marriage, but want to choose my own husband.

But not yet. So I warn Evan to behave himself and act just like a friend.

The five of us meet at a homey vegetarian restaurant with red and white checkered tablecloths. My stomach knots with nervous excitement.

"What do you do, Evan?" Naina asks.

"I'm a cook."

"A cook?" Amma's brow furrows.

"Yes, at a vegetarian restaurant," he smiles. He's proud of Pyewacket.

A wave of disapproval sweeps him into a pile of cowdung. Naina looks down at the menu. Amma takes a sip of water and clears her throat.

She looks at Kathy. "What do you do, Kathy?"

"I'm a cellist."

"I see," she says with a stiff smile and looks away.

She doesn't see. Musicians and cooks have no place in their world. To them, success looks like an engineer, doctor, or lawyer. A chill descends at the table.

Kathy and I look at each other, giggle, then talk about recent recitals and the latest gossip about the violin teacher who's dating a graduate student. My parents study the menu.

"Evan went to Wake Forest," I tell them, trying to get a conversation going.

"Oh?" Amma exclaims. "What was your major?"

"Biology."

"What do you want to do next?"

"I'm not sure. I traveled around Europe last year for a year. Now, Chapel Hill feels right." He looks at me mischievously. I look away.

"Were you studying in Europe?" Amma asks.

"No, just traveling," he says and launches into stories of his travels. My parents listen, nod politely at appropriate pauses.

When our food arrives Evan looks at me with a lover's eyes. I wish he wouldn't. I'm afraid my parents will see.

"This vegetable lasagna is wonderful. Try it." His eyes sparkle as he delights in my inner torment.

He has no idea how bad the wrath of my parents can be.

I feel afraid, then suddenly bold. I hate having to hide. Let them see. Let them see I'm close and friendly with men. I'm not stiff and polite like Indians. I rebelliously spear an asparagus off Evan's plate. "Yummm. Try my burrito."

We fork mouthfuls off of each other's plates. Naina glances darkly at us. My parents grow increasingly quiet and a cold dislike emanates from them. Evan rattles on about Europe to fill the coldness, as Kathy silently watches this disaster unfold.

After lunch, we stroll towards my apartment in the warm summer sunshine. Evan and Kathy walk ahead, away from my parents. I walk beside Amma and Naina in silence, impatient for them to leave. I hoped they'd like Evan, but this was an absolute fiasco.

In their eyes I'm still a child. Only when a father places an Indian woman's hand in her husband's at her wedding ceremony does she have permission to be an adult. He gives her husband the right to her body along with her dowry, and gives her permission to be sexual. Till then, she's a girl, his virgin daughter.

I feel part-child, part-lusciously sexual woman. The door between my two worlds swings before me, and I don't know how to bring these together without devastating my parents. I'm terrified to tell them about Evan. When I do, I will be betraying and rejecting them, their trust in me, and all they've done for me. For I will be leaving not only centuries of tradition and generations of ancestors, but I'll be leaving them.

Forever.

5
netted

1985

Looking out the blurry window as the jet violently shudders to a halt on the steel-gray runway, I go over my plan. I'm visiting Amma and Naina in Charleston, South Carolina, for ten days. They moved here from Winston-Salem, North Carolina, a year ago. I'm going to secretly take my passport and green card from Naina's mahogany desk in his bedroom. Their impromptu visit to Chapel Hill with the proposal a few months ago has unnerved me. Once I have my legal documents, they'll have no power over me. I'll slip into their bedroom when they aren't around and hide them in my suitcase pocket.

I take a deep breath. Brace myself. I'll need to have my guard up. It's going to be a challenge to pretend it's an ordinary summer visit.

Naina's waiting for me at the airline gate, slightly stooped, his long arms folded and black hair tousled with his usual worried expression. Arjun and Nikhil, my ten- and eight-year-old cousins from Lexington, Virginia, are with him. We hug.

I feel the bittersweet pang of my pretense.

At home, Amma gives me a cursory hug with a taut smile. I remember why I couldn't wait to leave home.

"How are you?" she asks.

"Fine," I reply. "How are you?"

She says, "Oh well, fine, you know," in a long-suffering tone which means, not fine. She turns away and busies herself cutting eggplant.

I sigh with a stab of guilt and resentment, and go to the guest bedroom to unpack.

The next morning when Naina's at work and Amma's on the phone in the kitchen, I sneak to Naina's desk in my parents' bedroom to search for my passport and green card. Top right drawer. Just as I remembered. Easy-peasy. I tuck the documents into my suitcase pocket. I write a note to Evan. "I got them. See you in a few days. Love and kisses."

I pause, sealed envelope in hand, before I head outside. I stare out the window at the burnished leaves of a Japanese maple. Should I mail it in a public mailbox away from Amma's prying eyes? Oh, I'm being silly. She's not *that* bad. The mailman will be here in an hour. Now that I have my passport, they can't do anything to me. I smile and step into the sizzling June midday, place my letter in the black mailbox at the end of our driveway, and raise its little red flag.

The next couple of days, I nonchalantly listen to music, sort through my clothes, read novels, watch movies, hang out with Arjun and Nikhil, and count the days. Hmm… strange. Why's Amma spending so much time in her room on the phone? Well, just as well. And thank God Arjun and Nikhil are here, so we can avoid conversation.

After dinner, we all go for long walks on muggy, sweltering evenings under magnolia blossoms that hang like huge cupped hands from broad-leafed trees. I hold in my excitement. Hug my delightful secret to myself. Only a few more days. Every step, every second, is taking me towards freedom, music, my Chapel Hill life, and Evan's arms.

"I've made an appointment for you to have a physical," Amma says.

I'm eating granola at the kitchen table. "Why?" I've never had one.

"It'll be good for you. You haven't had one in years."

Hmm. Odd. But I'd better play along these last few days.

Dr. Moore is in his seventies, tall and gauntly debonair. "I'll take good care of her," he warmly assures Amma after she introduces us. "How're you doing, Kamala?"

"I'm doing well, Doctor," she smiles coyly. "My medications are working and I go on my evening walks. Of course, my meditation and spiritual practice really help. I'll wait outside." She waves goodbye to him and leaves.

He smiles, watching her. He turns to me with intelligent, piercing blue eyes. "Your mother's a wonderful woman. She's worried about you."

My stomach prickles. I feel like a little girl before a school principal. "Why?"

"She's just worried. So, how's school?"

"Good."

"What are you studying?"

"Piano. I'm in graduate school."

"How's your health? I know how it is in college. Alcohol, drugs… people use all kinds of things. Do you use any?"

Why's he asking me this? He hasn't even checked my pulse or blood pressure. "No, I don't."

"You do know how bad those things are for your health, don't you?"

Why the lecture? Did Amma say something? "Yes, I do. I don't drink or do drugs. I'm not interested in them."

"Well, your mother asked me to test you for drugs."

"Test me for *drugs*?" I echo, bewildered. "Why?"

"I don't know. She asked me to. She's worried about you."

"Do you see anything wrong?"

"I don't. But she wants me to, so I'm going to, okay?" His tone is sharp.

He draws my thick red blood into a tube. Examines me. "I don't see anything. But the tests will be accurate."

Outside, I ask Amma, "Why did you have him test me for drugs?"

"I think it's good for you to have a checkup from time to time."

What's up with her? When I get home, I take my passport and green card from my suitcase and hide them in a stack of my undergraduate folders.

Two days later, she tells me the blood test results are negative.

Of course.

What *was* that about?

My two aunts Roopa Aunty and Vasupinni from Chicago suddenly visit. I'm surprised, because our family is anything but spontaneous, but Roopa Aunty, who's a travel agent, said she got discount tickets.

They're in their mid-thirties, ten years younger than Amma. The three of them grew up together and are close. Every weekend they spend hours on the phone talking about Amla's failing marriage, Arjun's grades in Math, the exact proportion of rice and *urad dal* to make their *dosas* crisper, which store in Chicago Tanuja ordered *khalakhand* from, and what her diamond necklace looked like at her recent party. They speak, as most in my family do, in sentences of woven English and Telugu, yet their main "language" is living Indian in America.

I'm happy to see Roopa Aunty, for she's my favorite aunt—gentle, warm, and caring—so very different from Amma. I loved her visits to India when I was a girl, when we baked Duncan Hines cakes from mixes she brought from the U.S. that melted in our mouths like chiffon. Trundled in cycle rickshaws in monsoon downpours to watch her favorite Hindi movies. Laughed as we dunked steaming samosas in mint and tamarind chutney on grimy steel plates we bought from street vendors. Excited to receive her exotic American gifts of T-shirts, stickers, and jigsaw puzzles.

On the other hand, I can only exchange a couple of forced pleasantries with Vasupinni. She's short and wiry, her hair cropped close about her narrow, olive-skinned face. Tightly wound with a nervous energy. She's very closed off, and I can never tell what she really thinks or feels about me. She cut her hair a few years after she got married and moved to the U.S.

I'm glad they're here. The next five days will pass more quickly. The house will bustle with their cooking, chatter, and interminable shopping sprees. I can retreat into the background, away from Amma's probing eyes.

The day after they arrive, Roopa Aunty and Vasupinni ask me to take them shopping. Amma doesn't want to go, which is strange, for she turns down shopping only when her asthma flares. But I have time on my hands so I drive my aunts to Northwoods Mall and desultorily accompany them while they shop for a couple of hours. Then we sit down to eat at the bustling food court.

"How's school, Mytrae?" Roopa Aunty asks, a plateful of Schezuan chicken before her.

"It's going well. I gave a recital last month. I'm growing as a pianist. After next year, I'd like to teach, perhaps get a doctorate."

"Don't you think it's time you got married?" She puts down her fork, tangled with chow mein, suddenly serious.

I look at her in surprise. She's usually so playful and friendly with me. "Oh, I'm not ready yet," I say casually, biting into my avocado, Swiss cheese, and tomato sandwich.

"You're twenty-*two*," her tone accuses.

"I know, but I want to finish graduate school and get a job. I want a career before I get married."

"Well, a proposal's come for you. It's a good match. We want you to consider it." She tosses it out flippantly, like she's talking about the weather.

My eyes widen. "A *proposal?*"

"Yes."

She dives into her handbag, pulls out a couple of printed stapled sheets, and slides them across the table toward me. It's a resumé! I can't believe my eyes. Two sheets in Times New Roman type, bullet-pointing an Indian man's educational qualifications and business management experience. His long dreary name and stiff, unappealing passport photograph make my sandwich lurch inside me. Surely they couldn't think I'd be interested in *him*.

"I don't marry resumés." I slide it back to her with disdain.

"Is it because of Evan?" Her serious black eyes penetrate mine.

Evan? A cannonball rams into my gut. How in the world do they know?

My letter!

My body freezes. *Amma read it!* I thought, being in graduate school, she'd grant me that much privacy. But then, how foolish I am to think she'll stop being invasive. I remember the times I came home from college to find my journal moved to a different place in my room.

"It's not because of Evan," I say casually, though I'm quaking. "I'm not ready for marriage yet. I have another year of graduate school. I want to have a career before I marry." I'm partly relieved. Now I can take responsibility for my life and relationship.

"It's time you got married, Mytrae," Vasupinni nasally chimes in from her fried rice and vegetables. "If you wait too long, all the good men get taken. You won't find one you like."

Is she regretting waiting too long for her own arranged marriage? She and her husband are oil and water, a stellar example of a mismatch.

Vasupinni continues, "Also, it takes time to find a good man. That's why we're starting now."

"I'm only twenty-two. I want to wait at least two more years. Twenty-four isn't old."

"Why don't you meet him?" Roopa Aunty presses.

"He's a good catch. Educated at Yale and already doing well," Vasupinni says.

"I'm not interested," I say firmly.

They persist for several more minutes but I am not budging.

We finish lunch and drive home in silence. *Now* I know why they came. Amma asked them to come to do what she can't. Of course, given our relationship, she knows I won't consider any proposal coming from her. Why on earth was I such a fool to use the home mailbox? I can't believe she read it. How dare she invade my privacy for the umpteenth time. Okay, calm down, breathe, you're out of here in a few days. There's nothing they can do even if they know. Just play innocent and unhurried. Soon you'll be free.

Arjun and Nikhil are watching a basketball game in the living room. Roopa Aunty hands Arjun a few bills. "Go to the movies with Nikhil and don't come home for five hours."

"Five hours? What's going on? We just *went* to a movie!" Arjun says.

"Just *go*, Arjun," she says in a don't-ask-questions-and-do-as-you're-told tone.

They look at me with raised eyebrows. They know I'm in for it. I shrug. They hurry out to the garage. I vanish into my room. Quickly check my stack of college folders. *Phew*. My passport and green card are still here. I sit on my bed, taut as a twisted rag. I know Roopa Aunty and Vasupinni are reporting back to Amma. The house seethes like a pot of milk about to boil over.

I'm ready as I ever will be for a fight.

"My-thre-yah," Roopa Aunty coos, reversing the vowels in my name like when I was a girl, her English rose perfume wafting in with her into my room. But beneath her English rose, a steeliness. "We want to talk to you."

My palms grip the edge of the mattress to brace myself. I take a deep breath. Swing my legs off my bed. The hardwood floor is firm and cool beneath my bare soles as I follow Roopa Aunty to the wood-paneled family room decorated with paintings of the monkey god Hanuman, and sailboats leaving a harbor that Amma brought from India. The June sun streams the hot South Carolina day through a French window. Amma wears a purple kaftan and rigidly perches on the mahogany leather recliner, her face an oncoming storm. My nostrils flare in battle. I lift my chin with determination. A box of tissues and her blue asthma inhaler are beside her, as always. The room is immaculate. Not a speck of dust on the gleaming cherry coffee and end tables. *Time, India Today* magazines, and Vedanta books neatly piled in descending sizes. The TV and VCR remotes lie beside each other like straight, stiff soldiers. Almost imperceptibly, I feel a net hanging above me.

Vasupinni hunches forward, nervous and titillated on the brown and beige checkered sofa, one bare foot over the other. Roopa Aunty sinks down beside her, and anxiously draws her *palloo*, the end of her sari, printed with violet garden sprays, close about her rounded bosom. They look anxiously at Amma. In this dragon's lair they're merely guards—efficient at Amma's bidding, but not powerful. The three women stare at me. I sit on the edge of a pea-green chair to face my mother.

"So you're dating Evan?" Amma begins. Her eyes are dark and hungry. Fierce.

"Yes." I boldly tilt my chin. Finally, I can be an adult instead of skulking about. "How did you know? Did you read my letter?"

"No. Hema's niece goes to Chapel Hill and she told her aunt she saw you using drugs and going around with him. I asked her to keep watch on you."

That doesn't make sense. Why hasn't she told me about her friend's niece? She always wants me to meet people she approves of. How could this niece keep watch on me when we've never met? I don't have Indian women friends. But now I know why Amma insisted I have a physical. Why does she think I use drugs?

"But I *don't* use drugs."

"Are you sleeping with him?"

Her question pummels my belly. We've never talked about sex. Her harsh, accusing tone makes the bliss I have with Evan seem like the filth on India's roads. I hesitate. Should I say yes? If I do, it's my final exit from her, from them all. I take a deep breath. Look her straight in the eye. "Yes, I am."

Roopa Aunty gasps, her jaw hangs open. Vasupinni's knees lock, her toes curl and clutch the tan carpet's strands. A sly smirk spreads on one side of her face.

Amma's eyes narrow. Her lips purse to a tight slit. The room caves into a silence that hangs forever.

Vasupinni and Roopa Aunty look back and forth, back and forth between Amma and me as though they're watching a tennis match.

There. I've taken my life from her hands. My armpits are slick as wet leaves.

"That's it! You're not going back." Her words lacerate the silence. Her eyes glint with revulsion.

"What do you *mean*?"

"Just what I said. You're not going back."

"How can I *not* go back? I have *school*!" My education was my protection. Nothing, I thought, could ever interrupt that.

"You're going to India for three months. If you still want to date Evan after that, you can."

"I don't *want* to go." My voice is panicked, outraged. "I have to finish school."

"You don't have a choice. You're *going*," Amma's authority and disapproval are like daggers of broken glass. "You'll write to Barbara Rowan and tell her you won't return to school this summer but will resume in the fall." She pauses and softens a bit. "It's only for three months. You can call and write to Evan while you're there. It's just a break. You'll be back in three months. If you still like him after that, you can be with him."

The room spins. I'm shaking. My body is evaporating into thin air. My mind races furiously to make sense of her plan. Faced with her wrath and authority, the only thing I know to do is to obey.

My throat clutches shut as when she scolded and beat me as a girl.

"Amma will go with you," Roopa Aunty says kindly. "We're very worried about you, Mytrae. Those seizures are alarming."

"They're *not* seizures. They're *kriyas*."

I'd told my parents about my *kriyas*, thinking they'd be happy for my spiritual growth, but they freaked out.

Amma says, "We trusted you when we sent you to Chapel Hill. You were supposed to be studying, not dating and doing drugs."

"I'm *not* doing drugs. If you don't believe me, believe the tests!"

"Who knows with those tests? It was a few days after you came home. The doctor said the effects could have worn off."

Who was this spy on campus who told her this?

I stare at her, speechless. I don't know whether I'm more surprised by how little she knows me to think I use drugs, or her obstinacy that doesn't hear what I say. It's all too familiar. I can never get through to her. It's like trying to swim upstream while my feet are tethered to a rock. Always sinking back, helpless and despairing with futility. Familiar as it is, it swallows me now as it did as a child. However much I tell myself I'm a fool to want her to see me, some part of me wanders around in a desert waiting and hoping. Maybe. Just maybe. Maybe if I somehow fit into her idea of me, she'll love me. Maybe if I do what she wants, become who she wants, she'll love me.

"Why did you go to that Muktananda cult?" Vasupinni nasally pipes in.

"It's *not* a cult. *Kriyas* are *kundalini* energy. I had a spiritual awakening."

"I wrote to Gurumayi after hearing about your drugs." Amma says. "Of course she wrote back denying it. But we've heard the stories about that ashram. Drugs and sex. That's what that cult's all about. You don't know the first thing about spirituality and are caught up in a sham."

"You *wrote* to her?" I'm outraged she wrote to Gurumayi. "I want to see her letter."

"There's *no* more discussion. *Go* write the letter to your teacher."

"What did she write? I want to see her letter."

"Some rubbish about your having a pure heart. Nothing much at all. *Go on.* There's *no* more to be said. We'll get tickets to leave tomorrow. I can't believe I have to face Daadi with this news." She clutches her head and moans. "What am I going to *tell* her?"

I'm surprised Gurumayi remembers me after our meeting in New York, and I'm flattered by her loving words. Yet they're sullied by Amma's distaste for her. I sit, frozen, in the armchair.

"Go *on!* Do you know how *shameful* this is?" She shakes her arm jaggedly, palm upturned, fingers thrusting her loathing at me. "To sleep with someone before you get married means you're like any cheap white girl. That you don't have any dignity as an Indian woman. We trusted you. We believed in you. Clearly, we were wrong. I'm *ashamed* of you. *Go! Go* write that letter."

Shame shudders and stirs awake in my belly. It crawls through me, its dark, cloud-like fingers curling and clutching, like a swarm of ravenous, black locusts that destroy everything strong, alive, and beautiful. My head bows. My shoulders stoop. I can't bear their eyes on me. With shame on my skin, I cannot think to come up with a different plan, a different argument. I do not believe I have a choice.

She is stronger than I am.

I freeze. I stagger out of the den, away from their gaze and fall on my bed.

Roopa Aunty follows me. She sits on an ivory straight-backed wooden chair beside my bed. Her worried eyes dart from me to Naina's begonias and impatiens outside. "It's not what we do, Mytrae. It's wrong. Here they sleep with anyone and everyone. They change partners at the drop of a hat. We're Indian. We're different. Sex is sacred. Marriage is the only place for it. We have that dignity. And it's different for us because we stay only with one man. Here they try anyone they can before they settle down. If Madhav dies, I won't marry again. I simply couldn't be with another man that way. There's no guarantee Evan will stay with you or marry you."

Because she's my favorite aunt, her disappointment falls thick and heavy upon me.

It's the first time anyone in my family's spoken to me about sex. I look down, embarrassed, and pick at my polyester floral comforter.

But limit myself to one man even if he dies? How severe! Why can't I have my own belief? Sex is exquisite pleasure, where I open to waves upon waves of love with Evan. It's a spiritual expansion.

Transcendent. Yet they make it seem repulsive, shameful, vile. And that *I* am repulsive, shameful, vile to enjoy it. Yet even as I question my family's rules around sexuality, shame, familiar as an old friend, seeps through me like a dark, spreading ink stain. It says, how dare you? How dare you enjoy something so bad? It wraps its dark fingers around my throat and mouth and silences me.

She pushes back the chair and stretches out her open palm. "Where's your passport and green card?" she says, abrupt and firm.

Helpless now, I rummage through my stack of folders on a shelf and pull out my navy blue Indian passport with its English and Hindi gold lettering of "Republic of India" and four lions standing back to back. Emperor Ashoka's emblem, the lions represent power, courage, pride, and confidence. I admired him for renouncing violence and wars and converting to Buddhism after walking through bloody carcasses on a battlefield. It's India's emblem now, with *satyameva jayate*, "Truth alone triumphs," in Sanskrit below. My green card, with my picture at fifteen, for which my family and I waited five years, is clipped to a page inside.

Limply, I hand them to her.

When Naina comes home that evening, I hear his outraged voice as he talks with the women in the kitchen.

I brace myself.

He blows into my room. His eyebrows are furrowed. His eyes flash with anger. His tight jaw thrusts out. He purses his lips and grits his teeth like he does before he's ready to beat me or Raghu. He stands over my bed menacingly, thrusting his hands at my face. "Have you no shame? You were both so disgusting at the restaurant in Chapel Hill. Falling over each other, eating food from each others' plates. Shame on you! We gave you so much more than other Indian girls. Freedom. Education. And *this* is what you go and do?"

I curl away from him, cringe into the corner of my bed, trembling. Will he thrash me?

"My blood is boiling. Do you know what you've done to our family? You've ruined our name and reputation. You're a *disgrace* and you've disgraced us," he shouts, his face black with rage.

"I have to call Evan," I say defiantly.

"No, you won't." His jaw is clenched. He knits his lips into a thin line.

"I have to return my library books. They're in his house. And what about my rent while I'm away?"

He leaves to talk with the women, then returns. "Only one call."

He watches me, seething, as I go into my parents' bedroom. I shut the door. Pick up the phone on their bedside table.

Please Evan, be home.

"Hello?" Evan answers.

I try not to sob. "Evan, my parents found out about us and they're taking me back to India for three months." I hear a click. Someone's listening in on the kitchen extension.

"Oh my God! Don't go, Nitro. You *can't* go!"

"They're saying I have to. Then they'll allow us to be together."

"If you go it'll all be over, don't you *see*?"

"It's only three months, Evan. We can do it."

"Can't you get out of there? I wish I could come get you." His voice is frantic.

Naina opens the bedroom door and walks towards me, clenching and unclenching his fist. "Put down the phone."

I stare at him. "I'm not done."

"Put *down* the phone." His face is grim. He stops a foot away from me. I feel the heat of his body. Smell his acrid sweat. The memory of him beating me after I cut my hair four years ago ripples through me.

"I have to go, Evan. I love you," I say in a rush and hang up.

Naina hovers two feet away, his sweat like rotting leaves. My body trembles. His eyes are daggers. My eyelids lower. I duck past him, and scuttle into my room.

Taut as a caged leopard, I sit on the edge of my bed. Should I leave? Jump out the window? Where can I go? We're way out in Charleston's suburbs. The closest 7-11 is three miles away. I could call Evan collect. Then what? It's 8pm. I can't be out alone all night. The bus station's at least fifteen miles away. I don't have money for a cab. If I walk, they'll find me soon enough. They'll call the police who will easily find me on the one road to Charleston. Then what? Visions of Naina chasing Raghu as a boy round and around our bedroom thrashing him flash through my mind. Raghu yelped and howled as Naina beat his face, shoulders, ears, and back. Raghu cowered for days after, head down at meals, not speaking to me, not even tossing his cricket ball up and down.

I shiver. Stare at my suitcase in the silvery moonlight. It gapes back at me, open-mouthed and silent.

The house seethes. Their voices rise and fall late into the night. Eventually, they turn in. If I tiptoe out, someone will definitely hear. Every creak can be heard in this old house. Amma and Naina's bedroom is next to mine. How close Naina was when I spoke to Evan. Menacingly close. His tall, broad frame and muscular shoulders. His fist opening and closing as he watched me. He'll thrash me to a pulp if I try to escape. My body sweats fear. I can't move. Can't think. Why do I feel so numb? It's like when I was little, when Amma said she would kill me.

Honeysuckle-scented night air wafts through the window, cools my burning face. I'll go to India. It's just three months. Of course Evan and I will stay true.

I'll be back.

Soon.

Part 2

Seetha's jaw drops. Her eyes open wide like lotus flowers in spring to stare at Rama. She cannot believe her ears. Did he, her beloved, just ask her that?

Rama repeats his question. "Seetha, are you chaste?"

Seetha takes a deep breath and draws herself straight. "I am, my lord," she replies. "I am pure as the river Ganga when she emerges from Mother Earth in the Himalayas. Ravana kept me in his palace garden surrounded by women servants. Every day he came to see me and ask me to bed with him. And every day I gave him the same reply, 'I won't. Have you no shame asking a married woman to your bed?"

Rama scratches his head. "But why didn't he just take you?"

Seetha replied, "He had his own moral code, my lord. Though he was a demon, he wouldn't take any woman by force, only if she desired him as well."

Rama cocks his head and strokes his beard. "Hmmm. I don't believe it."

"It's true, my lord. I wouldn't lie to you. I am Seetha, virtuous as any goddess. Why would I be with him when you're the only beat of my heart. With every breath, I thought of you and only you for eleven months and fourteen days." Her voice is like a sad violin. "Besides, if he'd taken me, I would be with child."

"You have to admit, it's hard to believe. I'm sorry, Seetha. It's not only for me, but for my people's peace of mind. I won't be respected if I take a woman who's been with another man for a year to his bed. I need you to prove it. I will organize a fire yagna."

He turns on his heels and walks away. Seetha stares at his retreating back. But she must do as he asks. He is her lord, her master. That is her duty and dignity as a wife. His wife.

She does the only thing she knows to do, and can do. Pray.

The yagna, ritual, is organized in the palace courtyard. Courtiers, ministers, and people of state are gathered. When it is time, Rama leads Seetha to the fire.

Dressed in white, Seetha closes her eyes, and lifts her hands in prayer. "Lord Agni, if I am pure, let me emerge unscathed."

She steps, barefooted, into the roaring flames.

Rama catches his breath. Everyone does.

The flames part. Seetha stands, her lips moving in prayer, in the midst of the roaring bonfire as the flames encircle her.

After a few minutes, Rama says, "Beloved, you may step out."

Seetha steps out, unscathed. Not a hair on her head was harmed. Her skin unsinged. Her sari white as Himalayan snow.

That night and for many nights, Rama takes Seetha back into their marriage bed and the long-lost lovers reunite.

But, much as she tries to put it behind her, Rama's mistrust of her words pulses through her like a haunting drone.

6
the first two months

1985

Surely, someone will see sense. They can't keep me indefinitely in a four-room cottage with my grandparents.

The relatives stream into the house like curious ants. The educated ones. The not-so-educated ones. Those who speak English. Those who speak only Telugu. Aunts, uncles, and cousins three and four-times removed. They're happy to see Amma. And, they smell scandal. I don't want to meet them but bow to Amma's insistence that I play along with her lie. No matter what, no one must sniff out what I've done. Their voyeuristic, suspicious eyes bore into me as I sit, eyes cast down, seething and panicked, the way Raghu and I did when we were scolded as children.

"How does someone who's been in a cult behave?" an aunt with bulging cataracts whispers to another, inquisitively looking me up and down.

"I wonder what really happened?" ogles another tightly wound aunt.

"How sane is she?"

"What drugs did she take?"

"Is their story true? Or was there a boy?"

"Poor Kamala. What you must be going through. So much worry!"

In India, there's license to talk about someone in front of them like a zoo animal.

Amma bemoans her fate. "What can we do? That country's such a bad influence. You have to be so careful with children there. Who would have thought this of Mytrae? We're so angry and disappointed with her."

When I can't bear the lie and their gawking eyes, I slip away into my room. But from under my door their voices point and murmur "bad girl," "shame on you for worrying your parents and disappointing your family" in an unrelenting *sussurando*.

This is Amma's outer circle. She won't tell them I slept with Evan. Family conversations, peppered with secrets, always confused me as a girl. "Don't tell so-and-so, but…" or "Keep this to yourself." Everyone was afraid of who knew what, but it always seemed like everyone knew everything anyway. They only pretended they didn't know, so they seemed like an ally and could hear their version.

But she tells her inner circle, a gaggle of cousins she grew up with, that there was a "boy" in the picture. Indians call men "boys" before they're married. Even when they're thirty-seven. "I have to tell *someone*," she'd said on the flight to Hyderabad. "I can't face Daadi's anger."

When she does, my aunts bolt upright on the edge of their seat, their eyes grow like saucers, nostrils flare, and tongues salivate. I'm the scandal of the decade.

"How disgusting."

"That country is terrible. They shamelessly sleep with each other."

"Yes, there's no respect. Men or women, they're like animals. No decency or dignity, I tell you."

"How *bad* we feel for you, Kamala. You gave her all the freedom. Let her go to graduate school. Encouraged and trusted her. You must be so disappointed."

"Yes, I really trusted her," Amma says. "We gave her the best of everything. Wake Forest was such a good school. She wanted to do music. Even that we let her do. I didn't imagine she would do *this*. But she's let us all down. Mother didn't want us to go to the U.S. because of this child, you know. And now… what to do? It's our karma."

"What's he like?" Gowri, her favorite cousin, asks, titillated.

"Oh, he's nothing. Long hair. Very ordinary-looking. Isn't doing anything. He's a cook. Can you believe it? A cook! He'll never amount to anything. What would people say?"

Evan's hair barely covers his neck. And what's wrong with long hair anyway?

Her inner circle invades my room. With each one, my heart flares with hope. Maybe *this* one will understand.

But they all sit on my bed and wheedle, "You can't base marriage on love. It simply doesn't work that way. He may love you today, but he won't tomorrow. Western men just want to have a good time, then leave you. What's the point of getting involved if it's not going to last? Marriage isn't the movies. Give this up, Mytrae. It'll be better for you in the long run. As you get older, you'll see the wisdom of what we're telling you."

Even a cousin only ten years older than I, with short hair, says, "My marriage may not be a Mills & Boon romance, but we're compatible and have a family. Our marriages are based on so much more. Family. Values. Tradition. And they work."

I stare at her. She's Westernized, with her haircut and clothes, but Indian inside. Does no one know what it's like to love? Is love inconsequential for Indians? Is marriage only practical? A transaction? My heart dims like a firefly in the night.

I need an adult—even one, just one—on my side.

And by adult, I mean someone married. Someone with power.

I must *do* something to get out of here. But what? I'm watched every hour, day or night. The servants have been ordered to be on guard. When I step out from my room, a servant hovers. When the phone rings, someone rushes to answer it. Every day I eagerly wait for the postman hoping to get a letter from Evan, but someone dashes to the door when the doorbell rings. If I step into the garden, the gardener shadows me. A Nepalese Gurkha patrols the grounds with a stout stick at night, a sheathed dagger on his belt.

I can't just pick up the telephone to call Evan. International calls must be booked in advance. There's no 9-1-1 or women's rights organization here.

I sit in the small bedroom of my grandparents' house, trapped.

What if I could escape? Grab Amma's keys from under her pillow at night? Even if she wakes up, fight her off, rush to her *almirah*, unlock it, take my passport and run out the front door? I won't get far, not without money. I'd probably be raped.

Could someone take me in? Not family. My school and college friends are abroad. Besides, no one will go against my family. Everyone believes parents know what's best for their children, no matter how brutal their ways. Can I become a maid or a tutor in someone's home? No, I'm too well educated and look well off. They'd be accused of kidnapping. The police? No, they won't listen to me—I'm unmarried and my family's well known. Besides, Vikram Uncle is Hyderabad's police commissioner. They'll bring me right back.

I'm not a U.S. citizen. Going to the Embassy isn't an option.

With each dashed idea, my prison bars choke me tighter. At twenty-two, unmarried, and in India, I have no rights to my body, my freedom, or my life. I haven't lived here as an adult. I get up from my bed and stare desperately at the ten-foot-high compound wall outside. Is this it? The end of everything?

I must *do* something. Escape. Find my way back to the U.S. But *what*?

Afternoons when Amma, Daadi, and Thatha nap, I creep to Roshan Uncle and Leela Aunty's elegantly furnished house next door. It's a refuge from Amma and Daadi's patrol. In the same compound as the cottage, it's the only place Amma allows me to go. I can listen to music there. Maybe if I can convince them to help, they'll speak up for me with Amma.

After studying at Cambridge in his twenties Roshan Uncle returned to India with British mannerisms and a clipped accent. Though brusque and somewhat intimidating, I hope, with his Western education that he'll take a stand against me being locked up. Weekdays, he's at his factory that manufactures conveyor belts. Leela Aunty's usually out socializing with her friends or shopping. Most mornings, their home recovers from late night parties where alcohol, rich food, music, laughter, and dancing abound. Servants sweep and mop the marble floors, roll up emerald and cream silk hand-knotted carpets, dust mahogany furniture, polish the silver, and water houseplants.

I slip in through the back door and take refuge in their study. One wall is lined with golden teak shelves filled with books, LPs, and CDs. An auburn corduroy sofa sits across from two fern green armchairs, a large teak desk with neatly stacked piles of papers against a third wall. Slipping off my sandals, the olive granite floor feels cool against my bare feet. I browse Roshan Uncle's prized Western classical music selection. Some recordings are from the '50s, some from this decade. Carefully handling an old LP, I place Beethoven's Fifth Piano Concerto on his turntable.

Rudolph Serkin.

The music transports me. My eyes close. My body remembers. Tears well. *This* is home. But I cannot return. The more music suffuses my cells, the further freedom seems. I can't make sense of it all. Isn't it human to feel and love such beauty? Is it because I love something so beautiful that I'm being punished? Why am I not allowed to love music just as they love their clothes, jewelry, parties, and social status? Limp with grief and despair I crumple over the emerald arm of the armchair, sobbing.

Evan. His warm searching eyes float into my mind. His tall, lean, strong body. I can smell his muskiness against my skin. Taste the sweetness of his long, succulent kisses. I long for your arms around me, your soft nuzzling and whispers. Our rides to ecstasy.

Are you out of your mind with shock and worry? Will you come for me? What would they say if you just showed up and knocked on our front door? What would they *do*? Though they would scream and raise a ruckus, I'd fling my door open and rush out with you. But India's too far. I don't expect you to come. We'd just begun, hadn't even talked about our future. I can't imagine life without you. I'm fool to have gotten on that stupid plane instead of listening to you.

As I'm wiping my tears, Leela Aunty floats in unexpectedly in a cream and magenta Bengal woven cotton sari and a cloud of exquisite floral perfume. I startle to see her. I quickly blot my cheeks with the sleeve of my salvaar-kameez. Get up and turn off the record.

"Sit, sit. Was it an affair or a crush?" she asks inquisitively in her strident voice. Slim, tall, fair, and pretty, her curly hair falls to a blunt cut below her ears. Sinking onto the sofa, she shakes one leg over the other, her manicured feet tapering into fashionable slippers.

I curl my toes under me. I don't think of Evan and me as an affair. But terminology aside, perhaps she'll understand. "An affair."

"So many people have affairs," her thin lips smirk, "and their families never find out." She pauses. Looks at me with marble eyes. "Were you in love with him?"

I nod and blubber uncontrollably. Even if she's nosy, at least she's talking to me. At least she asks about love instead of thinking it was just sex.

She hands me her cotton handkerchief embroidered with posies. Waits till I stop heaving. "I had an affair too before I was married."

I blow my nose. Look up at her in surprise.

"I met him in college and we got together a few times. My mother found out and stopped us from seeing each other."

"Why?"

"Because I was so young and he was still a student. My mother had my two younger sisters' futures to think about as well. So I didn't see him again."

"Were you in love with him?"

"At eighteen, what did I know about love? I liked him. I think I was infatuated."

"How did you marry Roshan Uncle?"

She explained how Daadi's friend had seen her while visiting a mutual friend. "The proposal came to my mother a few months after she stopped me from meeting the man I was infatuated with. I met Roshan Uncle and he was interested. I wasn't into him but my mother convinced me. My sisters talked me into it too. It was a good match. It's because of my marriage that my sisters have done well too."

Daadi had told me years after Roshan Uncle returned from England, he didn't want to get married, yet people alluded to his affairs. But a man's past is his own and no one questions him about it. After years of Daadi pressuring him, he agreed to get married on the condition that his future wife "be a dish." He was thirty, oh so late for a man, according to Daadi. In their wedding photograph, he looks eagerly at Leela Aunty while she leans back, hesitantly biting her lip. Eleven years older than her, he groomed her to be his mate at his social level. They have two lovely daughters and a whirlwind social life. But I wonder about their relationship when I hear loud fights from next door.

"Don't tell Daadi about the affair, okay?"

I nod.

"Look, you'll get over it soon," she says kindly. "Amma doesn't want you to go back. You're young, beautiful, and have your whole life ahead of you. Come over anytime you want. I know it can be really difficult with both of them. Borrow any books you like."

She leaves for a friend's house. I blubber some more, grateful for her kindness. And wait for Roshan Uncle to return from work.

He breezes into the study, a tennis racquet slung over his shoulder. Short and wiry, his hairy spindly legs stick through starched white shorts. His swarthy face is topped by a thick gray mop. "Had a bad day?" His black eyes peer at me through thick spectacles, then, as though he's irritated I'm there, he turns to busy himself with a small pile of post on his desk.

I nod, tears brimming.

"You'll have to get over this," he clips sternly in his British accent, without turning around. "You're not going back." Without a look, he strides out of the study to his bedroom and bangs the door.

His words slam in my face. My heart sinks. I hurriedly get up and turn off the record player. I don't want to stay here a minute longer. I slink back to my room. Everyone, it seems, has hardened against love and freedom, even if they tasted it. Maybe especially if they have.

The next day, Amma scolds, "So you told Leela Aunty you slept with Evan! If you tell anyone else, I'll kill you."

I'm stung by Leela Aunty's betrayal. I'd better watch my mouth. Whatever I tell anyone will worm its way back to Amma. Do I have to learn this a million times? They're on *her* side, not mine.

I watch Thatha stroll in the garden every evening. He walks on the lawn under the *gulmohar* tree, winds through the rock garden, beside hibiscus and zinnia flowerbeds. Then he sits on a bench to watch the flaming orange sky fade into blue-gray twilight. Huddled in a cornflower blue cardigan and billowing white pajamas, he hasn't spoken more than a few words to me since I came. What is he thinking? He's disappointed in me. Deeply. He barely speaks to me. When I turn to him he looks away. But he's my final hope. Surely, he won't want all my years of dedication to my music reduced to ashes?

I join him on the teal iron bench on the lawn as he gazes at the changing Hyderabad sky, the long green limbs and vermilion blossoms of the flame of the forest. Crows caw and mynahs chitter as they flock to their nests. City traffic hums in the distance and an occasional motorbike rips through the neighborhood. The earth and stones sigh, surrendering their heat to descending nightfall. A patch of garden, a pinhole of hope.

"Thatha, can I have an aerogramme?"

A koyal calls hauntingly. He looks at me, then away. His hearing aid crackles, so I know he's heard. We sit in silence. I wait, barely breathing, as the coral sky bleeds into indigo. Then, he stands up and shuffles inside.

The next day, Amma chastises me. "Don't *ever* ask anyone for an aerogramme again. *No* one will give you one. It's all over and you'd better accept it. You're *not*. Going. Back."

Nights, I startle awake drenched in sweat. Desperate. Helpless. Longing for Evan's body entwined around me. His soft breathing in my ear. I sob into the dark arms of night, so much softer than day's glaring eyes. I tug its black shroud tight about me. In the thin silvery moonlight, with the light rustle of leaves, I can be alone with my grief. Muffle my gasps into my pillow so Amma won't wake on her twin bed beside mine.

One night she does. "You know why you can't sleep, don't you?" she spits.

I choke a sob back down my throat. I won't cry with her.

"You want *that*," she hisses at my curved back.

My body flames. She thinks I was with Evan just for sex.

Her words ring in my ears. *All your education is nothing compared to your virginity.* The tortured wisp wafts up in me... *but I was never a virgin to begin with.*

Would she set me free if I told her? Told them all? Splatter my secret and watch it spread like ruby blood from a just-broken hymen upon the white sheet of the family's name and pride?

She'd slap my face, my mouth. Pummel my cheeks left to right to left again, till I redden raw. Pulverize and grind the truth back into my mouth and back down my throat. Till she draws blood.

She'd scream, "Have you no shame? After what you've done?" That I'd accused her son.

Daadi would gasp, her jaw hanging slack. Her hands would rise, shaking, to cover her mouth, "*Ayyo*, I wish you were never born."

They would huddle and whisper in Daadi's bedroom. Daadi would break, eventually, like a Hyderabad summer swells red hot and taut, and just when you can't bear it any longer bursts into ribbons of monsoon rain. She'd cry for me and be torn inside, but I'd always be defiled in her eyes.

Amma won't break. If I think she hates me now, she'd turn on me like a wolf mother with raised hackles and bared teeth defending her cub. I don't even know what they'd do to me. Any memory of me blackened for sure. Any talk of me stifled into a deep well of silence. They'd cover the blood-stained sheets with silk *razais*, quilts, and embroidered cushions. Daadi would hang her head with sorrow and shame for months, years. Amma would come up with something, anything, to hold her head up high. There would be another lie. And another.

Until I no longer existed in their minds, like I'd never been born.

I have the trump card to set myself free but the truth is, the long shadow of my past pins me down, squeezing the air out of my lungs as he did, then. I cannot say the words. Cannot do it to them. Cannot bear to lose what few scraps of virtue I have in their eyes. Better the shadow's pitch-black mouth swallow me up whole.

The Gurkha's stick rattles against the compound wall in the still night on his watch. Thwack-thwack. Thwack-thwack.

You're bad.

I'm bad. Bad. Bad.

Thwack-thwack.

Amma's presence fills the room which is stuffed with remnants of her vivacious Hyderabad life before she immigrated. Two twin beds each piled high with three cotton mattresses. Her hand-cranked Singer sewing machine. A big round teak table rammed into a corner. A white bookcase full of her dusty classics and spiritual books. Two steel *almirahs* crammed with cotton saris for daily wear, and silk ones for parties and weddings. Tarnished silver platters and dishes for parties she threw for over a hundred people at a time. Vases, porcelain curios, and knick-knacks that decorated *Laughing Waters*. There's nothing "laughing" about them now. I look at two figurines I loved as a girl. A shepherdess tending her flock of sheep. A cherubic boy and a girl kneeling to pray and holding a book open to "Our Father." Every passing year, chances of my parents returning permanently to India fade, yet Amma clutches her old life. I, another once-loved dream, have joined them in storage.

I sit on the cold, green-tiled floor and open the bookcase. Georgette Heyer, Daphne du Maurier, Jane Austen, Thomas Hardy. Her more recent spiritual acquisitions of Ramakrishna Paramahamsa, Vivekananda, Eknath Easwaran. I pull out a thick navy-blue bound book without a title. It opens to black parchment pages and the musky smell of her past. Before she got married she worked at the *Indian Express*, a national newspaper, in Madras. A picture of her at my age falls out. I look at her young, beautiful, and laughing, sitting at a table in her office surrounded by her journalist colleagues. Her eyes like stars. Everything ahead of her.

I would like to have known her then.

Pasted in the black pages are articles from her weekly column, A Woman's Angle. I turn page after page reading the titles. "Why Women Need to Be Educated." "The Ills of Our Dowry System." "The Dangers of Our Caste System." "Why Women Should Vote." "Women Have Minds Too, Yes They Do!"

This was the mother I was so proud of. *These* were the ideals she instilled in me. She stopped working after she married. It wasn't appropriate then. But after Raghu and I were in school, she taught journalism part-time at Osmania University. She was so Westernized. Liberal. Progressive. Or so I thought. What *happened*? After we immigrated, she started going to Hindu philosophy lectures in Winston-Salem, becoming more Indian than she'd been in India.

"Come out," Amma yells, entering the room. "How much longer will you stay here? Come out and be with everyone."

"I *won't!*" I scream. "You've ruined me. Ruined my *life*."

"*You're* the one who ruined it."

"Why did you educate me just to rip it all away?"

I lift up the scrap book and tilt it towards her. "*This* is who you used to be. You believed in women's education. You wrote about it."

Her thick eyebrows furrow. She gasps. Shakes her head. "Of course we do. We sent you to the best schools. But look what you've gone and done."

"You can't keep me here against my will."

"You know nothing at all about life. You're going to stay here till you get married."

I can't bear to be in the same room with her. My only refuge is the bathroom. I dash in. Bolt the door. Slide to the floor, my back against the white tiled wall, shaking. Head on my knees, I sob my heart out. My rage. My heartbreak. My lost freedom. Snot oozes in long jelly strands to the gray granite floor.

I want to go back to where I belong. To the music department, Hill Hall, to my practice, study, and teaching. I close my eyes and take myself there. The corridors and rooms singing with pianos, clarinets, and violins. Warbling with sopranos. An occasional honking tuba or trumpet. I smell the musty manuscripts stacked on pine shelves in my office. Beethoven's Op. 110. Debussy's *L'isle joyeuse*. I see the uneven cream and black keys of the faded teak Steinway I use to teach undergraduate students. When I sit down at the piano and my fingers rest on the keyboard, I become one with it and enter worlds of beauty, my body suffused with music. On that black chipped piano stool is where I'm most deeply myself. Hear the sublime first movement of Beethoven's Op. 110. *Moderato cantabile molto espressivo.* My fingers play it on my arms. Don't they know such beauty? Where your soul rises like gossamer to the heavens? Where you disappear and all that exists is great, great beauty. Where you *become* Beauty?

"Open up, Mytrae!" Amma, Daadi, and the servants bang on the door and window's iron grill.

Slowly, through the din and my tears, it dawns on me.

It's over.

Everything I've loved is over. My music. Evan. My life in the U.S. I'm never going back.

The world goes dark. Nothing matters now. Nothing at all.

I may as well be dead.

Amma tries to marry me off.

"We're going to visit Mukesh Uncle. Wear something nice," she orders, rummaging in her almirah. "It's been two months since you've been here. Time to get over that boy. Here, wear this. I wore it when I was your age." She pulls out a yellow chiffon, the color of whipped egg yolks. Flings it on my lap.

"I don't want to go."

"They've invited both of us. You're going."

"They're *your* friends. I'm hardly feeling social."

"I don't care. You're going and that's that."

"Well then, if I'm going I don't want to wear a sari."

"You have to. You're in India now. No more running around in pants."

I just want her off my back. I can't think. Can't feel. I pull on the thick beige cotton petticoat that falls to my ankles. Slip my arms into the blouse that stops just below my breasts. It's one of three sari blouses I had tailored when I visited two summers ago. It's loose now. I'm skinnier by ten pounds at least. Pin it in the back with a safety pin so it doesn't flap. With each turn of the sari's six yards around my body I feel like I'm suffocating. Never liked saris. Midriff bare, neck scooped low, everything else tightly sheathed. I can't walk with long, loose strides, the way I do in jeans. I look at myself in the mirror. This isn't me.

At Mukesh Uncle's plush home I sink into the corner of a sumptuous sofa. Don't want their eyes on me. Hope no one talks to me. Parvathi, his gracious wife, plies us with onion *pakoras* and cucumber-mint sandwiches. Amit, their son, and a couple of other guests are there for dinner. Mukesh Uncle cracks silly jokes. I smile wanly, feeling like a distant echo of myself. Drift in and out, mostly out, of conversation. Answer only when I'm spoken to. Don't care what they think. Somehow, the interminable evening ends.

The following day, Amma asks, "Are you interested in seeing Amit again?"

"For what?"

"You know…"

I stare at her, aghast.

"He likes you a lot. He's a good boy. He's an engineer and studied in the U.S. We know the family. They're good people. He's not the best catch, but good."

And what kind of a catch am I, with my broken hymen? Amit was a slender, quiet man who let his parents do the talking last evening. His years of freedom in the U.S. didn't show. He sat with his head bowed deferentially, hands clasped, reaching for mixed nuts now and then. Four months ago he would've failed Amma's lofty standards but now he's good enough. And what about him? Isn't he expecting an unbroken hymen?

I shake my head and roll my eyes. "Don't you understand? I'm not a cow you can shop around. There's no way I'm getting married, whomever you introduce me to."

One freedom I have, even now, is that women in my family are allowed to say "yes" or "no" to proposals that come their way. Most Indian women, especially ones less educated, don't have that freedom. They're simply told whom they have to marry. So Amma can push all she wants, but I'll have to agree.

Amma asks Daadi, "Can you believe it? She hardly spoke to that boy."

"Enough, Kamala," Daadi says, with a frown. "Leave the child alone. She's not ready. Why are you pushing her? And he's so bla-a-ack!" Distaste engulfs her face.

Thank God for Daadi. And her obsession with color. In an arranged marriage the first consideration, after family, is looks. Like most Indians, she categorizes everyone with her caste system of color. There's black, brown, wheatish, fair, and very fair.

I'm relieved when Amma heeds Daadi and stops badgering me.

I decide to kill myself.

Oblivion's better than this. I can't live here, not like this, in a coffin.

But how? Slit my wrists? How long will it take? How painful will it be? How much blood will pool? Will someone find me before I die? Break down the door? I don't want to end up in a coma but anything's better than *this*.

I take my toilet case into the bathroom. Lock the door. Unscrew the single screw of my pink Bic plastic razor with a nail file. The cool, slim blades fall into the shadowy hollow of my sweating trembling palm. So small, so sharp, so lethal. I step down into the bathing area. Sit cross-legged on the cold marble floor. I shiver. Stare at the blades for minutes of hung time. Deep breath. Okay. *Now*. Feel the cool steel silver on my left wrist. Close my eyes. Really? Am I *really* going to do this?

I open my eyes. Look up. Through the grimy window mesh, the peepal tree's branches and leaves rustle *whoosh whoosh* with a soft breeze. With life. Look around the sparse tomb-like bathroom faintly smelling of disinfectant. I can't. I simply can't. Can't bring myself to put blade to flesh regardless of this horror. I'll get through it somehow. Don't know how, but life—or whatever this is—is too precious.

Music and sex opened me to utter beauty and ecstasy. Something no one else in my family seems to feel. No matter what, I won't let them touch or break that part of me.

I stand up. Toss the blades and razor in the dustbin.

I step out of my bedroom into the living room suffused with caramelized onion, ginger, and garlic and halt. I overhear Daadi and Amma talking in the kitchen. I pause in my bare feet to listen. "Why did you take that child there?" Daadi says angrily. "I told you not to. She was only fifteen. Such a sweet child. So impressionable."

"I didn't know, Mother," Amma says. "I thought if she stayed at home with us she'd be fine. I thought our values were well rooted and she could withstand that country."

"It's all your fault. You should have kept an eye on her. You were playing with fire, taking her there at that age." A steel spatula scrapes angrily against a cast iron tureen.

A long pause. Good that Amma's getting a dose of what she dishes out. But I also feel for her—I know what it's like to receive a tongue-lashing from Daadi.

"Why'd you think I didn't let you go to England?" Daadi's voice softens like ghee warming in the sun.

"I know, Mother." Amma sighs, her voice hollow. Her Ventolin inhaler rattles as she shakes it, followed by her long, struggled inhale.

The usual whiff of worry flits through me.

It's her biggest regret. Not being allowed to go. She was a star college student in her early twenties when she applied to Oxford. I can see her, young and slender in her half-sari, opening the envelope with the blue and gold Oxford crest, hands trembling as she reads it and dashes, her thick, hip-length braids flying behind her, to tell Thatha. I can see him jump up from his desk, beam with pride and joy, and kiss her three times on both cheeks. *His* firstborn. *His* daughter. He went to Cambridge. Now *she* will go to Oxford. And they rush to tell Daadi.

But Daadi's face sours like day-old milk, and she says in a voice like iron, "You can't go. You're unmarried."

Amma's face changes, a watercolor of puzzlement, disbelief, shock, frustration, and outrage. "But…" she begins.

"No buts. That's that. I won't allow it. Forget about it now. Time to get married. We're looking for a boy. Gowri's getting married. It's time for you, too.

And so the matter is sealed. Everyone knows you can't argue with Daadi and even if you dare, you won't get anywhere. Even Thatha would raise his hands helplessly, bow and shake his head to say, "If your mother doesn't want it, I can't go against her."

So Oxford rattles around in Amma, shrieking like an old, lost ghost caught in between worlds. She doesn't speak of it much. But our early years in the U.S., she'd tell cashiers at the drug store, the fabric store, Sears and JC Penney's that yes, she could indeed speak English and had been accepted to Oxford. They didn't know what she was talking about. Sometimes, she'll say about Roshan Uncle in a tone thin, dark, and wistful as an oboe, "He went to Cambridge."

I always felt sorry for her that she couldn't fly.

But I will. Somehow.

Fly.

7

a month, a swami

1985

Tens of thousands sit cross-legged on large *dhurries* in a New Delhi cricket stadium, eagerly awaiting Swami Chinmayananda's arrival. Stalls stacked with his books and brochures border the stadium. He arrives in a gleaming, black Mercedes-Benz heralded by a cavalcade of army men on motorcycles. Human barricades—dual rows of men holding hands—make passage through the pressing throngs as he walks to the dais, a bowing, scraping retinue trailing behind.

Amma brought me here to her favorite guru, with the hope that a modern swami will know what to do with me and I might "get purified."

I came just to get out of the house. And with the hope that, if he's modern, surely he won't allow anyone to be locked up. But I wonder, can I *really* be purified? Was I *ever* pure?

Regal and austere, Chinmayananda strides onstage on two-inch *padukas*, wooden platform sandals, to the chanting of Sanskrit *slokas*. Tall and lean, he's magnetic as a leopard, commanding as a king. The only things soft about him are his flowing silk ochre robes and foot-long tapering gray beard that he thoughtfully strokes while he thunders fortissimo on the *Bhagawad Gita* and *Mundako Upanishad*.

I'm skeptical. Why is he so ostentatious? But, along with hushed thousands, I listen spellbound to his passionate, profound discourses. This is no ordinary, milk-sweet swami. This is a lion. A colossus come to shake the world. I don't know much about religion but his Advaita Vedanta teachings ring in me clear and true as a temple bell. They are familiar as music I've heard aeons ago. As I listen, it dawns on me that I'm not hearing these truths for the first time, but remembering what I've known for lifetimes.

However reluctant I am to open to anyone Amma wants me to meet, this swami has a wisdom, brilliance, and power that I cannot help but admire.

I enter the spacious five-star hotel suite. Very plush for a swami. I hover nervously by the door. My heels dig into the Persian rug but Amma shoves me from behind. She was able to get a private audience with him, as a few people in our family are long-time devotees.

The room vibrates like a live wire. Chinmayananda sits, his spine like a lightning rod to heaven, on an emerald paisley armchair.

"Come," he nods to me. "Nothing is wrong."

Then why am I here?

"Prostrate," Amma says before my seat hits the floor.

I bow on the crimson paisley rug. Why do I have to do this? Why is Amma relinquishing her power to him when she doesn't with any man? His presence is like the aftershock of thunder. I reel from his force. I sit up, cross-legged and wary. Three lines of *vibhuti*, sacred ash from the fire of his austerities and penance, streak across his broad forehead. A fiery vermillion, turmeric, and sandalwood *tilak* on his third eye marks his Divinity. But his gaunt seventy-something face is neither warm nor loving. His hooded coal eyes bore into mine. Is he reading my mind? Peering into my heart and soul? Does he see the blackness I hide? I feel stripped. My eyes lower to the rug. And wait. I know not to speak first with elders or teachers, certainly a swami.

He wags his foot and strokes his coarse gray beard. "You didn't commit a crime," he growls, his voice like thunder. "You wanted a boyfriend."

At least he's more understanding than Amma. To her I may as well have killed someone. Will you tell her to let me go free? At least leave the house? But the questions only rattle around in my head like dolls in a box, unable to find my throat.

"In that country there's so much freedom. *Too* much freedom." His tone is like a scythe. "But you're Indian. Things are different for us. I don't have to tell you that. That's why you've been brought back. You have to learn what it means to be an Indian woman."

A silent shriek of terror rips through me. It is all so final. I can withstand Amma, my family even. But this… his spiritual judgment… shreds me. I feel his power like a wrestler's brawny arm bending my will to his as I struggle to hold on to myself.

I'm *impure*.

He waits for me to speak but I can't. He's given his verdict. What's left to say? Who am I, after all? A little mouse from Chapel Hill beside his spiritual giant-ness?

"Tell me about the *kriyas*," he invites.

I look up, surprised he still talks to me after his judgment. "I don't really know, Swamiji. I go to a Siddha Yoga meditation group and get *kriyas* when I meditate."

"What do you feel?" His eyes tunnel into mine.

"I'm not aware of anything. My friends tell me I shake and sometimes do *yogasanas*." Yoga poses.

He stares out the window and strokes his foot-long beard. "Kundalini yoga is an accepted path. But the teacher must be in close contact with the student. Otherwise, things can get dangerous. I knew Nityananda, Muktananda's teacher. *He* was a true teacher. But Muktananda… and now the brother and sister team of Siddha Yoga…" his voice trails skeptically. "It's not a path I follow. My path is *jnana yoga*, the path of knowledge."

Is Siddha Yoga a false path? Was I foolish to choose it?

He pauses and stares out the window, still wagging his foot.

What is he thinking?

"You can go now," he orders.

My forehead brushes the carpet at his feet. I flee his hotel room and wait in the hallway for Amma.

When Amma emerges she says, "Swamiji wants you to travel with him for six weeks. His secretary's ill so he wants you to help him with his correspondence."

I stare at her in surprise. "You're letting me travel alone with him? For *six weeks*?"

"He's asked for you. Who knows why? It's a great honor and blessing. You won't be alone with him. You're not that special. He has so many around him. You're Indian, Mytrae, and you've forgotten that. We're all helping you return to who you are."

Why does *he* want *me* around him? Because my great-aunt and great-uncle are his longtime devotees? Am I, as a wayward woman, a challenge to him? Well, it's better than being locked up. And perhaps… after… who knows, maybe I'll be purified enough he'll tell her to set me free.

On the outskirts of Bombay, at Chinmayananda's Powai ashram, a *brahmacharini*, woman novitiate, knocks on my aluminum door at 3:30 a.m. for meditation. Dipping a brass jug in a cracked iron bucket of icy water, I hurriedly bathe. In my small, austere room, I wrap a sari around myself and follow the wafting sandalwood incense to the Shiva temple. On its altar a few mud lamps coax forth the dawn. Cross-legged *brahmacharis* chant *stotrams*, hymns. The cold air reverberates with sounds of sacred Sanskrit, and my body crisps to alert on the hard marble floor.

The large marble Shiva in the temple enchants me. Blue-skinned, the crescent moon ensconced in his beautiful black hair coiled high on his head, snakes milling about his neck, garlands around his bare torso, Shiva smiles through half closed eyes with such sweetness and love at me that I can see his lips move. A transcendent bliss and peace descends upon me. My heart flowers open. I've found what Chinmayananda calls *ishta devata*, my personal deity.

After two hours, scalding milky *chai* warms me as I wander through the ashram's sprawling banyan and peepal trees, enchanted, as daybreak swathes the sky pink, and ochre, then gold. *Brahmacharis* and *brahmacharinis* in white cotton robes stroll, radiating purity and stillness. The earth throbs with time-worn wisdom, purity, and truth. The morning's chants reverberate through me. It slowly dawns on me what Chinmayananda's introducing me to.

As I stand beneath the magnificent banyans, my blood and being fill with pride to realize what India's been through the ages—an offering of sacredness to the world.

I reach towards its truths with both hands. And hope, above everything, that this might clear my deepest, darkest shame.

A woman devotee, her eyes wide with fearful respect, tells me I have to go to his room at four o'clock every morning for a couple of hours of dictation. Then I have to type them, get his signatures, and mail them. He gets bags of letters every day, she says, and replies to each one. After that, I'm free to attend his lectures, sit with him in *satsang*, and go with him to *bhikshas*, meals in people's homes. Her nervousness warns me not to mess up or upset him.

My first morning, I hover apprehensively in front of his door, then lightly knock.

"Come," he calls.

I enter. The room is fragrant with sandalwood incense. Electric with his presence and concentration. The flame of an oil lamp dances at a Ganesh statue's feet. He's been up for a couple of hours already. His back to me, he hunches over a large mahogany desk, an empty teacup by his elbow. I prostrate nervously.

"*Om Namah Shivaya*," he intones in his resonant bass.

Without glancing at me, he nods toward a big rose silk cushion on the floor by his desk. I sit gingerly on its tasseled edge and pick up the notepad and ballpoint pen on it. He says, "I'll dictate letters and you'll type them."

"Yes, Swamiji," I reply, sotto voce.

We work through stacks of letters from devotees all over the world. I'm surprised how many hundreds of professionals and serious seekers crave his wisdom on every possible issue. Vedantic concepts, spiritual experiences, family fights, marital and parenting problems. Where to buy a house. Whom their children are to marry. How to grow mission centers, build a temple, get donations, untangle political knots.

I do what I'm told but refuse to treat him like he's the King of England. At *bhikshas* and *satsang*, women fawn over him in their best silk saris and glittering jewelry. Jostle against each other to sidle up as close as they can to him. Compete with each other to serve his next spoonful while he slurps their food. Titter, hands to their mouths, when he compliments their *payasam*, rice pudding. Wait with bated breath for a look, a nod, a smile, to wash or massage his feet. The men stand, shoulders respectfully bowed, hands folded, and receive *prasad*, blessed food, beaming like it's a gift from God. His every sentence is cherished and analyzed.

I'm suspicious about almost everything. Why does he court wealthy, corrupt Bombay magnates at *bhiksha*s? Why does he wear silks, gold watches, and slip plump envelopes he's handed into his pocket with a big grin? Why does everyone bow and scrape before him, relish every look and word like they've won a lottery? And why would any swami wither his *brahmacharis* to cowering heaps with sarcasm and rage? Devotees say he gets angry to wake them up. He knows everything, they say. He can do anything because he's Realized. *God*-Realized, they say wide-eyed, in hushed tones.

That awes and frightens me. That he sits beside God—a mysterious, powerful being to whom I've never really said hello.

"Western music's too emotional," Chinmayananda's lips curl with derision as he looks at me across a crowded living room. We're at a *satsang* where devotees cluster around him like grapes. A *Bhagawad Gita* chant plays in the background. I wish I could disappear into the wall. I don't want his attention in public. "Western music is of the heart, panting, desperate, heaving." He pants and heaves, his tongue hanging out like a dog. "Only Indian music is spiritual. Westerners are too emotional. They don't understand real music." He points at me. "And *you* don't understand."

My cheeks flare. *You* don't know what you're talking about. You're not a musician. Have you ever listened to a Beethoven symphony, a Rachmaninoff piano concerto, the Archduke piano trio? Mozart or Bach? Have you soared on sounds that vault you into delight and ecstasy, into otherworldly planes of being? Has sound ever pervaded your every cell so that you don't know where you end and the music begins? Where you dissolve into a vast exquisiteness and become that sacred beauty? You haven't.

But I pause with his authoritative conviction. Does Indian music have something that Western music doesn't?

"*You* are too emotional. Too *rajasic*," he jeers, his face in a condescending sneer. He abruptly stands up as though he cannot bear the sight of me and goes to his lunch.

I feel like I've just been crumpled up and thrown in the trash. Everyone turns to stare. Am I unevolved because I love Western music? Are my emotions shameful? Is something wrong with me because I feel so much, love so much?

Hinduism characterizes people into three types. *Sattvic* people are serene, pure, and mindful. *Rajasic* people are energetic, vital, and passionate. *Tamasic* people are slow, dull, and heavy. In his talks he tells us to rise above our passions and desires and become *sattvic*. Before I met him I hadn't an inkling what category I was in, and didn't care.

His disparaging certainty unnerves me. Am I bad if I'm *rajasic*? *Music* too?

You don't know what you're talking about, I fume silently, my head down and cheeks hot, twisting and untwisting my handkerchief into a ball.

His public humiliations continue.

At a devotee's home I crouch to stroke a German Shepherd and fondle its ears. I croon, "You're so beautiful, you lovely guy." Seeing me, Chinmayananda loudly proclaims, "These Westerners love animals more than people. *Tchah!*"

Everyone stares. My face burns.

After a *bhiksha*, some devotees lead Chinmayananda to the verandah to rinse his hands and mouth. I stand some twenty feet from him and the crowd. He gargles loudly, looks up at me, then aims the water from his mouth at my feet. The water splashes against my ankles and I step back. He does it again. And again. How *dare* he? Furious and shamed, I turn on my heels and walk away.

Walking away is the only way I know to rebel against him. But over time his public shaming serrates my core. It confirms my dark secret that I'm bad. Shameful. Impure. I wish I could slink away from his and his devotees' eyes into a cave to hide.

Gradually at first, then more feverishly like a mouse clutched in a hawk's talons, I begin to scratch and claw and tear at myself. Doubt what I love. And what I know.

The bus rumbles and teeters up the Himalayan foothills as the plains drop away along with their heat, dust, and city bustle. Simple hamlets and villages speckle the hillsides. Mud-patted homes painted terracotta, leaf green, and turmeric. Rural folk with sparkling eyes, wide smiles, and an easy, pliant warmth carry baskets of kindling, vegetables, and fruits on their heads. I inhale the cool, crisp air, fragrant with eucalyptus. *This* is the India I love.

I alight from the bus with the other devotees in Chinmayananda's ashram. Slowly, I rotate, drinking in the astounding beauty of the snow-capped mountains. We're in Sidhbari, a hamlet in the lush Kangra valley in Himachal Pradesh. Sidhbari means the valley of sages. This, people say, is his favorite ashram. It's where he's most at peace. I can see why.

In the ashram, a red, yellow, and green 23-foot idol of Hanuman, the muscular monkey deity, kneels, a mace on his shoulder. On the roof of Chinmayananda's *kutiya*, cottage, a massive black granite Shiva *lingam* rises erect, turgid, and bold into the sky.

Powerful. Male.

Our first evening Chinmayananda looks at me sternly and orders, "You'll eat dinner with me every night. I won't eat unless you're there."

"Yes, Swamiji." I bow my head, still hating his control and authority.

So every night, a ten-year-old boy and I sit at his table surrounded by devotees. Chanting a few mantras, he tears a piece of *roti* and wraps it around curried vegetable. The first he places in the boy's mouth; the second in mine. My hands wring with shame under the tablecloth. He isn't gentle but grimaces with repulsion lest his fingers touch my saliva. Why, if this is his blessing, should he do it with such disgust? But his devotees look at me with envy. For they push and shove to grab his plate after he eats so they can eat on it without washing. To them his saliva, his look, everything he touches is with the hand of God.

But one night, I stay in my room. I won't go. Not tonight. I hate him. Hate him feeding me. He wants my heart. Wants me to surrender to him. I won't. Maybe he'll forget.

Half an hour after dinner time, a woman rushes in, "*Here* you are! I've been looking all over! Come, come! Swamiji sent for you. He's angry! Why didn't you go for dinner? He won't eat without you. Hurry, hurry!"

I leap off my bed. As we scurry to his *kutiya* I ask her again and again, "Why can't he eat without me?" She glares at me like I'm a fool. The devotees frown at me when I slink into the dining room. Chinmayananda sits before his untouched plate, his thick eyebrows furrowed. *No* one makes him wait. He glowers at me as I slide into my chair. My resolve to challenge him crumbles. I've made him wait. Him, with his ill health. Him, an illustrious swami. Him with all his glory, power, wisdom, and realization.

"You wanted to see what I would *do*? You wanted to see how *important* you are? You wanted me to send for *you*? *Here*!" He thrusts a mouthful angrily into my mouth.

I flinch at his harsh, angry fingers. Wish I could spit out the *roti*, bread. But I swallow it without tasting. Sit with my head bowed. When he gets up, I cower and quake more than usual against the wall to let him pass.

I hate being here. Hate that I'm supposed to adore him like his fawning devotees. Hate his attention. His power. Being so close to him.

After dinner the devotees scold me, "Why weren't you here? Don't disobey him. You're so blessed he's feeding you. Don't do it again."

"I forgot," I mumble, looking down, so they can't see the hate in my eyes.

I enter his room one morning to refresh his water flask. He's at his desk, the tea I brought earlier untouched. I pick up his cup.

"Leave it," he growls.

"It's become cold, Swamiji. I'll bring you a fresh cup."

He swills it in a gulp.

"You've become so sweet." He swivels toward me. Wraps his arm around my waist. Draws me close. Buries his face between my breasts.

What is he *doing*! I freeze. I want to push him away but don't dare. He doesn't move for the longest time. Is he blessing me? Or... *what*? I stare at his oily gray hair that falls in thin strands below his shoulders. After what seems like ten minutes he releases me, then swivels back to his writing like nothing happened. Like I'm not here.

I leave his room feeling like I did when I crawled into bed after Raghu finished with me. Too ashamed to tell. Was it a blessing? Or a curse, I wonder, as I whisk buttermilk for his mid-morning drink. I want to tell his inner circle, don't you see the Emperor isn't wearing any clothes?

I haven't heard any sexual rumors. But I've wondered about the erotic frenzy of the women around him. The only whispers are that he uses snuff, sometimes smokes cigarettes, and speaks at clandestine Hindu political fundamentalist meetings.

I crush curry leaves in a mortar and pestle to flavor his buttermilk, waves of fear and doubt seething and churning in my belly. How can I possibly speak about sexuality and him in the same sentence? *No one will believe me.* Why did he paw at me? Am I sending out something that I should be ashamed of? Even the scriptures, apart from the Swami, warn against sexual pleasure.

Maybe if I let go of my desires, I will become pure?

Day after day, I feel the tornado of him bending the tree of me. I twist and turn to hide everything I know is beautiful. Everything I know is true. I curve away from him to shield myself from his eyes, his words. His black cow-dung words. Others' eyes.

But his tornado blows relentless that month. I feel his force, his spiritual authority bending me. I obey. Type his letters.

Sit quietly, like a good girl.

We're told to attend the village nurses' song and dance event. After dinner we stroll into the valley, as the moon rises over the snow-capped Himalayan foothills, as deodar, pine, and conifer trees stretch their green arms into sunset's golden embers. Across the Kangra valley, through the distant mist, yellow lights of Dharamsala and McLeod Ganj twinkle. The air bites cold but the bright-eyed, ruddy-cheeked nurses have a bonfire blazing. They sing their cheerful modal tribal songs, clapping and swaying like merry wildflowers.

Chinmayananda reclines long and lean on a lounge chair covered with an amber blanket. His thumb turns his *mala*'s *rudraksha* beads. I hover behind the crowd. But his eyes seek me out over heads of black hair. "Everyone dance." He glares at me. "And I mean *everyone*."

I step into the circle, self-conscious and embarrassed. Try to ignore him. Turn my back to him as I gyrate and undulate. Let go and whirl as if to say fuck you and your religion.

But I feel his eyes travel up and down my moving body, strip me naked while saying "Shameless whore."

He sees *it*. The blackness in my soul.

Still, I dance. I don't want him to touch the beauty of me. I bend and turn and twist against his power, his lust, his loathing. But, with a great groan, the tree of me rents in two, splits, and flies off into the night. Half a tree, wings like a torn leaf, shrieking, into the wide lost cold darkness. It's my soul, my fire, my truth, and my power. Slowly, amidst the clapping and songs, I wind to a standstill. My steps slow, falter, and stop. My body a crumpled, crinkled movement.

I slowly back away from him into the crowd. And do the only thing I know to do. Turn my hate of him towards myself. Hate my femininity, my twenty-two-year-old body which whirled and cupped and curved to rock and reggae in Chapel Hill. Ways my body flows when I play Schumann and Debussy. Ways my body rode, tumbled, shivered like gossamer. Shuddered with ecstasy while making love with Evan.

Only one thought rattles inside me… *I cannot even hear the music.*

I grovel and fawn like a slave now. Massage his left leg, another woman on his right. Feel happy when he says, "You do that well." Take the slap of his public humiliation and clasp it to my breast. He scorns me *for* my good. Each lash loosens my mortal ego. Only a guru can do that. *Gu-ru*, dispeller of darkness.

My darkness.

Destroy them all. Destroy my desires, my *vasanas*, my *samskaras*. My passions. My wants. My loves. My desires. I offer them up to you, O Lord. Cleanse me clean, O Chinmaya.

"Swamiji, will you bless my *mala*?" I ask, handing him my wooden prayer beads the color of dried ginger.

Cupping my *mala* in his palms, he closes his eyes and prays over it. Loops it around my neck. When I pull away, he tugs my neck towards him like a cowherd does his cow. "*You* will need a second twist to hold you." His lips purse determinedly as he loops a second time around my neck.

I grin to hide my shame. I'm so bad I need two twists. Grin to tell him that I'm grateful he's helping me.

"Swamiji, I'd like to travel with you," I ask as my six weeks with him come to a close.

"I don't have people like you around me," he whips.

My smile fades. It's true, then. My karma can't be erased. I'm not pure enough to be around him. I'm just one of the many "sick" people he asks to travel with him to purify them.

"Then can I join the *brahmachari* course?" His Bombay ashram teaches a two-year course for spiritual initiates.

He looks me up and down with surprise. "Really? *You*? Alright, but get your parents' permission. Both of them need to agree."

To my surprise, Amma agrees. "It will be good for you," she says.

But Naina refuses when she asks him over the phone. "I don't want my daughter giving up the world. Why can't she do something like everyone else instead of all her nonsense ideas? Like engineering or medicine?"

I've hoped Chinmayananda will at least advise Amma to let me go outside the house. But when it's time to say goodbye at Hyderabad airport, he curtly says, "You'll go home now and live as your parents ask you."

His sentence slices into me like a guillotine. I prostrate numbly. When I rise he draws me into the crook of his shoulder, his long, gray beard rasping against my cheek, and whispers in my ear, "I've become so fond of you."

My mind whirls fuzzily, my heart like lead. If you are fond of me, why sentence me to be locked up?

Dazed and numb, I stare out the window as Amma and I are driven back to Daadi's and Thatha's home. Something happened these past weeks. I feel rearranged, crumpled, and as twisted as a *dupatta*, a chiffon scarf, looped around my own neck.

8
my scarlet sin

1985

"Evan's moved on." Amma says smugly, walking into our room.

"He's moved?"

"No, he's moved *on*. He's dating someone else." Her eyes glint triumphantly. "That's how American men are. They use women briefly and move on. It would never have worked out."

I stare at her, reeling. How does she know? My body feels cold and limp as a mollusk. I last lay in your arms in August… it's only November. Did you forget me so soon, Evan?

"He told Naina," she says as though reading my mind. "Naina called him to get your library books. You see, Mytrae, we love you, we want the best for you. It was in your best interest we put an end to it. Sooo, write and tell him it's over. Finished. You're not going back. Come!" She hands me a sheet of paper and gestures to the living room.

I can't breathe. My mind is fuzzy. Can't think to question why I must write to him if it's over. Only that I *can* write to him after so long. My legs like lead, I stand up and follow her to the living room.

"Write!" she orders, settling behind me into a black leather chair.

Numbly, I sit in the straight-backed wicker chair at Daadi's writing desk in the living room. A faded picture of roses in a milk jug hangs on the wall. My eyes glaze over the black rotary telephone, dog-eared directory, her tattered leather address book. Under the table's glass top are my cousins' crayon drawings: a house with a happy family, two girls playing hopscotch, a vase of flowers. Will they be prevented from love, too? I peer at myself at seven, smiling, in a family photograph at *Laughing Waters* with Daadi and Thatha, their three children and six grandchildren.

Everything seemed possible in that beautiful garden.

The world flows through Daadi's living room. It's a day like any other. The maid and her grass broom rustle through, *huuusk-huuusk*. The driver rings the doorbell for the car keys. Thatha shuffles in, his slippers slapping the white and gray marble floor as he dodges tile cracks to ask Daadi financial questions, answers to which he forgot he wrote down two days ago, for her sharp mind stores every detail. He'll scrawl them in his wobbly handwriting into hardbound ruled ledgers with blue, green, and red ink. Daadi chats with the cook about vegetable prices, the gardener's daughter's marriage, and the maid's alcoholic, cheating husband. Mustard seeds pop and cumin seeds sizzle in hot oil. The aroma of sautéing onions wafts through. Roshan Uncle breezes in to say good morning to them in his British accent, and out.

It is a public place in which to write a very private letter. Amma will scrutinize it, slip it in an envelope, seal, stamp, and post. Evan will open it, his hands trembling with worry. His long expressive fingers, indelible in my mind, stroking my waist, my breasts, my hips, my thighs. In me. Or maybe he isn't worried anymore because he's with someone else?

Evan! Was our love so fleeting? Is it true, then, what they say about American men, that it's easy for them to love and leave? I don't want to believe it, but the truth of it lodges like hard, cold granite in my chest. I've yearned to write to you but not with Amma, hawk-like, three feet behind me. And not to tell you *this*. I stare at the white sheet, empty and void.

I take a deep breath. Take a pen from Daadi's frayed plastic pen holder.

Dear Evan,

I'm not returning to the U.S. I don't know if I ever will. I want you to know that you know me in ways my parents never will. Our love is one of the most precious things I've ever felt. The times we shared were the most blissful and wonderful I've ever known. I want you to be happy. I will always love you.

Though it feels like I'm sticking a dagger in my chest, I release you. Love again. Be happy. Free.

Have what I cannot have.

I write on both sides of the sheet and hand it to Amma. As it passes from my fingers to hers something in me shudders to a violent death. I'm not just letting go of Evan, but letting go of love. Of music. Of my dream for my own life.

I feel like a widow who just heard her husband died. She must disrobe herself of her jewelry. She tugs the gold bangles from her hands, unfastens her *mangalsutra*, wedding necklace. Lets them clang, along with her radiance, then shiver into silence on the floor.

"God, let me learn from this, whatever this is."

But God doesn't answer.

It's because I love you so much that I hurt.

The hot afternoon air breezes through the iron mesh windows and ruffles my cream and green salvaar-kameez against my skin. They can have my body, but not my soul. They can lock me up but they will never touch my music. My tongue, parched with what I am to do, sticks to the roof of my mouth.

If I cannot kill myself, I will kill what I love.

I must bury it. Put it away where they'll never find it. Like a man buries his wife's jewels under a tree when fleeing a war. When I'm free I'll find it again.

I push it down into my belly like a mouthful of gulped moss. It sinks without protest, soft and soundless. An abyss within opens wide. It drops deep, deep, deep. So deep I don't know into which shadowy crevice it lodges. There it will not be hurt. There *I* won't hurt. I will return for you when the time is right.

The earth closes over.

Every week Daadi hands me the brown string-tie envelope that arrives in the post from Chinmaya Mission, Bombay. It's the only piece of mail Amma allows me to receive. She returned to Charleston three months after bringing me here.

It's been almost a year since I've been here, and nine months alone with my grandparents. The long, swollen days with unending hours and minutes beat a steady ostinato of *bad, bad, bad* into my cells. I cannot make sense of my family's silence. No relative from the U.S. calls me. No one in India thinks it's wrong for me to be shut away. I don't go next door to Roshan Uncle and Leela Aunty's house to listen to music anymore. It sears me too much.

The only thing that makes sense, now, is that I deserve this.

The gray granite floors are gloomy like a sulking child. Two large windows with diamond-shaped iron steel grills keep out hungry, whining mosquitoes. Green curtains dangle with unfastened hooks like mouths with missing teeth. A faded painting of ships docked at a harbor hangs crookedly on a wall. Wall lamp sconces with askew beige linen shades are beleaguered by layers of dust, and glow a dim, bleak 30 watts at night.

Seven feet beyond my window the world moves on. Fruit vendors bawl selling mangoes, *sapotas*, custard apples, as the fruits change season after season. The roll of bicycle wheels in the dust. Bhajans and movie songs blare from the *basti* at dawn and dusk. The gypsy Lambadi women laugh and chatter, and in my mind's eye I see their feminine sways down the road, their arms linked together, in their bright red, yellow, and green dresses with sewn-in mirrors. Listen to the clinks of their ivory and glass bangles that cover their forearms and their bawdy songs. I envy them. I envy everyone their freedom. I will never regain the light Amma dreamed of for me. In her eyes, I can never erase the stain of my scarlet sin.

I settle down cross-legged on the floor beside my bed for my morning ritual of reading and meditation. I untie the envelope's brown twine and pull out the sheaf of pages with small single-spaced print.

To purify myself.

You are not your desires. You are not your thoughts. You are not your emotions. Sublimate your desires, your emotions. How dare I be angry? At Daadi. At Amma. Naina. Sublimate hate. Turn it into love. They put you here out of love. Because you don't know what's good for you. *You are not the ego. The world is maya, illusion. Free yourself from it. Don't be attached. When you are attached you suffer. Desire causes suffering.*

Only the *Bhagawad Gita* and the *Upanishads* quiet the roars inside me. Push down the searing pain which, thank goodness, has been numbed. Everything is deadened now. It's better to let mornings slide into afternoons, and afternoons into evenings, as I stare out the window at the compound wall. I have learned to just exist. Until night's sweet oblivion. It isn't unnatural for me not to protest or fight back more.

My cells throb with visceral fear.

You can't go against them, they say.

I have long given up trying or even thinking about how or when I will be released. I no longer think about how long I will remain here. After almost a year, I cannot imagine freedom. I cannot imagine wanting anything for myself. I doubt everything I knew to be true. I have let go of hope. My only battle is to still my feelings when they rise, like forbidden lovers, however much I try to sublimate them like the teachings say.

I am grateful for Daadi. At least she, unlike Amma, bears witness to my sullen bitterness, numbness, and heartbreak. When she invites me to come out of my room and watch *Ramayana*, Hindi, or Telugu movies with her, help her make *chapathis* for dinner, or go sit with Thatha in the garden, I feel her care. Even when I cry, shaking with frustration and rage, and wish I were dead. She is at least *here, with* me, in my unbearable now.

But every few weeks my frustration, hate, rage, and helplessness surge like red, molten lava and all of a sudden I scream at

Daadi, "I wish I was dead! Death would be better than this!" She stares at the screen where Seetha and the women dressed in silks and bedecked with jewels hang their covered heads, demure, dutiful, and obedient to their elders and men. She turns, looks me squarely in the eyes, and says, "I wish you were, too."

9

marriage liaisons

1986

"What's he like?" Daadi quavers to Amma, who sits on her mother's maroon sofa drinking tea.

"They're Brahmins," she says proudly, a higher caste than ours. "He's in his thirties, a businessman, very good looking according to his mother, Janaki. He's turned down ten or eleven girls." Amma came to Hyderabad a week ago with a marriage proposal for me.

"Our child is very good looking also," Daadi says protectively. "She'll have to like him too. Why didn't he get married earlier? He's old! Is he fair?"

"I don't know, Mother!" Amma says, exasperated. "It's come through Swamiji. It's such Grace."

She says Grace like it's the word of God. I tremble. What if Swamiji, with his powers, knows who I'm supposed to marry but I don't like him? Will I be bad in God's eyes?

"It may have come through him, but it has to be right. We just can't throw her away," Daadi retorts sharply.

I relish their bickering and Daadi's protectiveness. I'm grateful I can choose. Right now, it feels like my only power. But after living in this cottage for over a year, I'm ready to entertain a proposal. Marriage is my only way to freedom, and I feel myself both reluctant and hopeful as I turn to meet it.

Matchmaking swings Indian women into exuberance. Now that a proposal's in play, Leela Aunty visits often and the three women buzz about Vishwanath's successful career, his picky taste in women, and that, like us, he's South Indian. Daadi makes enquiries about his family. Amma takes our horoscopes to the family astrologer who says the stars are good for our union. Leela Aunty says she'll take me shopping to the best sari stores. Everyone's been waiting for my life to move from idling into first gear and Vishwanath, it seems, is the ticket. And whatever am I going to wear when I meet him? The four of us comb through Amma's saris and finally settle on her lavender chiffon.

Daadi plans high tea all week long. On the big day, her teak table is crowded with samosas, cucumber and mint sandwiches, cutlets, trifle pudding, and *kheer*, rice pudding. And her prized homemade mango juice. I watch her fry *gulab jamuns* then transfer them, sizzling, into sugar syrup. When I see the amount of food I ask, "Are they coming for tea or dinner?"

The rolls of her belly jiggle with laughter as she spoons dough into hot oil. "We have to have good food. That's how they'll know our family's standards. They're Brahmins. Their food's quick and light. Bland. Our house may be small but we have good food!"

In India's complex caste hierarchy, we're Vaishyas, the agricultural caste, third on the totem pole. Brahmins, the priestly caste, are the highest. But in Daadi's eyes, our good food, luxurious homes, and education make us superior. In arranged marriages, caste and subcaste are very important, but when a guru suggests a match, it outranks everything.

The doorbell rings. "They're here!" Amma says, nervously adjusting the pleats of her navy blue silk sari in the mirror. "Are you ready?" I nod. We wait for Daadi to greet the visitors. Then, after an appropriate pause, we enter the living room.

A chunky man sits, legs splayed wide, on an armchair. How rude! Surely he knows to stand up for a woman, especially for Amma. But he sits, looking me up and down. I stare squarely back at a round balding face, small eyes in distant retreat behind spectacles, and a protruding stomach.

No! is my instant response.

Over tea, Daadi jabbers about the weather, soaring prices, her life in Madras, their life in Madras, probing inquisitions into their family history. Amma tries to be important and humble at the same time, talks of her spirituality, our family's education and status. Vishwanath's eyes roam over me. His mother, Janaki, has permanent worry lines on her forehead and smiles at me with long teeth. I smile back at her with painful falsity.

"Why don't both of you go into Roshan's garden," Daadi suggests, leaning back in her armchair after she's exhausted her topics.

I shrink into my chair.

"Yes, let's." Vishwanath eagerly puts down his cup.

Reluctantly, I lead him to the lawn where we sit on white wrought-iron chairs with emerald green cushions. "What do you do?" I ask. At least give the man a chance.

"I run my own business," he says arrogantly. "And I'm writing a book. I have some friends, but mostly, I'm busy. I live with my mother now."

He's pompous. I can't bear the idea of marrying him but I must give it a try, spiritually ordained as it is. Proposals don't come every day. "What do you want in a relationship?"

"I want someone educated who can talk to my friends, entertain, and understand what I do."

"How do you feel about a working wife?"

"I'm okay with that, but she must know her family and home come first. What do you do?"

I squirm. If he's telling me my place now, the noose will only tighten later. "I'm here in India, but I was doing my masters in piano performance in the U.S."

"Do you like it here?"

"No."

"What do you do all day?"

"Mostly nothing." It's quite acceptable for unmarried women my age to do nothing.

"Where do you live in the U.S.?"

"I don't. My parents live in South Carolina."

He likes me. I don't like him. Are these the kinds of men I'm going to be expected to marry? Unattractive, arrogant, looking for someone to take care of them? My heart sinks. We have nothing more to say. I watch the sun slowly slide below the blushing horizon. Mynahs chitter and cheep as they fly over eucalyptus trees to their nests. Coral blossoms hang like open, wide bells from the flame of the forest tree, weighing down its boughs. The evening hushes into a quiet peace.

"So what do you think?" He breaks our silence. "We'll have to give them an answer."

"I don't know. I need to think about it. What about you?"

"I'm interested. If you like, we can meet again to talk."

We return to the others. Soon, our guests leave.

"What do you think, child?" Daadi asks.

"I don't like him."

"Now, don't say that," Amma retorts irritated. "You've just met him once. He may not like you either; he's turned down several girls."

"Our child's not like other girls," Daadi counters. "He's very old. And fat. Everything's not based upon your Swamiji."

"What do *you* know? Swamiji's a *Realized* soul. Mytrae doesn't know how fortunate she is to have this match. It's so rare and blessed to have your life partner chosen for you by a Realized guru." Amma walks away in a huff.

"Swamiji, Swamiji," Daadi grumbles as we gather the dishes. "That's all your mother can think about. I don't know what's happened to her. Well, maybe you should meet again."

So I meet Vishwanath two more times, chaperoned by Amma as it would be scandalous to meet him alone. Each time she wheedles, "Swamiji suggested it. *Try* to like him." But, sitting across from Vishwanath, however much I long to leave my shut-in life, I shudder imagining life, let alone lovemaking, with him. No matter how blessed the match.

"Child, if you don't like him even ten percent, tell me and I'll handle Amma," says Daadi. We're engaged in our nightly ritual of making *chapathis*, flat unleavened bread. Making balls of dough between her palms, she flattens and rolls them. With a forefinger, she smears ghee over the dough, folding it into a triangle then rolls it out again. She peels the translucent dough and smacks it on the smoking iron griddle. I let one side heat till little bubbles form, then flip it with my fingers. When this side bubbles too, I press its tips with a steel spatula as the *chapathi* puffs into a sizzling golden prism.

"I don't like him even one percent, Daadi," I say, grateful down to my toes that she'd speak up for me. I smear ghee on both sides of the rust-speckled *chapathi* and slide it in a steel container.

"I'll tell her, don't worry. She's gone a little crazy with this Swamiji business. It's always Swamiji this and Swamiji that." Her round shoulders heave as she rolls. Tears well up. I'm surprised by her fierce protection. I love that she wants me to have a happy marriage. I feel her love. It makes me see her strictness in a different light. She's a lioness about family, but cares about each of us. Not like Amma, who doesn't give a fig about my happiness, just that I'm respectable in other people's eyes and off her hands.

She tells Amma at dinner. "It's all fine for your Swamiji to suggest a match but it doesn't mean it's God's word. Our child has to be happy. I'm not going to let her be thrown away if she's unhappy."

"She's unfortunate, ill-fated," Amma rants. "She doesn't know what she's doing turning down such a blessed proposal. Now I'll have to consult the astrologers again. What did I do in my past life to have a child like this?" She storms off to our bedroom.

I feel guilty to let her down again, but marrying Vishwanath is unthinkable.

There's no music in him.

"I'm leaving in a few days. Since you're here, you may as well do something. Swamiji says you're ready to understand Indian music. Do you want to learn an Indian instrument?" Amma asks we eat breakfast with Daadi and Leela Aunty. We sit at the white linoleum table in Daadi's kitchen, processing the demise of the Vishwanath proposal.

I can't believe my ears. Anger flares through me. How can he possibly know what I'm ready for in music? A stab of fear. But does he know more about my soul than I do? I look up from my toast and nod. I long for the piano but a beautiful Indian instrument's better than nothing. "I'd like to learn the sitar."

Leela Aunty says, "My friend, Poonam, wants to learn. Mytrae can go with her?" She sips tea from a porcelain cup with rose bouquets. Ah yes, a warden's necessary.

"Yes, Poonam's a good woman. She'll be a good companion." Daadi slathers her toast with soft cream butter.

"Why don't you learn Sanskrit too? It'll purify you," Amma says, crunching her toast.

"Okay." I don't mind being purified as long as I can get out of the house.

"I'll take you to enroll at the Ramakrishna Mission tomorrow," Amma says.

"I'll go visiting those days. I'll drop her off and pick her up," Daadi says through a mouthful of scrambled eggs.

Leela Aunty offers, "There's an aerobics course up the road, too. How about that? She can walk there."

Incredulous, I look at Amma. "You're letting me go outside?"

Amma nods. "Will you find out when it is, Leela?"

"Yes, I will," Leela Aunty smiles at me.

Delight slowly spreads through me. My almost–solitary confinement's over!

Even if only to await an arranged marriage.

Poonam, a traditional Tamilian woman in a fuchsia sari, and I drive to Atma Ram, a sitar *pundit*, teacher. Poonam has olive skin, limpid eyes, full lips, and a huge red *bindi*. I warm to her husky alto as she chats about her family.

Atma Ram's sprawling compound is an oasis in the middle of teeming Hyderabad. Enormous banyans offer their lush coolness from the searing sun. A small, ancient temple with a *tulsi* plant in front hallows the ground. The home is humble and unassuming. Atma Ram emerges, a heavy-set balding man in his mid-fifties in a white cotton *kurta* and loose pajamas. His wife and son appear on the terracotta verandah and stare curiously at us. Greeting us with a peaceful smile, he leads us slowly, deliberately, to two ancient rooms in the compound. Something in my body deeply relaxes. This is the India I love.

We lower our heads to enter the room. Twenty cedar and mahogany sitars of different sizes lean like sinuous damsels against the whitewashed walls. The air is hallowed, like practice rooms at school, only simpler, devoid of display. It is a space in which to tunnel into the sanctity of sound. I vibrate as though I've been strummed.

Atma Ram sits effortlessly in *gomukhasana* and picks up a sitar, which blends to him as if it were a limb. Closing his eyes, he lightly runs his fingers across the strings as if in prayer. I reverberate to the exquisite sound. He shows us how to hold it, strum it. "The string must cut in. It will have to make a groove in your finger. It will hurt the first few weeks, but you'll get used to it. The flesh must harden, then it won't hurt," he says, showing us his forefinger which is almost sliced in two. He teaches us our first *raga*, which seeps into my cells like long-awaited rain into parched brown earth.

"The only payment I want is your dedicated practice," he says quietly at the end.

"But we must pay you!" Poonam and I exclaim in chorus.

"No, no. I cannot accept. I come from a lineage of teachers. I was taught by my father and he by his. It is sad people don't appreciate classical music anymore. Only a few are left who do true justice to the art. It is a great joy to me that my little son wants to learn."

I am profoundly moved that he's a true teacher of the *guru-shishya* tradition. We're wealthy enough to give him more than what he might ask for, and yet, he wants nothing. Instead, we take fruits or sweets, saying they are for his children. He accepts, reluctantly.

"Why do you have to take them so often?" Daadi shrills each time I ask her for money to buy our offerings.

"He's not taking any fees, Daadi."

"Well, he can ask if he wants it, can't he?" she grouches, handing me a few rupees.

I practice for hours. Exercises, *ragas*, and simple tunes. The taut string cuts painfully into my forefinger but I don't stop, for I'm beginning to feel music again, like a sunflower waking up to the sun.

I like the Ramakrishna Mission ashram, with its green lawns, tall eucalyptus, wide peepals and banyans. Even the air hushes as if readying for meditation. Swamis and brahmacharis stroll on dusty trails in white and orange robes clasping well-worn scriptures as they finger *malas*, prayer beads, and silently mouth mantras.

I join six other students in a modest classroom with wooden benches. Sunlight speckled with chalk dust streams through a tiny, barred window. Our teacher explains Sanskrit *slokas* and *suktas*, hymns about Krishna and Lakshmi, with a honeyed devotion reminding me what I love most about India—pure, simple people.

Over weeks, I become friends with one of the students, Sujatha. A frail woman my age, her fearful dark eyes are the most enormous feature in her delicately boned face. Despite our different lives and social status, we share our nervousness about our impending arranged marriages.

She confides, "My mother died when I was eleven. My sister's been on the marriage block for years but nothing's worked out. She's almost thirty. Our father's frustrated and anxious. The only proposals that come are from impotent or decrepit men. I worry he's begun looking for me which means she'll be left unmarried. She feels pressured because she's been so much trouble but her chances of marrying after me are almost nil. And since she's unmarried, it will affect my proposals." Her hands flutter nervously to clutch her *palloo*, the end of her sari, to her chest.

So many Indian families feel unfortunate, even cursed, to have daughters. When a family has multiple daughters, the younger ones wait for their older sisters to marry first. Otherwise people think something's wrong with the older one. As I listen to Sujatha, it seems all Indian women are born for is marriage with clouds of shame surrounding the process. Shame to be born a woman. Guilt to be a burden to your family. Shame to be married off like a transaction. Shame and guilt if you aren't married.

I don't tell her my story. At twenty-three, I've dared and lived so much more than she has. She'd be scandalized to know I slept with a man, an American man at that, before marriage.

"I, too, am nervous about an arranged marriage," I tell her as we sit on a bench under a banyan tree, jasmine perfuming the ashram air. "Who knows whom we'll end up with?"

The hunt for my bridegroom continues. The process is like a spider preparing for supper. Spinning, the endless waiting, then the swift snap and catch.

"What do you want in a husband, child?" Daadi hangs up the phone after talking with a favorite family gossip. She's announced to her wide network that I'm on the marriage block.

The news spreads like wildfire.

Evan. Do you think about me? Are you happy? Have you given your beautiful heart to another? Lying on Daadi's mahogany *divan* covered with a *Kalamkari* bedspread with peacocks and elephants, I think about the men I've been attracted to. "Someone tall and lean," I answer. "Color isn't important. Someone who's his own man and not tied to his family. And he must be okay with me working."

"Yes, yes, we'll check all of that. We're not going to throw you away. Several have come but we've turned them down for one reason or another. Amma's in a rush but you needn't worry. I'm not going to let her do that. Remember Vishwanath?"

I nod, trusting her. She's in her element with matchmaking, on the phone enquiring with charm, diplomacy, and a boldness that makes me blush. Finding a groom is a complicated investigation. She and the family will probe as far back as they can (seven generations being the guideline), sleuthing for lineage on the father's and mother's sides. Caste and subcaste. Pedigree. Social status.

Skin color. Looks. Education. Professional achievement. Wealth. Sophistication. Health and mental health. Integrity. Values. Bone structure. Teeth. Thatha seeks self-made men. Amma includes baldness in the mix of what to sift out.

"It's like choosing a racehorse," I groan.

"You don't mind if he's non-vegetarian, do you?" she asks.

"That's fine. But I'm not going to cook meat." I became vegetarian at eighteen after I ran over a rabbit. My meat-eating family raised an eyebrow but understood, as many Indians are vegetarians. Weary of my marriage talk, I ask, "Tell me about Amma's proposals."

"*Oooyy*, your Amma," Daadi sighs, settling her soft rounded body into a high-backed white wicker chair, its cushions the color of succulent mango. "She wanted to get married. She was twenty-four, you know. It was getting late. Her cousin, Gowri, married two years before so your mother was eager. But you know how picky we are. Thatha turned down a few proposals. Finally, a family friend suggested your father, who just returned from college in America. He came to see your mother and she immediately agreed!"

Did Amma decide because she really liked Naina or because she was desperate? Hardly romantic. In arranged marriages, affection and companionship develop over time. But no one expects love, though it happens occasionally. I strain against my inevitable destiny, which I can feel hurtling me forward like the Ganga into the Bay of Bengal.

"Tell me about you and Thatha," I ask, snuggling into a primrose silk bolster, though I've heard their story many times.

She smiles at me. "*Ayyo*, that was such a drama. My father was a lawyer, not as rich as Thatha's, who was a landowner. But we were neighbors in Vijayawada and they were best of friends. As children Pushpa, Thatha, Naresh, and I played in the forest and swam in the river together." Pushpa is Daadi's sister, and Naresh, Thatha's brother. "After Thatha returned from Cambridge, he asked my father's permission to marry me. I was sixteen. And Naresh wanted to marry Pushpa. But their father was livid and rejected the match. He threatened to disown them. But Thatha didn't care. You know how your Thatha is. Once he makes up his mind, that's it. He left his father's house.

"Now my father always loved Thatha. 'This is a *real* man!' he'd say about him. He helped Thatha make wedding plans in secret. Two days before the wedding, Thatha's father found out and locked up Naresh. But the night before the wedding, Thatha sneaked into the house, unlocked Naresh, and spirited him away in their horse cart. They arrived just in time to the marriage pandal. The two couples had to get married at 12:23 a.m., as it was the only auspicious time that month. That's why I was given only one pendant on my *mangalsutra*. Thatha's father disowned and disinherited them. We were poor, but always had enough. Ten years later, we saved enough to buy me a second pendant."

She pulls her *mangalsutra* out from under the folds of her sari and shows me the thick gold chain with a tapered design at the end. Flanked by a couple of black and coral beads, two pendants hang, the size of gold sovereigns. One shaped like a round golden breast with a ruby for a nipple, the other a flat disc with a golden nipple. This *mangalsutra* is her radiance, her glory, her dignity as a married woman, the equivalent of the wedding ring for Western women. *Mangalsutra* designs vary family to family. In my state, Andhra Pradesh, one pendant is given by the bride's family, the other by her husband's family, each with the family's design. It's an anomaly to have just one so I can only imagine how Daadi felt as a young wife, tucking her one-pendant *mangalsutra* into her blouse so people wouldn't stare.

I lean forward to see it closer. It weighs heavy and foreboding in my palm. I can have only one husband in my lifetime. "So romantic," I sigh, as she trundles off to make more phone calls. In a country of arranged marriages, such stories of love bloom rare as cactus flowers. I feel so lucky to have known love. I may never love again, but I want to at least like my future husband and enjoy his company.

"Amma says he's tall and thin, nice looking. Good features. A little on the dark side." Daadi fills me in on Aditya, the next potential groom. I can always count on her undiluted truth about appearance. "Leela Aunty says he's very good-looking, but then she says everyone's good-looking!" Her face puckers with distaste, as she rarely passes up a chance to dig at her daughter-in-law. "He did his master's in engineering in the U.S. and returned to India two years ago. He lives with his parents and works in his father's factory."

Aditya comes for tea. Much, much better than Vishwanath. Bright black eyes, dark chocolate skin. A lithe build. Pleasant, sensitive, and gentle, slightly unsure of himself.

We're both unsure. We talk about the U.S., our families, and our interests.

He likes me. I'm not attracted to him, nor do I feel a connection, but am open. After all, it isn't exactly raining bridegrooms.

We meet a couple more times. Daadi keeps her pulse on my feelings. "What are you thinking, Mytrae?"

"He's nice, like a friend, but I don't feel anything more."

"They're a good family. Not great, but good. His mother's all about money and dressing. His father's a good, serious man. You'll have to decide soon. He likes you. One or two more meetings more, then that's it."

His mother visits one evening. Over-eager with a protruding stomach, large breasts and a well-oiled bun adorned with jasmine flowers, she drools at me, her lips red from chewing betel nut, as though I were a prize cow. I smile back uncomfortably. Daadi keeps the conversation flowing with prices, gossip, and her favorite sari stores. Aditya's mother tries to wedge in potential dates and details of the marriage ceremony but Daadi resolutely keeps her at bay: "Let's see what the two young people decide."

"What do you do in the evenings?" I ask Aditya at our next meeting over tea and store-bought pound cake.

"Not much. I'm usually tired after work and go home," he answers.

"Do you have friends? What's your social life like?"

"I don't have many friends since I returned from the U.S. I don't go to parties," he says softly and hangs his head.

For a twenty-something man he doesn't seem enthused by life. As I sit across from him in Daadi's living room, I ask myself whether I can live with him. Nothing in me leaps with excitement. Sleep with him? My stomach turns. I know. But I need to be certain.

"What's your relationship like with your parents?" I ask.

"It's good."

"My mother has strong ideas. But she does it out of love."

He seems too docile for me. "How long will you live at home?"

"I don't have plans to move out any time soon. I'm working in my father's factory. After a few years… maybe… I'll see how things go."

"Maybe" seals my decision. I want fire, a spark going somewhere.

"I can't, Daadi," I say after Aditya leaves.

"Alright, child," she sighs. "I don't know where your man will come from. But the time has to be right. It still isn't." When all else fails and human will seems puny, Daadi surrenders to fate and time. I love her for not pressuring me.

Thatha double-checks. "You've seen two men and you're turning them down. Are you sure you aren't making a mistake?"

My gut churns again. "Yes, Thatha, I'm sure." He shakes his head, his forehead creased with worry.

The next time Aditya visits, I say as gently as I can, "I like you but I don't think it will work out. We're different and want different things."

His face darkens. He looks crestfallen. "Then there's nothing more to talk about," he says abruptly and leaves.

As we discuss the end of Aditya's proposal with Leela Aunty that evening, Daadi clutches her head with her hands. "Poor chap, he was so disappointed!"

"I think he was very good-looking. Where are we going to find someone? There's nobody good enough. I tell you, nobody's going to be good enough for our girls," Leela Aunty squawks desperately, thinking of her two teenage daughters.

After Leela Aunty leaves, Daadi bristles. "Leela thinks everyone's very good-looking. What does she know? We raise our girls giving them so much, exposing them to so much. We can't just throw them away!"

I love her for not throwing me away.

Poonam persuades Daadi to let me teach at Nasr School for girls. Daadi and my parents agree. They trust me now. So I get a job teaching English and History to third and fifth graders. I feel alive to be out in the world again and working. I see myself in the girls' bright eyes and innocent ways. Grading tests, preparing for class, teaching them songs and dances I write and set to Western tunes. I love the girls to pieces, and they love me back. I learn about their lives, ask about their dreams, and encourage them to reach for the stars. I know which ones will go on to college, for their parents want them to study. But there are many, like Anees, for whom school is a mere passing of time till they marry, often shortly after puberty. Anees will study only as much as her traditional, religious father will allow. Her dream is to be a doctor, she tells me, her coal-black eyes gleaming, but her head hangs and her voice falters. "My father won't..." My heart breaks for her. She's one of my most brilliant students and would be an incredible physician.

I begin to form a plan. I will earn enough to be financially independent, move out of my grandparents' house, and eventually, find my way to the U.S. Every month I count the few hundred-rupee notes I've saved in my sanitary napkin box at the back of my closet. I call travel agents. A ticket costs 80,000 rupees. I'll be gray before I can save that on my paltry salary of 600 rupees a month. But if I travel through the Middle East instead of Europe, they tell me, I can get a ticket for 60,000 rupees. Buy soon, they urge, prices are going up.

Fly via the Middle East? How will I ever get my passport from Amma's cupboard? That's a question I haven't answered. An even larger problem is how not to be recognized at the airport and get past airport security? Our family is so large, Daadi runs into at least ten people everywhere we go. And Indian families are aggressively nosy, especially with young women. They make it their business not just to know, but to be our caretakers and guardians. Someone would surely rush over at the airport and ask me what I was doing. Take me right back to Daadi's and Thatha's.

The only way out is incognito. Maybe I can get a *burkha* made and travel in it. It won't cost much. I smile to myself.

I like that idea.

10

stepping stones

1987

"What happened to your face, Myt?" Nina's, my childhood friend's, eyebrows arch high with surprise when she sees me at her parents' Christmas party.

"These? Pimples." They're dime-size, despite Leela Aunty's advice of "put baking soda" and Daadi's "try *channagapindi* and *pasupu*." I smeared the pale yellow garbanzo flour and turmeric paste on my face day after day for months, but they only multiplied—red, angry manifestations of what smolders inside me.

I'm delighted to see Nina and that Daadi allowed me to visit. I haven't seen her since we were teenagers, when I cut my hair. Now, twenty-four, newly married, and radiant, she's visiting from Bloomington, Indiana, where she's getting her Ph.D. in Economics.

Nina takes my hand and leads me to her bedroom. Sits me down on her bed. She looks shocked. "You've become so thin, Myt. You don't look the same. I've been so worried about you. I can't believe you're not continuing grad school. What happened?"

I tell her my story, concluding with, "It's been two years now."

"Your mother called me after she brought you back. She told me you were in a cult and on drugs. That you're here in India to dry out."

"But I *wasn't* on drugs. I've never tried them. I've never felt a need to. And it wasn't a cult. I had a spiritual awakening."

She's silent. Her mouth purses with doubt. She doesn't believe me! I clutch my glass of pineapple juice, feeling dark-despairingly alone. An acrid taste fills my mouth—Amma's swayed even my closest friends.

"Come." She stands up. "I want you to meet Nupur. Both of you live so close, you must get together." She weaves me through the guests to an attractive woman whose soulful eyes and wide smile meet my gaze.

A week later, when the doorbell rings, I open the front door to Nupur, her lithe body in a loose yellow shirt, tight jeans, and sandals. "Want to come to my home to hang out?" she lilts warmly like we're already friends. Her huge, mischievous eyes sparkling with self-confidence and life rivet me. Seeing her, I remember what laughter and fun felt like.

"I have to ask Daadi."

To my surprise, Daadi agrees. "Okay, but be back in an hour." It's the first time she's let me go out with someone she doesn't know.

I walk awkwardly with Nupur who talks non-stop about Nina and the Christmas party. She doesn't walk—she bounces—as though her buoyant body can't contain her aliveness. We enter her family's huge compound with lawns, a rose garden, and gazebos.

A wave of anxiety rushes through me. My social skills are rusty. What can I talk about? Will we connect? She's unfettered as her bob-cut, while I feel old and lumbering like those I live with.

She leads me to her bedroom. She has a huge bed and a mirror just as wide, a massive dressing table strewn with makeup and jewelry, and a row of wall closets that could hold all of Daadi's possessions. A small hillock of stuffed animals, a boom-box, books, small piles of fashionable clothes, and strewn high heels celebrate the sheer fun of being a young woman. Coming from my straitlaced, spartan space, hers is a room my imagination can barely hold.

Nupur chats about her undergraduate student life in Bloomington, where she knew Nina. I tell her of mine in Chapel Hill, leaving out Evan and being brought back. In that hour and the following months, we become fast friends, and discover a shared love of walks, badminton, music, and books. I can laugh again, for her vivacity is contagious and her spirit bold. She confides about past boyfriends and her hopes for a husband. Her parents, too, are looking for a potential husband for her. But my jaw drops, incredulous, when she tells me they allow her to date and that they know she lived with men. I'm amazed they treat her like an adult and allow her to make her own decisions.

They trust her, and she them.

In her mansion with ornate mahogany furniture and many servants, her family easily fills its walls. In their ease I taste something foreign—an irresistible warmth—which draws me to them like honey. Her boisterously teasing father, effusively hugging mother, and captivatingly feminine sister with almond-shaped eyes, express many shades of love—exuberant, joyful, and unabashed. I can't help but compare her family with mine. It's because they're kind that they're so good to me, I think, not because of who I am.

And I become a frequent visitor, feeling like a stray, starved and undeserving of their sweetness.

"Have you thought about writing to him?" Nupur asks when I finally tell her about Evan. We sprawl on lime and mauve paisley cushioned wicker chairs, as the afternoon sun streams into her verandah. Outside, a fruit vendor bawls prices of custard apples and papayas.

"I don't have his address."

"Don't you have an old letter, a friend's address, anything you can remember?"

"Only a friend's card from a year ago, which Daadi opened before giving it to me."

"Why don't you write and ask her for Evan's address? I'll give you an envelope and stamps. Use my address for the return address."

Solutions to my insurmountable problems seem trifles for her, my own hope long buried like a frozen cadaver. But a couple of weeks later, Nupur hands me a letter. I rip it open. My friend is happy to hear from me. She became a massage therapist and is married. Evan, she writes, moved to Munich, Germany, a year ago, and she includes his address. She doesn't mention a girlfriend.

What in the world is he doing there?

"Use my address to receive letters. I'll give you stamps," Nupur offers. "Would you like to write now? You can use my room. Here's some paper."

I stand frozen, staring at her. Write to him? Will he even want to hear from me? Linking my arm in hers, Nupur leads me to her room. "I'll be downstairs if you need me."

Sitting cross-legged on her rose carpet, I stare at the white sheet, pen in hand. What *can* I write after all this time? What is he doing? Whom is he with? I close my eyes. Breathe him into my mind and heart. Hear the timbre of his voice.

I open my eyes, put pen to paper, and write in a gush:

Dear Evan,

I know you'll be very surprised to hear from me. I hope you're well. I got your address from Anna.

How can I begin to tell you everything? I don't know what you thought of my earlier letter, which my mother made me write. She told me you had moved on. Of course, I'm happy that you did, not knowing when or if I'd return.

I describe all that's happened since that fateful summer in 1985.

I don't have access to my passport or the outside world. It's been so long I don't know if it's okay for me to turn to you now as a friend, but I need help so I can stand up and walk again.

Love,
Mytrae.

I walk downstairs. Nupur hands me an envelope. "Seal it. I'll mail it. Did you put my address as your return address?"

I nod, tearfully, unable to speak. We hug each other tight.

"Come over," Nupur telephones, her voice urgent.

She opens her front door before I walk up the marble stairs leading to her house, and hands me a thick airmail envelope. My heart lurches to see my name in Evan's slanting, capitalized handwriting with a fine-point pen. Memories of his notes flood through me. For days I've hoped that he'd write, but was also afraid he wouldn't. Why would he, if he'd moved on?

"Go up to my room and read it. No one will disturb you," she says, as I stand dumbstruck, staring at the envelope.

I go into her room and close the door. Leaning against a wall, I slide to the floor. I carefully open the envelope and inhale, trying to smell his hands that placed the thick sheaf inside. From the sheer number of translucent pages, I know he still cares.

Dearest Mytrae,

Tears spill down my cheeks. *Dearest!*

I was devastated when I realized you weren't returning. I tried so hard to convince you before you left for India, but you believed your family. I knew they wouldn't let you return to me and I begged you not to get on that plane. But you trusted them.

I got your grandparents' telephone number through AT&T with great difficulty. I tried calling you several times but your family wouldn't put me through. I wrote several letters, which I realized you didn't receive. I asked Jeannette, your friend, to make a three-way conference call but she wasn't allowed to get through either.

After you left, I couldn't bear to live in my rooms—everywhere I looked, I saw you. So I moved to a house in the Pittsboro woods near Chapel Hill where I lived alone for two years, growing vegetables, chopping firewood, working on my VW Bug and at the restaurant. A German shepherd kept me company. You would have loved him. Nights, I sat under the stars visualizing a golden cape shielding both of us, and sent you love, energy, protection, support. I knew that someday, somehow, you'd find your way out.

David's been a wonderful supportive friend. I continued going to the Siddha Yoga meditation group. George and Patty have been amazing. George helped me find a job in a German lab a few months ago. It's been good for me to move here. I've made some great friends.

I read the eighteen pages four or five times, barely breathing. Even though he doesn't say he loves me, he loved me then. *Really* loved me. More than I imagined. He *hadn't* moved on like Amma said. He'd ached and grieved for me just as I had. He didn't write to convince my parents he'd moved on, but instead, he unintentionally convinced *me*! I cry at his loneliness, at his beautiful nighttime ritual. I wish I could hold him, and him me.

I knew the letter your mother made you write was a hoax. I know you wrote in between the lines for me. You wrote that I saw you in ways they could never even begin to see you or know you. That some of the best times in your life were with me. I'm so glad I could give you that. I didn't reply hoping that if they thought I'd moved on, they'd release you.

There's a lot more, of course, than I can write you in these pages.

If you can get to the U.S., I'm willing to help in any way I can.

Love,
Evan

I clutch the pages to my chest, trembling like a leaf.

I run downstairs to Nupur. She hugs me. "Is it what you wanted to hear?"

"Yes." My face is wet.

"I'm so happy for you!"

And so my correspondence with Evan begins. Every two weeks, I begin to expect Nupur to hand me an airmail envelope with red and blue stripes addressed in his slanting hand, and to unfold a thick sheaf of creamy airmail paper. I stuff it in the front of my *salwār*, my breasts warming it as I walk home. I lock myself in my bathroom to read it again and again, holding the leaf-thin paper to my cheeks, lips, and face, knowing his hands—his beautiful hands with long fingers touched them. I stow it deep inside my closet, under the newspaper lining of the top shelves, out of reach of Daadi's short legs.

I want to be with him. I don't care what he does for a living. I don't care about marriage. I just us want to be together.

How can I possibly get out of India? He's asking the impossible.

I'm not the only one dreaming of new possibilities. Indians are as well. Two years before, for the first time since our independence, the government opened the gates to foreign exchange, investment, and collaboration. India, like an eager bride, is spreading her thighs to receive Western technology. Students are flocking to mushrooming institutes like devotees to temples on religious holidays, and companies, piranha-like, are snapping up newly trained workers. Software development is a phenomenon spreading like wildfire, and Daadi's visitors, television, and newspapers are abuzz about quick money to be made.

"So-and-so's doing computers," Daadi reports after her latest phone gossip session. "Everyone's doing it. People are making sacks of money after a six-month or one-year course. So-and-so says how simple it was, and *she*'s no bright spark!"

That gets my attention. Though I loathed computer science in college, if almost all of India is able to earn sacks of money, surely I can manage some version of it?

"I'd like to take a computer course, Daadi. It'll be good for me to learn something practical." I hate succumbing to my family's byline. Practicality. But it's my only way forward. And I want them to think I've come around, think the way they do.

"Why not? Very good money. A year of training, and in a year or two people are doing so well. And they want them abroad too. Let me check with your mother."

Hmmm… maybe that's a way for me to get to the U.S.? To my surprise, my parents agree. I take a six-month training then apply to the National Institute of Computer Education, its imposing title and sign belying its fly-by-night reality. In Khairatabad, a busy neighborhood, I climb a narrow stairwell lined with freshly watered potted plants fragrant with damp earth. Upstairs, a wiry young man, his unkempt mustache the most prominent feature on his gaunt face, sits at a Formica desk in a small, darkened room.

The power is out. The propped-open door streams in mid-morning sunshine, honks, swirls of diesel smoke, and dust. It doesn't take long to survey the two-room Institute with two computers and classroom. Business doesn't seem great, I think, as I take in the man's wavy hair, long overdue for a cut, and spare frame lost in his clothes. But I need a job, as I've been already rejected by established companies.

The man tells me they're hiring a part-time instructor and programmer, and I sign up for an interview.

On the appointed day, I go half an hour early.

"You're early," the scraggly mustached man remarks. "I'm Ashok." I sit down across from his desk. He pelts questions at me but I can only answer a few. I grow increasingly flustered.

He flings his pen on the table. "How do you expect me to hire you?" His self-assuredness and lightning intelligence challenge me.

"I know I don't know all the things you've asked me. But I really need a job and I'm a quick learner."

"Why don't you take a few courses here?"

"I don't want to keep spending money on courses. But I want to learn. If you'll teach me, I'll learn in half the time for half the money."

We eyeball each other.

"OK. Start next week. I'll pay you 600 rupees a month."

It's a deal. I have a foothold in the software world! We formulate a work-study position for me to teach and develop software.

Soon, the Institute becomes my haven from Daadi's home. Ashok is kind and friendly, though I'm a little intimidated by his intellect and confidence. Singu, our office boy, is a sweet soul who fetches us tea and biscuits. Fifteen, dark and pockmarked, he's fiercely loyal to Ashok. He studied up to primary school and his dream is to open a street-side kiosk and sell *paan*, a digestive made with betel leaves, spices, fruits, and sugar.

"*Aur kuch khao*, Madam." Eat something more, he cajoles with surprising warmth. "*Idli lana? Dosa?*" Shall I bring you steamed rice cakes or a crepe made with fermented rice and lentil batter?

"*Nahin*, Singu," I answer, "*yay bus hai.*" No, this is enough.

I feel cared about in these dusty two rooms in a way I haven't for a long time.

I have a new job, I write Evan. *I'm hoping to save and become financially independent so I can leave my family and make my own life in India. Eventually, I hope to save enough to make it to the U.S. I don't know how long all of this will take.*

Evan writes back.

I'm so happy to be in contact with you again. I can't imagine all that you've been through. I know there must be so much more going on than you can write in your letters. Nupur sounds like a great friend. I'm glad you have her. I feel your pain across the miles. I know you'll find a way out soon.

I give my letters to Singu to mail and ask Evan to write me at the Institute, instead of going through Nupur. I don't want to keep bothering her. She's been so generous and I don't want to impose on her any further.

One morning on *chai* break, Ashok asks, "Why are you here in India when you've studied in the U.S.?"

I feel like I can trust him. He seems like a nice guy. And he doesn't know anyone my family knows. So I pour out my story.

He leans back in his chair, plays with his mustache. "*That* explains it. I didn't understand why you have a driver but don't eat, only drink cups and cups of tea."

I even confide my wild fantasy. "I'm trying to leave India. I'm trying to save money and fly to the U.S. via the Middle East. I'll wear a *burkha* so no one recognizes me at the airport."

His eyebrows rise high as they can go. "A *burkha*?"

"A *burkha*," I say decisively. "I'm in touch with Evan who's in Germany, who says he'll help me once I get to the U.S."

He sighs. "I really wanted to go to graduate school in the U.S. Two of my best friends went there two years ago," Ashok confides as the power goes out. The entire city screeches to a halt during the two-hour power cuts every morning and afternoon. India's teeming millions strain its straggling infrastructure and the cuts are necessary to conserve resources. Larger offices have generators. Singu fetches us tender coconuts, oblong jade buckets of delicious coconut water, which we sip from pink and mauve straws. Ashok continues, "I applied but didn't get in because my family didn't support me in the process. My father didn't give me the financial paperwork I needed. My mother's a housewife and doesn't have a say in such matters. I've resigned myself to staying here, but I'm still upset with them." He grimaces.

I feel sorry for him. "So that's why you often sleep here." That's why the bare-boned two-room Institute gathers waifs. But he's street-smart, ambitious, and not weighed down by family status like me. And, he's a man. I say, "You're so bright. You could go really far. There are plenty of assistantships there. Don't give up just because your family doesn't support you. Anyone can soar as high as they want there. You just need to believe in yourself. They want people like you—bright, young, hard-working, and enterprising." We slurp the dregs of our coconuts, then scrape their succulent translucent flesh with a hacked half-moon of green coconut shell.

Ashok leans back in his chair and is quiet for a few moments. "Perhaps I should try again. After all, I have the Institute to show for financial collateral and don't need my family's support." He puts down his coconut and smiles at me, "Thanks for your encouragement, Mytrae. If I get in, I can help you after I go there."

I smile at him.

I won't take him up on it but am moved by his kind offer.

"Leela's been enquiring about the Chowdhary boy for you," Daadi says. "You have to go to the U.S. in May to renew your green card so you can meet him then. Your parents will buy you a ticket."

I gulp down a squeal but keep my face poker straight. *There's my ticket! I don't have to save for years.* I make sure my tone's casual. "Oh? When?"

"He's studying in Chicago," Daadi continues. "Leela says he's good-looking. His sister's coming next week from the U.S. and wants to meet you."

The Chowdharys live up the street from us. Mrs. Chowdhary is a Bharatanatyam Indian classical dance teacher. Her stick whacks time on her terracotta-floored verandah, punctuating our mornings and afternoons. I see her walking in her garden sometimes, swaying like a jacaranda, her arms and hips speaking a sensual tongue foreign to the uptight women in my family. I like that she isn't in Roshan Uncle and Leela Aunty's party crowd, and is passionate about her art. I often pass Mr. Chowdhary on his evening walk, cane in hand. He's stout, has a shock of gray hair, enormous ears, and always offers me a beaming smile.

I play along, enquiring about the Chowdhary boy's studies, plans, and do they have a picture?

"He's really handsome," Leela Aunty's voice rises excitedly. "And they're a very good family. So cultured. You'd better get married soon or else you'll be on the shelf, Mytrae. Then you're done for. Nobody better is going to come along. I think he's the one. Yes, this is definitely going to work out!"

"No more meetings in my house," Daadi says definitively. "My house hasn't been auspicious for you. Leela, let them meet in yours. And wear something nice, Mytrae!"

I buy a new *salwaar-kameez* at a shop Leela Aunty recommends, the first clothes I've bought since coming to India. I meet the sister, Sonia, in Roshan Uncle and Leela Aunty's home. She's sweet, warm, and down-to-earth. We talk about living in the U.S., art, and music. I feel deceitful because I really like her, her parents, and their artistic bent. She likes me and tells Leela Aunty she wants to take the next step.

I write to Evan.

I'm going to the U.S. in May to renew my green card. My parents want me to meet a prospective groom. I don't know where to go. Is there any chance you might be in the U.S. then? If not, do you know of anyone I could stay with for a few days till I find my feet? How do you think you can help me once I get there?

My ticket is via New York to Charleston, South Carolina, where my parents live. Their plan is that after a few days I will go see Chowdhary boy or he will come to meet me. But I plan to use the ticket to JFK, then buy my own ticket to some small town, I don't yet know where. Some place I can make a fresh start, and where they won't find me.

I desperately need money but don't want to ask Evan. I hope he'll offer. All the few thousands of rupees I've saved will get me is a night or two in a hotel.

But I'm determined that this will be my chance.

One afternoon, while Ashok and I work on an accounting project, he puts his hand on my thigh. I look at him in surprise. He leans forward to kiss me and I kiss him back, surprised by his impatient mouth, unlike Evan's unhurried, attuned sensuality. I'm impure anyway, so I have nothing to lose and now that I have my plan, I'm my own woman. He's not a good kisser, but I'm curious and things heat up. We make love standing up, our clothes still on, my right leg propped wide on a plastic chair, my back bumping against the whitewashed wall. He comes all too quickly in a couple of minutes.

The next few months, I go early to work. We make love in a hurry on a red and green patterned jute mat on the grimy granite floor. His kisses are abrupt robbings, not the slow, delicious sensuality I knew with Evan. His fingers inside me are rough, rushing to get somewhere. He thrusts inside me before I'm fully aroused, yet I'm grateful for some comfort and touch. He pumps, heaving for a few minutes as I stare beyond his shoulder at the maple Formica desk and turmeric yellow cubicle. After he comes, he rolls over to get a little sleep. I sit at his desk, legs propped, and smoke one of his Charminar cigarettes. I stare out the iron grilled window at snarling traffic, Bollywood billboards, dust-laden trees, and think wistfully about Evan and our rides to ecstasy.

Will I ever have that again?

Suddenly, Evan stops writing. Right after I wrote I was going to meet the Chowdhary boy. I write a few more times but don't hear back. For the sixth time, I write.

> *It's been two months since I heard from you. If you can't help, just let me know. I'll completely understand. I have a plan B. A friend, Ashok, is trying to go to the U.S. and he can help me when I get there.*

Radio silence. Was it the prospective groom? Or Ashok? Surely he understands I have to get out any way I can? Maybe he's moved on, though he's been considerate enough not to mention anyone. I'm not expecting anything more than friendship. I just need his help.

What did I say to make him stop writing?

The full moon wanes to a slivered, silver crescent. My period, always in rhythm with the full moon, is late. I begin to fret. Ashok and I haven't used protection. The next full moon, I throw balled up unused sanitary pads in the trash hoping ever watchful Daadi won't check.

"I think I might be pregnant," I tell Ashok.

"What? Are you sure?"

Jittery of being recognized, I have a urine test at a lab under a false name. The test comes back negative. I'm relieved but the nurse says, "It can be confirmed only after three months."

Two moons grow full, and waste. My breasts enlarge, sore. I'm slightly nauseous at times. Worried, I comb Roshan Uncle's encyclopedias on pregnancy. A second test is positive. I'm horrified—I don't want a child now, and certainly not Ashok's.

If I wait three months till I get to the U.S. my stomach will show even in my loosest *salvār-kameez*. If I go to a hospital, a doctor or visitor will certainly recognize me. Just the other day Daadi said, "Leela said she saw so-and-so come out of outpatient surgery. So-and-so didn't say what she was there for. Must be an abortion!"

I don't know of any discreet, safe place. I don't want to ask Nupur. The expense worries me. Ashok falls silent when I bring up an abortion. I have to handle this on my own. In answer to my worries, I open the newspaper one morning to a small advertisement: *Marie Stopes Clinic. Safe private first trimester abortions. Your choice for reproductive healthcare.*

I make an appointment at the small, surprisingly clean clinic where several other young women, some clearly unmarried, anxiously wait with me. The clinic manager explains, "A British woman started this clinic decades ago to offer safe abortions. A doctor does the procedure and it's completely safe. We have a 98% success rate. Only 2% of the time we have emergencies, then we transfer you to a hospital."

I can't worry about the 2% risk.

"We have two options, with or without anesthesia," she continues. "Without anesthesia is three hundred rupees. With, five hundred rupees."

Definitely with. And I can afford five hundred rupees. What I can't afford is the luxury of what this is for me emotionally. So I shove my feelings down and tackle it like any task: practically. Early one morning I trundle in an auto-rickshaw to the clinic. As I change into the blue robe the aide hands me, blood-curdling screams and howls erupt from the procedure room.

"This is what happens when you do such things. This is what'll happen if you do it again," a male voice harshly scolds.

My blood runs cold. My legs clamp. I squeeze my eyes shut and stick my fingers in my ears to shut out the harrowing screams. Soon, a nurse leads a young woman, faint and hobbling, out. A man, I assume is her father, follows. Whimpering, she lies down on a cot a few feet away. Curling into fetal position, she rocks back and forth, yelping and moaning. My worries erupt. I haven't bothered to think of physical repercussions. I was more worried my family would find out. Suddenly, the clinic and aides look primitive. In the stark, grim waiting room, I hug my chest, as doubts spew: What will it be like? Will there be complications? Will I be able to have children? Am I doing the right thing?

When it's my turn, a stern, taciturn nurse leads me into the tiny windowless procedure room, tells me to lie down on a cold, stainless steel surgical table, and roughly slings my legs into the stirrups. Soon, a disheveled, seedy-looking doctor enters.

My anxiety increases.

"I'm going to administer anesthesia," he says. "It should be fine. But if there are any complications, we'll have to transport you to the hospital."

Now *that's* reassuring. I clutch the sides of the surgical table.

"Here, hold my hand," the nurse stretches out her arm. I grip her dark sinewy warmth, look at the whitewashed wall as the doctor slides a needle into a blue vein on the back of my hand. Questions race. What if he's one of India's many medical school failures? What if I end up in emergency and someone recognizes me?

"Breathe deeply," he directs.

I do. The world blurs.

I awake, weak and foggy, to cramps on the same narrow cot with an eggplant-colored bedspread on which the screaming woman had lain. The nurse appears. "The procedure was successful. You'll bleed for a couple of days. You have a sanitary pad on. Lie here for half an hour then you can leave. Is someone coming for you?"

I nod. I had asked Ashok to pick me up.

When Ashok arrives, he's concerned but impatient. "How are you? Sorry I'm late but I got held up at a meeting. I have an auto waiting. Come on, hurry up. Let's go. I have another meeting." He fidgets, playing with his keys, clearly uncomfortable.

"You can get up and go," the nurse encourages.

My head swirling, I hobble out of the clinic holding Ashok's arm and climb into the auto-rickshaw. He climbs in after me. "Are you okay?" he asks, gripping the iron frame of the auto-rickshaw as it jounces vigorously on the rough roads. I nod though I'm cramping terribly. He looks away, his mouth grimacing like when he's angry. Checks his watch again. My head bumps against the vinyl headrest as we ride, interminably, to the Institute.

Singu jumps up and holds my arm as I get out of the auto. "*Kyaa huaa*, madam?" What happened?

"I'm not well, Singu," I lean, dizzy, against the railing. Slowly, we climb the stairs.

Ashok leads me into the classroom. I lay down on a grubby jute mat on the cold granite floor, cover myself with a grimy faded peach sheet.

"Do you want anything?"

"No, thanks."

I drift into a still anesthetized slumber. When I wake, Singu brings me strong black tea. Ashok is out. I go home.

"What happened?" Daadi asks, surprised to see me back home mid-day.

"I don't feel well. I got my period."

She feels my brow. "Didn't you just get it two weeks ago? You don't have the flu!"

"I just don't feel well."

I change my pads the next two days. Thank my stars it's over without complications and that Daadi doesn't suspect anything.

I can't believe I had an abortion.

Another secret.

The following month, Ashok flies into the office, his face beaming. "I got in to Ball State University, Muncie, Indiana!" He thumps the table, raises his arms in a V, and whoops with joy.

"Oh! Congratulations! I knew you'd get in!"

"I'm going the same time as you. You can stay with me until you decide what to do."

"Thanks. You deserve it. You'll do very well." I smile, happy for him. He believes in himself. He's got guts and a feverish drive for achievement. They're qualities I wish I had. I feel grateful to have him as a friend, lover… I don't quite know what we are.

But my heart hollows. *Why* did Evan stop writing?

I don't want to, but I might have to take Ashok up on his offer. At least I'll have a place to stay till I get settled. After three years I feel vulnerable and mangled. He'll look out for me like a banyan's shade in scorching May. But my belly twists. What will he expect? I ignore my belly. I'll stay with him, get a job waitressing, then figure things out. I don't have to have everything planned now.

    I am finally heading to freedom.

11

freedom

1988

I'm so excited I could fall to my knees and kiss the navy blue carpet at JFK Airport.

Ashok's waiting for me at the gate. He arrived yesterday.

I run to hug him. "I'm free! I'm free!!"

He laughs. "I wasn't sure you'd come."

I breathe the hustle and the bustle in. America! I've ached for you for so long. Now, I can go anywhere I want. Do anything I want.

A pang goes through me. I last spoke with Evan here three years ago.

As I planned, I stow my one of my two suitcases filled with silk saris Daadi and Leela Aunty chose for my trousseau and as wedding gifts in an airport locker. I'd felt guilty shopping with them. They were so excited for me. But I want nothing to do with my family—not saris, not an arranged marriage, nor their expectations for me. Raghu lives here in New York City. He can collect it. I scribble a note.

Amma and Naina,

I'm not returning because I don't want an arranged marriage. I want to make a life for myself. I've left the suitcase with new wedding saris in JFK Airport's locker #51. The ticket's enclosed so Raghu can collect it.

Mytrae

I drop the envelope in a mailbox, throw my ticket to Charleston in the trash, and beam at Ashok.

He goes with me as I buy my ticket to Indianapolis.

"I wasn't sure you'd come," he repeats, his eyes soft and vulnerable.

A weight descends in my heart. He likes me. More than I like him. It makes me feel like I have to take care of him. We're not sure what type of relationship we will have. I don't want to depend on his kindness, but I just emptied my wallet for my ticket.

We stay at an Indian-owned motel our first night in Muncie. Ashok suggests we say we're married so we don't shock them. He also suggests it's a good way to get married student housing. I squirm at the lie, but go along. It's only for a while, I tell myself. Once I'm earning enough, I'll get my own place. We rent a one-bedroom apartment in the married housing complex and the International Students' Association loans us a saggy green couch, mattress, desk, two chairs, and cookware.

I get a job at a Mexican restaurant. Every evening after my

shift, Ashok meets me and eagerly counts the forty-something dollars I earn. They'll go toward our rent and groceries.

I introduce him to all things American. How to use an ATM, traffic rules, social etiquette, and choose clothes in discount stores. He's in awe of Americans' confidence, accent, and men more muscular than he, so he's happy to let me lead. Yet when I take him to the computer services department to ask if they have an assistantship, he walks out half an hour later with a jaunty step and an assistantship that pays his tuition and stipend. He's a lightning-quick learner, savvy, with an enviable fearlessness about his career.

He says, "They *help* you do things here, instead of making everything complicated and difficult!"

I'm happy he, too, is free to live his dream. This connects us. We're kind and caring with each other in ways our families haven't been.

I wonder how my parents and family have received my note. They must be shocked and angry. They must have called off the proposal with the Chowdhary boy. People's tongues must be wagging.

Good. Let them. After holding me in India for three years, what do they expect?

I apply to the graduate music program at Ball State and am delighted to be accepted for the fall semester and get an assistantship. I know I won't be able to get a job with music, so I enroll in a second graduate degree in computer science.

Freedom tastes like golden wildflower honey. I gulp it in big mouthfuls. Every morning I wake up to the delicious luxury that the day ahead is mine and mine alone. I'd never heard of this obscure town, but my life in Muncie is paradise. Away from my family's clutches, I feel rich to be free to waitress, ride the bus, and return to my music study. Much more than if I was bedecked with all the rubies and diamonds my family wanted for me.

I push through the double doors of the music department and halt, holding my breath. Rows of practice rooms resound with familiar sounds of piano, violin, clarinet, and flute. Schubert. Chopin. Bach. A soprano warbles arpeggios. My body vibrates. I walk to an empty practice room. Inside is an upright piano, its brass pedals tarnished and worn. I stand before it, lightly brushing my fingers across the keys. Press one. Close my eyes and let its soul sing into mine. This, is heaven. When the note fades, I sit down on the bench.

My fingers ripple through scales and arpeggios, Beethoven and Debussy. But… something's wrong. Very wrong.

I can't feel.

My fingers remember. But I don't *feel* music the way I used to. The way melodies and harmonies seeped into my cells. The way music flowed and danced in my body like lilacs swaying in the breeze. Though I'm playing the right notes I feel numb, as though a thick wall separates me from the music. My fingers fly frantically up and down the keys. My heart pounds.

What happened?

I know nothing about trauma. I don't know that physical freedom isn't emotional freedom. I live and work like a normal person, but have no idea how much emotional damage has occurred the last three years. I don't realize how afraid I am, how hard it is for me to trust myself, others, or life, and how my self-esteem drags, face down, on the ground.

Perhaps, I tell myself as I play Beethoven's Third Piano Concerto with growing desperation, I'll be able feel again if I just give it enough time.

"Let's get married," Ashok says as we sit on our couch watching TV.

"Married?" I echo and stare at him. His face looks even more narrow since he shaved his mustache to fit into a world of mostly mustache-less men.

"I don't like living like this. It's not right."

"Why don't we wait? We've just begun life."

"Why wait? Besides, I need a green card." His tone is aggressive, irritated, and urgent. "I really need one."

My stomach twists. He's asking me to marry him as though he's inviting me to eat at Long John Silver's. Does he want to marry me for me or to get a green card? I'm a green card holder so I could sponsor him if we do marry. But I'm just catching my breath after India. It's been only two months since we arrived. As we discussed, I wanted to stay with him till I feel strong enough to be on my own. But I'm not ready. I'm not myself. Still feel numb, shaky, and broken.

He's kind and protective. And I feel safe with him in a way I haven't felt in a very long time. I remember the two times he boldly knocked on our neighbors' door when we heard the couple yelling and fighting, flinging pans against our cardboard-thin walls. A tall, brawny American man opened the door and glared angrily at us. I stood behind Ashok as he held the screen door open, small, brown, and slight, yet his protection filled their living room. He asked the woman if she was okay, his fierce tone letting her know he meant business. I knew, then, he'd protect me no matter what. Safety and protection are what I most need now.

Despite his boldness his insecurity shows, like his chipped front tooth when he laughs. He's embarrassed about it so he quickly closes his mouth to a beaming smile. But that's when I see who he really is, a brown waif in a white world, and it makes me want to take care of him. Just like I want him to take care of me.

Besides, Evan doesn't want anything to do with me anymore. I can't imagine loving anyone else. Not like that.

I am an untethered boat. I don't know what I'm doing or where I'm going. Without my family's iron will, I don't have my own. I wanted to take it slow, but Ashok's urgency and aggressive tone startles me, drown out my hesitations, and makes me feel like I must decide. Now. His irritation makes me feel like I must please him and give him what he wants. I don't want him to be angry with me. I can't think when someone's angry with me. And I'm too guilty to leave. He's given me a roof over my head when I most needed it. Shouldn't I help him in return? I don't want to seem ungrateful or like I'm using him. I don't know what I want. But he does. He's a train going somewhere, and anywhere's better than the station I've been idling at for so long.

I find myself saying, "Okay." My shoulders sag. I should offer a smile, but it can't find its way to my lips.

The next week we ride the bus to the courthouse. A clerk marries us and we sign the forms, as unceremoniously as when we applied for married student housing. I wish he'd kiss me, but he doesn't like to display affection in public. We return on the same bus, side by side on the navy blue vinyl seats, looking out the window at the small, reliable town of Muncie. I wish he'd hold my hand. Anything so I feel like I did the right thing.

He gets off for his Data Structures and Algorithms class. I go home alone. The day is no different from any other. I serve burritos at the restaurant and cook spaghetti with bottled marinara sauce for dinner. We watch TV and have hasty, unsatisfying sex with the lights out.

After, I lie in the dark, thinking, "I'm married. *Married!* Shouldn't I feel excited?"

But I feel ordinary. Just ordinary. And resigned. Is this what being married feels like?

The following week we ride the bus to Indianapolis to apply for his green card.

Ashok isn't adventurous or eager to explore, as I hoped. I know what it's like to immigrate and gave him some time. But after six months, I'm ready for more than school and waitressing.

"Let's explore Muncie," I suggest, as we sit on our couch and the walls of our living room with gray linoleum floors close in on me.

"There's nothing to do in this one-horse town. I don't want to go to bars." Ashok frowns, lounging on a black vinyl chair, engrossed in a *Dukes of Hazzard* rerun.

"Then let's borrow a car and drive out to Delaware County."

"No, let's stay home and watch TV. Hey, adjust the antenna. You know how to do it."

Our 14-inch TV has a wobbly knob for twelve channels and two antennae he asks me to adjust when the signal falters. I stand, slowly swiveling the slim steel rods, asking, "How's this? What about now?"

He's reluctant to socialize with Americans. So we join the small group of Indian students and faculty for potlucks ending with canned Alphonso mangoes and dollops of vanilla ice cream or pistachio *kulfi*, Indian ice-cream, watching Bollywood or Indian art movies. The get-togethers are like warm body hugs from back home, yet he often declines those invitations too, saying he doesn't have much in common with them.

I adjust the antenna, thirsty for the life I had. I've introduced Ashok to music and dance concerts and literary readings, but he yawns through them all. He doesn't like to walk or hike. He pours himself into work, assistantship duties, television, and football. He makes friends with a few Greek students who invite us to dinners of succulent roast lamb, souvlaki, or moussaka, followed by raucous beer tubing and Turkish cigarettes, trying to conceal my distaste and judgment.

We're so different. Much more than I thought. As I look at him, absorbed in the show, I realize with a sinking feeling that this is what my marriage will be like. I married too soon. I didn't give myself a breathing chance to be free, but felt guilty and pressured to give him a green card.

Worst of all, I married someone much like the prospective grooms my family suggested.

I share my regret with Caroline, a pianist friend. She has alabaster skin, exquisite musicianship, a refined sensibility, and incredible baking skills. She's also empathetic. Her eyes sparkle with fun but reveal her lonely weariness—she's divorced and a single mother of a disabled daughter. We talk about music, department goings-on, hairstyles, and of course, relationships. We've brainstormed ways to arouse a couple of colleagues' interest in her, without success but with many laughs. She emerges after each attempt, sunnily optimistic about love.

She says, "You don't seem happy. What do you like about your marriage?"

"Not much. I think I've made a mistake."

"Have you thought about leaving?"

"I can't! I'm married." I'm shocked. "I can never leave."

Later, I realized she's Western, so has a different view about marriage. She lives from her heart and won't settle for just any relationship.

But I can't. I can marry only once, till death do us part. It's a belief that fills my pores, like watermelon juice fills the crisp pink cells of the green-rinded fruit.

When a package arrives in the mail from my parents' South Carolina address, I freeze. *How did they find me?* I unwrap it, my hands trembling. It's Amma's copy of Chinmayananda's commentary on the *Bhagawad Gita*. There's no note, just the book, its flaming ochre hardcover binding torn and loose, its title inscribed in golden letters. His flamboyant signature in thick black script sprawls across the first page. I ruffle the wafer-thin ecru pages. Its margins are filled with Amma's notes, the letters of her cursive like prim Victorian women sitting upright on straight-backed chairs. It's a book she's studied deeply. As have I. But it's her copy. It sears my hand like a red-hot iron. I fling it on our bed's navy blue comforter. Step back to stare at it, my body surging with panic.

She sent it to remind me who I am. *Their daughter!*

The book reaches its long, fiery orange arms into my depths. It's Chinmayananda, the Hindu scriptures, and everything holy judging me and what I've done. It's God on my bed. I ran away from my family to do what I wanted. I married a man much beneath my family's status and outside our caste without their permission.

I've brought shame to them all.

Trembling, I walk to my altar, a wooden shelf with a brass dancing Ganesha, a black and white picture of Shiva in meditation, a silver lamp, and an incense holder. I light the lamp and *champa*, magnolia, incense, fold my hands in prayer, close my eyes, and with a perilously wavering sense of self, pray.

"Please help me hold on to myself."

Naina's letter arrives a few days later. He writes they got my address from a friend I spoke to after I came. Why *ever* did she give them my address? He and Amma are driving up in two weeks to see me, then on to Raghu in New York. I'm shaken, but not surprised. The ground was prepared with the *Bhagawad Gita*. And Amma made Naina write. This is her signature plan of attack. She always gets others to talk to people before she enters the conversation, like she had my aunts fly in when she found out about Evan and me.

Trembling, I show Ashok the letter. "I can't talk to them. I don't want to see them."

"They just want to see you. They're driving a long way."

"Yes, but you don't know them."

"You can't be rude. They would find you sooner or later. Don't worry. I'll be there."

"Do you think they'll send me back?"

"Don't be silly. How can they?"

I'm terrified. What will they do to me? The idea that I could ask them not to come doesn't even occur to me. For two weeks, I'm tormented, sleep fitfully, and barely eat. The day before they arrive, I clean and tidy our apartment. Twice.

When the doorbell rings, my hands shake as I open the front door.

"Hello," Naina says.

"Hi." We stare at each other. I haven't seen him since I was taken back to India three years ago. The lines in his broad face are deeper, his hair grayer. His eyes are warm but I don't trust him. Amma looks grim, fatigued, and older. Her short black hair frames her fleshy face, once oval and angular. Her pudgy body tells me she's on steroids. She wears a floral blouse, polyester pants, and a rust paisley shawl around her shoulders. Our eyes meet and quickly dart away. As always, I look for warmth, for love in her eyes, but only find criticism and accusation.

Naina takes a step forward to hug me but I step back. They exchange glances.

"Come in," I say in a shaky voice.

Ashok is in class.

Amma takes in the shabby couch, nicked desk, vinyl chair, and Indian wall hanging of two women dancing. Her disapproval suffuses the room like cow dung. Naina folds his arms and sits on the couch. Amma gingerly lowers herself on its edge and draws her shawl tight about her, taking care not to let it graze the couch.

"How are you?" Naina's forehead furrows with worry.

"I'm fine," I say in the flat tone I often use with them that says "I'm not fine but I don't want to tell you anything. Because you won't understand."

Naina looks at Amma. He always matches his emotional state to hers. Seeing her down turned mouth, his face droops. After three years we don't know where to begin.

"So this is where you live?" he asks.

"Yes." I feel their judgment. After another awkward pause, I ask, "Would you like to check into your hotel?"

They nod, and we drive to Holiday Inn in silence. Inside their room I ask, "How was your drive?"

Naina says, "It was fine. It's a long drive. We broke journey in Kentucky, near Louisville. Amma helped drive. She's tired."

Amma digs in her handbag and pulls out her gray-blue asthma inhaler. She shakes it vigorously then inhales sharply. I try desperately not to feel like a bad daughter because no matter what, her health always trumps any situation. She unpacks her medication bottles, neatly lines them up on the bureau, and goes into the bathroom.

"Amma hasn't been well." Naina says in a low voice. "She had an attack."

She emerges in a black and white *ikat* caftan and sits on the chair furthest from me.

"Why're you going to see Raghu?"

"Oh, we're just going to see him," Amma says brusquely. Too brusquely.

"What's wrong?"

"Nothing, nothing. We're just going to visit him." Her forced casual tone gives her away. They never visit him. Something's up.

"Why are you going to see him?" I ask again.

They hesitate, then look at each other. Amma says, her voice low with shame, "His marriage is shaky. It's all very sad. I've been talking a little with Melissa because you know Raghu, he won't talk to us about these things. We want to see what we can do."

Raghu married Melissa, an American woman, while I was in India. He didn't tell my parents or invite them to the wedding. I can understand why. Lies and secrecy are the only way he and I can live our own lives. I wonder how he feels about them visiting? Does he really want their help with his marriage?

The room is full with what we can't say. But I don't want to bring up anything big after their long journey. "You're tired. Why don't you get some rest?" I say.

"Okay," Naina says. "We're here for three days. Let's meet tomorrow morning?"

"Okay. I'll come at 11. Bye." Naina gets up to hug me but I move swiftly to the door. Amma remains on the armchair.

Outside the hotel, my body quivers like a brittle fall leaf. I feel as powerless as when I was locked up. How strange to feel like this about your parents, I think. I'm free and in a free country, yet my body's quaking uncontrollably.

I phone Ashok when I get home. "They're here!"

"How did it go?"

I tell him in a rush. "Will you come with me tomorrow when I see them?"

"Yes, of course."

The next morning I'm enormously relieved to have Ashok with me when we knock on their door. Naina opens it.

Amma looks him up and down. Her disappointment is obvious. "Hello, Ashok!" she says in the falsely cheerful tone she uses for people she doesn't like.

"Hello!" he says boldly.

Naina and Ashok soon launch into conversation about school, engineering, and career plans. Amma listens, one thick well-shaped eyebrow raised sardonically. When their conversation falters she asks me, "So is this all we'll talk about?"

"What do you mean?"

"You know, about this and that, but not about why we're really here."

"Why *are* you here?"

"To see you," Naina replies.

"You've seen me," I feel bolder with Ashok there. "What more do you want?"

"Don't say that," Naina says.

"What else is there to say? What do you want me to say? Something you want to hear? Something I don't feel? Like you always have?" my voice rises.

"Calm down, Mytrae," Amma cajoles.

"Why should I calm down? You locked me up for a year. You kept me in India for three. You tried to marry me off so you wouldn't have to deal with me. You didn't even write or call me for three years. You destroyed my career in music."

"You're playing piano now," Naina pacifies.

"Yes, after all this time, after I've lost touch with it. You've no idea what three years without practice can do."

Ashok holds up his hand to tell to me to stop talking. "Mytrae, let me explain." He turns to my parents. "I don't think either of you really knew what was going on for her in India. You thought you left her with Daadi and that she was fine, that she was being taken care of. You didn't even call or write to see how she was doing! Do you actually know what was going on? I saw her the last year she was there. Her clothes were torn, they had big rips. She actually came to work dressed in those clothes. She wouldn't eat anything, only Marie biscuits with tea. Did you know that?"

I quiver at his passionate, firm tone. They look at each other. "We didn't know that," Naina says shamefacedly.

"No, I didn't know that," Amma mutters, embarrassed.

"Why did you leave her there for so long?" Ashok persists.

"Swamiji told us to," Amma defends weakly.

"She told me she was locked up for a year."

"She wasn't locked up!" Naina is indignant. "She stayed with her grandparents. She was fine."

"How could she be fine when she wasn't allowed to leave the house? To take or make phone calls? To do anything?"

"Why weren't you eating, Mytrae?" Amma accuses. "You ate fine when I was there."

"I didn't," I mutter, relief and gratitude washing over me alongside terror. I inch my chair toward Ashok, moved by his fierce protection. Moved that he can get through to them. He says what I've tried to for years, but they hear him in a way they never heard me. I see how tightly my parents grip their fantasy of me, those three years, what they did and didn't do. They don't see what it was like for me.

They don't *want* to see.

Amma and Naina look down, their faces pained. I glance at them, scared, angry, and relieved. Ashok looks expectantly at them, waiting for them to say something, anything. But our silence swells, big and round like a leech's belly, filling with everything we don't talk about. With Amma's rigid rightness, rendering her unable to see me or what my past has been. With her need to always be a good mother in her own eyes. With Naina shoring up her idea about herself so he won't be harshly criticized or shamed. With their upcoming trip to Raghu in New York, so embarrassing they can't speak of it, worried his marriage to a white woman is heading for divorce.

My arms wrap around my chest in the thick silence. I'm so grateful for Ashok.

Finally, Ashok asks in an irritated tone, "How's Raghu?"

"Oh, he's fine," Amma says quickly.

More silence.

Ashok says, "Well, I guess we'll leave. We can come back tomorrow."

We say our awkward goodbyes, looking down at the hotel carpet more than at each other. After we leave I thank Ashok, saying, "No one's ever done that for me."

He puts his arm around my shoulders. "I feel bad you had to go through all that. But I'm here now. I'll take care of you."

I smile at him gratefully. He can protect me from my parents, and that's what I need most right now.

12

a good Indian wife

1990

After Ashok and I graduate we move to Billerica, Massachusetts, and find work as software professionals. We make new friends, mostly Indian, explore Boston, and rent a home in a sweet neighborhood. I buy an upright Baldwin piano, but only occasionally do I open its lid to play for a while, then close it with a heavy heart.

A year into our new life Ashok walks into our kitchen and announces, "I got a job offer in San Antonio, Texas. We're moving."

"What?" I swing around, wooden spoon in hand, dripping tomato dal on the kitchen floor.

He sits at the kitchen table and stretches his legs. "A recruiter offered me a consulting job. I'm taking it."

"I didn't know you were looking!"

"I wasn't. She called. Apparently, these head hunters have lists. It's a great opportunity with lots more money. Hey, your spoon's dripping."

"Oh!" I put the spoon in the pan and turn off the stove. "But I just got a promotion. I don't want to leave my job. And the last place I want to go to is Texas!"

"You hate the cold. And I've already accepted."

"How can you accept without talking to me? Moving is a decision we both need to make. I don't like the cold but I'm learning a lot."

"Well, we're going. It's a better opportunity for me." His voice is like iron. He pushes back the chair and strides out of the room. I stand open-mouthed, staring after him.

I call my parents, whom I've made some slight peace with, to help me reason with him. But they say, "After you're married, you must follow your husband. Don't worry, you'll find another job."

Reluctantly, I resign. Pack and tape moving boxes. Grumble to myself that I can have an opinion about *idlis*, coconut chutney, paint, furniture, and even his clothes, but not this. I'm disgruntled, but I must go along. Support him though I don't like that his career is more important than mine.

Because this is what I must do as a wife.

Sacrifice what I want for his dreams.

Our families somewhat accept us. My parents are hugely relieved I've married an Indian. Naina relates to Ashok's unpretentious background, self-sufficiency, and down-to-earth simplicity. But Amma scoffs at Ashok's humble background, family, and accent. She can't brag about him to family and friends.

I'm relieved to finally feel some measure of approval from my family. I start speaking with my parents every week and visiting them in North Carolina a couple times a year. Our relationship is comfortably superficial. I share details of Ashok's and my success and our weekend activities. They share family goings-on and about Amma's health. It's a ritual that holds us together. It makes me feel like a good Indian daughter and wife. And so, my life feels and looks like enough. I've quieted my fever for Evan and music. Brushed them away like yesterday's dust sweepings into the closet of my past. With Ashok, my turmoil is finally stilled. With him, I can have a quiet nothingness. Still, a shadow haunts me, like a *palloo*, the end of a sari, shrouds a traditional Indian woman's face.

I don't speak with Raghu but on one of my trips to my parents' house, he's visiting too. We don't have much to say to each other. My body stiffens like a wooden board and my skin crawls when we're in the same room. I sit as far from him as possible. I don't trust him. Not the smile on his lips, his soft voice, or any interest he shows when he asks about Ashok or my life. I know he's judging my marriage. I know he's scoffing at my simple life. I see through his slimy pretense. He says one thing but thinks another. Yes, we both pretend to get along for my parents. But I sense a whole life behind who he reveals himself to be.

One day, the four of us watch the British Open. When it ends, I stand up to stretch. Watching tennis isn't my favorite thing.

"What shall we do now?" I ask.

"What do you want to do?" Amma asks.

"Shall we go for a walk? Naina suggests. He stands up and walks to the sliding door that opens to their backyard. "It's a nice day."

It is a beautiful day. The sun streams down on green maples, emerald grass, and brightens their garden's pink and white dogwoods, azaleas, and pansies.

"Yes, let's go." I say.

"Good idea." Amma walks to look out the sliding door. "How beautiful the azaleas look."

Raghu remains in a green armchair. He puts down the remote on the table. I stand a few feet from him. He looks up at me and smiles, a strange look on his face. Pats his thighs. "Come sit on my lap," he says.

My breath catches in my throat. *What?* Is he crazy? I stare at him, eyebrows furrowed, stunned.

He pats his thighs again like it's the most ordinary invitation. His fingers are mere inches from his crotch.

I'm so creeped out I can't speak. What is he thinking? What does he want from me *now*? Has he no shame? What sister sits on her brother's lap? And in front of our parents? It's as though he's dangling my secret in my face, like the tail of a mangled, stinking dead rat, laughing and toying with me the way he did when we were children.

I spin on my heels and hurry to my bedroom. Sit on the bed, trembling with rage and disgust. Stare at the wall between us, which seems all too flimsy to keep him out. But I cannot say anything. It would dismantle everything my parents believe about our family. I go on the walk. Though the sun's golden arms embrace me, my skin crawls, and I walk as far behind him as possible, a slimy, green frog stuck in my throat. That night and for the rest of my visit I lock my door and sleep with my head at the foot of my bed.

When Ashok's decisions to constantly move from job to job, city to city, go from confident to manic, and without my input, I grow increasingly resentful. Over the next twelve years we move eleven times, three times between India and the U.S. I go along because we have a plan to return to India to make a difference. But over the years, I give up art, music, literary events, and instead sink onto the couch to watch TV with him. I have less and less to say to my friends, and they to me. I rarely play the piano but always make sure to move it with me. It sits gleaming black, silent, and closed.

"You're an Indian wife. A wife follows her husband," my parents say when I seek their counsel. "Life is about doing what's needed. It's not always what you want."

Our third stint in India, I leave software to volunteer for a spiritual organization. I'm excited to work on projects that integrate spirituality with education, management, and the environment. Soon, I'm offered an opportunity to create and teach workshops all over India.

I tell Ashok excitedly over lunch, "They want me to teach seminars to schoolteachers!"

His hand pauses en route to his mouth. "There's no way I'm letting you go. A woman traveling alone? No way!" He eats a mouthful of rice and squash dal, then snaps a crispy *papadum* in two.

"But this is why we've returned to India!" I lean forward, aghast. "To do something meaningful. Now that I've found something I want to do, why don't you want me to do it?"

"If you do, I'll divorce you." He wolfs down his meal, disregarding my arguments, then walks away to wash up.

I grumble to Daadi, but she says, "You have to listen to your husband. That organization wants young people to do all kinds of work for them for free. Why should you? It's not decent that a young woman like you goes traveling all over the country."

"See, even your Daadi agrees with me!" Ashok crows.

My colleagues understand. It isn't at all uncommon for husbands to prevent their wives from traveling alone.

But I'm sick to my stomach to realize his talk about making a difference was hollow. Just like he told me he was an adventurer. I thought if I supported his dreams he'd support mine. His protectiveness, which initially made me feel safe, muzzles me now. His threats, angry outbursts, and put-downs about my friends have made me doubt myself. I thought being a good Indian wife would purify the murky eddies of shame and badness in me. But after twelve years our marriage is empty. The only thread holding us together is a piece of paper.

"Return to who you are." I hear the words spoken aloud a foot from my ear as I dust the black Ganesha statue in our living room.

I jump, startled. Who said that?

But there's only silence. And the morning sun streaming in through the windows. I shake my head.

Return to who I am?

Who *am* I?

I don't even know.

"I really think you and Ashok should reconsider having a child," says Swaroop, Ashok's younger brother, as we lounge in the living room after lunch. The warm December sun streams in the window, over papaya and coconut trees, telephone lines, and teeming Bangalore beyond.

"Oh, Swaroop, we've gone over this so often." I straighten the bolster on our chocolate and auburn paisley patterned divan.

Early in our marriage, Ashok and I agreed we didn't want children. With India's teeming population I didn't want to bring another child into the world. Though our families grumble and nag, my biological clock neither ticks nor tocks with Ashok.

Swaroop says, "No, really, listen to me. You two have everything. Money, spirituality. You'd make such great parents!" I like Swaroop. He's part-friend, part-brother.

"But we don't need to have children when we can help other children."

"All that is rubbish. Look at your lives. All you both do is work. You don't go anywhere, you don't travel, you don't have fun. Work, work, work. You only do for others. Nothing for yourselves. When was the last time you had a vacation?"

Though I've rejected my family's coaxing for years, as I look at Swaroop sprawled on a mauve and rose silk sofa, spooning creamy rice *kheer*, I know he's right. We have all the trappings of success, but our home doesn't feel like one—it's part software office, part morgue. My family and friends keep saying, "You don't really know what life is until you have children." Is that why I still feel like a girl, not a woman?

"What do you think, Ashok?" I ask.

"I don't know," Ashok says without looking up from his software magazine.

"Don't ask this guy. All he thinks of is his company. *You* have to decide. *You're* going to be the mother. Think about it, okay?"

I nod, clearing up the dishes. "Thanks, I will."

After Swaroop leaves, Ashok lolls on the divan and asks, "Do you want one?"

"Maybe we should. He's right, we don't have a life. Everyone has kids. It's how people connect and we don't connect with many people. We don't socialize much. Perhaps this will give us the grounding we need."

"Okay, if that's what you want. At least we'll have sex!" he grins.

So we try, hoping it might solve the morgue part of our lives. Hoping it might fill that dull, meaningless hole that nothing else seems to. We approach becoming pregnant like we do everything else: practically. Without emotion. As a task.

One night abdominal pains rip through me. Two days later I'm in surgery for an ectopic pregnancy and my left fallopian tube is removed. *I can't create!* becomes a mantra I pummel myself with. I can't even have a baby, I whip myself. After years of spurning children, I desperately want one now.

I can't create! I can't create! rips me over and over and I sink into a tsunami of tears.

Friends and family rally to my bedside and I'm grateful for their support. Give yourself time, my friends say. It will take at least six months. You'll bounce back, Amma says from Danville, Virginia, it's just a little procedure. Ashok doesn't want me to tell his family because they'll worry.

What do I do with this tidal wave of emotions that I can't seem to squelch?

I look around for women like me who've had ectopic pregnancies, miscarriages, and abortions but they're all indoors, veiled with their secret. There aren't any groups. The last thing my family, spiritual community, and culture wants is to hear my feelings. They want me to return to who I was, and quickly, as though my ectopic was a scraped knee.

It dawns on me that Indians have a gaping blind spot: *We don't speak about emotional issues.* It's effortless for us to talk about death, illness, bone-chilling poverty, violence, reincarnation, and enlightenment. But incest, rape, miscarriages, and ectopic pregnancies are taboo. So I go online where I join ectopic pregnancy support groups. There, I connect with Western women who talk about their experience and feelings, and can hear and support me when I share mine.

"Why did you want me to join your company legally?" I ask Ashok. We're at our kitchen table in our one-bedroom apartment in Campbell, California, near San Jose.

Ashok invited me to travel with him on one of his business trips because I was depressed after my ectopic pregnancy. "Come with me for three weeks and do some light administrative work. It'll be a nice break for you." But as Ashok's fledgling company struggled to survive the 2000 market crash, three weeks stretched into three months, then six, then an indefinite stay in the U.S. We fought for months. I wanted to return to India for my work but he said, "A wife must be with her husband." Once again, I gave in, resigned from my work, and administered his company full-time. That was a year ago.

Yesterday, for the first time, I read through the company's contract with the investors. I was shocked. We're bound to the company for four years and can't leave because Ashok invested money in it.

But Ashok's unperturbed. "The papers were drawn up by the investors." He spoons cornflakes into his mouth, staring vacantly through the window at pine trees in our apartment complex.

"But you didn't really need me. It's *your* company." I had initially refused to sign them when he thrust legal papers at me soon after my emergency surgery. I didn't want any part of it.

He had been furious and insistent then. "You have to sign. The investors want you in it. Your spiritual and social work appeals to them. You bring integrity."

I couldn't think straight at the time. Over the years I'd grown afraid of his volcanic rage and had learned to do what I could to appease him. So I signed. Once again, I went against what I wanted.

I stare at him, horrified and betrayed to realize what he'll do for money and success.

I feel sold. Pimped.

Now *I'm* legally and financially responsible for a company I have absolutely no interest in?

13
handfuls of truth

2002

I have a dream:

> *I'm lying naked on the gritty sand at the edge of an ocean's shore, its waves lapping my hips, whoosh-shush whoosh-shush. It's nighttime. The ocean is a shimmering, luminescent, silvery gray that stretches out forever. I drink in the sky's beauty, darkly speckled with a million different sized stars. Utterly magical. My body opens, sensual. The ocean makes love to me, entering and penetrating me wave after wave, slowly, powerfully, rhythmically. I rock up and down the shore with each incoming and outgoing wave, as I take all of it into me then release it. And I want nothing more than to make love to the entire ocean forever.*

As I awake, I'm aroused. When my mind kicks in, I'm embarrassed, even shocked, by my sexuality.

It's the ocean of life outside my brown puddle. It's life calling to make love to me. And my longing to make love back to it.

It's who I am.
It's what I want.
But how do I get there?

I peer at my reflection in the bathroom mirror but can't recognize myself. I'm a thirty-nine-year-old woman with a blunt cut. My face is tired. My eyes are sad and listless. My body's lost in my baggy clothes. I wear a polo-neck mid-thigh knit shirt that hangs like a sack over polyester-blend trousers.

At home I'm a cook, whipping up *chapathis*, vegetable curries, *dosas*, and *dals* twice a day. At Ashok's company I'm administrator, web designer, public relations liaison, and HR consultant.

Much as I peer under the bathroom vanity lights, I cannot find my face.

Evenings, I walk on the Los Gatos Creek trail in search of my forgotten face. Messages from Vedanta, my family, and culture clearly aren't working. I look to nature, and remember the rugged landscape I roamed as a child. I look to earth's moist brownness, her craggy mountains, coarse bushes, tall emerald grasses, poppies spilling open orange, and wetly patient snails. I look to the murmuring translucent lake, gasping fish breaking its surface. To the blue-gray sky with its wind face and the curving moon engulfing day's goldenness.

One tree draws me to her. Feminine, she's a mother tree. Her trunk is split in two, one branch grows this way, the other that. Her brown boughs reach up into the sky then bend, heavy. Her rustling stems drip with small emerald-green leaves. My steps slow as I approach and stand beneath her. I burrow my face in her jade coolness and let her shoots stream around my cheeks and neck. She holds, soothes, and murmurs to me. I close my eyes and drink her in. This is what a real mother must feel like. She is beautiful, noble, and wise, a tree spirit reminding and beckoning me to a feminine wisdom I've long forgotten.

Once I begin looking, I encounter grace. A forgotten fragment of my face returns with every encounter.

I question the religious teachings I studied, rooted in Indian culture. Why does Vedanta consider Prakrti, the feminine creative and material energy, to be less than the masculine? Why are women treated as inferior to men? Why is motherhood and pleasing one's husband revered but a woman's power, body, and sexuality demonized? Why does Vedanta reject the life energy of a tree, a mountain, a swallow, a whale? Why did Chinmayananda and my family spurn and destroy my love of music?

Grace.

One day a large, feminine presence arrives to occupy the space a few feet from my office desk. She is powerful. Dark. Fierce. Instinctively, I know it's Kali, the Hindu goddess of destruction, though I don't know much about her. Each day, I return to find her still there, unbudging and unwavering. Curious and in awe, I visit San Jose State University's library to learn about her. I walk through the stacks towards the section on Hindu goddesses when a few feet from me, from a shelf two feet above, the book *Kali: The Feminine Force* half slides out, as if pushed by an unseen hand. I stand staring at the cover, my mouth open, mesmerized by her fierce black and red face and lolling tongue. She speaks to something in me beyond everything I know to be true, beyond my culture, beyond what I know as spiritual. An inchoate something stirs in me. I leaf through the pages, its mysterious pictures more powerful than any femininity I know. I prop the book in front of my bed, so she's the last image I see before I sleep and the first when I awake. I feel her around me. With me. And I hunger for her ferocity, her unbowing, wild power for myself. I don't understand why she's here, but she lends me strength. Help has arrived.

Grace.

Two employees approach me with their concerns about Ashok. They've never been treated like this before. He proofs their emails before allowing them to send them to customers. He criticizes them during public presentations. He harshly rebukes them for their work. Their self-esteem is in shreds.

"He's emotionally abusive," one woman says. "It's completely unprofessional. I've never been in such a humiliating environment. Because it's a small startup and he's Director, he can get away with it. Otherwise, he'd be fired for unprofessional management."

"I used to be assertive and confident but after working with him, I've never felt so bad about myself," says a man. "After work, I feel so demeaned it's hard to face my wife."

They say what I haven't been able to find words for. I thought I was supposed to swallow how he treats me because he's my husband. Perhaps not.

More grace.

I talk Ashok into going to Point Reyes for a whale-watching boat trip. We haven't taken a day off our eighty-hour weeks in two years.

As the captain steers the catamaran from shore into the ocean's expanse, I breathe in deep lungfuls of salty sea air. Stress evaporates from my body with the lull and swish of the waves.

The ocean shimmers blue, green, and turquoise. Sunlight glistens each wave from indigo to sapphire to emerald. Like jewels, each wave sparkles one into another, fluid, changing, ephemeral.

Then I see them. The dolphins. At first, they're a few heads bobbing in the distance. Within seconds, hundreds surround the boat. Soon, they're all I can see apart from the iridescent ocean. Their wet domes and long noses bob up and down. Their gleaming, muscular bodies arc through air and water. And the squeaks, oh the squeaks. I smile at their delight as they fill the air with play, dance, and joy. Something long asleep in me uncurls and stretches, after years of slumber, and remembers. I watch them, transfixed. And I know as an orange poppy knows orange, a tree knows shade, or a seagull knows flight, that the universe is joy. It's made *of* joy and *with* joy. Not suffering. But a joy wide and deep as an ocean sparkling with the light and play of a thousand suns.

This is who I was before I was taken back to India. *This* is how I felt when I played the piano. *This* is who I was when I made love. I thought I had to sacrifice myself to be accepted, be a good wife, and spiritual. But sacrificing myself only made me unhappy, unfulfilled, and miserable. Life is not about sacrifice, but about joy, delight, and pleasure.

My heart flutters open.

Grace.

Every month, Ashok asks his investors for money for which we sign documents. I grow increasingly resentful and nervous. As the dot-com market crashes, the investors draw up a new document that says if the company is bought, they get first dibs on any profit and we'll get the remainder, if any.

I'm furious. We've slogged for three years on one salary and poured in huge amounts of our savings. I gave up my dreams for this. "I'm not signing," I tell Ashok.

"You have to," Ashok raises his voice.

"I won't." I sit on the carpet of our apartment, arms folded, my back stubborn against a used sofa with a baggy green slipcover. I'm tired of our vagabond life, of being uprooted every year, living with used furniture, and not making any lasting friends.

"You're legally bound. You have to." Ashok leans forward on a wicker chair.

"It's worked out well for you, hasn't it? It's convenient because I'm your wife. I'm free labor."

"Just another few months," he wheedles. "This customer is really interested."

"Yes, before it was that customer, then another one. They were all interested, but it's been three years, Ashok. The market's crashing. I've left everything. My life is reduced to your company."

"It'll be over soon. You *have* to sign." His tone is desperate.

"No, I don't. I don't have to do anything! I'm not going to."

His face contorts with rage. He stands up. Picks and swings up the wicker chair he was sitting on. Its black iron legs gouge a chunk out of the white ceiling. Fragments of plaster fall on his head.

I look him in the eye calmly. Throw it, I dare him in my mind. At least I'll have proof on my body to show how I feel on the inside. Go ahead.

He flings the chair to a corner and throws himself at me. His body bears down on mine. His hands circle and squeeze my throat. I slide to the floor. I can't breathe. I gasp, my legs kicking and flailing. My hands struggle to loosen his grip. My eyes roll back into my head. My grip slackens. After who knows how long, he releases me, storms into the bedroom, and slams the door. I roll into fetal position and hold my throat, coughing and heaving. I sit up, gasping, go to the kitchen, and drink some water. Lean against the counter, heaving.

What. Just. Happened?

I hear him in the bedroom talking to the company's advisor. He comes out and says, "Mr. Gupta wants to speak with you. Do you want to?"

I take the phone.

"What happened?" The advisor's warm, reassuring voice fills my eyes with tears.

"You know I've never wanted a dime," I cry. "I've worked and worked and this new document means my sweat and sacrifice is worth less than the money they've put in. I simply can't accept that. I can't take this anymore because I've given up everything. And I really don't have anything else to give up now."

"I know you didn't want any money from this. Are you open to talking to Arun?"

"Yes."

When we meet with Arun, our venture capital investor, he asks, "What's going on?"

"It's not fair that my work, our work, is worth less than the money you put in," I say. "Why should we wait to get money after you?"

"I agree," he says. "It isn't fair. Would you be okay if I modified the document so we all get an equal share?"

"Yes, I would."

I sign the papers. But Ashok's physical abuse has shaken me. His company and insatiable hunger for money are more important to him than I am. I'm grateful to finally see.

Grace.

I look up the term "emotional abuse." I take an online questionnaire and speak to a counselor who confirms it. But, I wonder, does emotional abuse apply only to Western women?

So I call Maitri, a San Francisco Bay Area organization for abused South Asian women. A warm, sensitive counselor confirms that the term applies to women of all cultures, that I've been emotionally abused for a very long time, and that I am indeed, very sane and healthy to question such treatment.

I pore through books at the Santa Clara Public Library, relieved to find a term for what I've experienced, and to read about other women's experiences. I'm liberated to read that Ashok's ridicule, control, rage, jealousy, coercing me to do what I don't want, limiting my choices of friends, work, where I want to live and what I want to do, isolating me from others, exploitation, and Jekyll and Hyde behavior isn't my fault.

Not my fault!

The books on emotional abuse lead to others. I sit on a library bench in the May sunshine as lilac wisteria drapes above me, poring through a pile of books on incest and trauma. I'm stunned to read descriptions of everything I've thought was strange about me but couldn't find words for. Dissociation, numbness, shame about my body and sexuality, lack of trust and self-worth, isolation, difficulty with relationships, passivity, feeling invisible and unreal, unable to do anything meaningful.

I'm relieved to find words for it. Incest. Trauma. PTSD—post-traumatic stress disorder, a term I haven't considered since Chapel Hill.

And that trauma isn't only for Western women, but for women everywhere.

For the first time in my life, I realize I'm not bad. Only wounded.

And that I can get help.

I go on a Vipassana retreat in the Yosemite foothills. For ten days, I live in silence with other women, wind through sequoias and firs, and lower my eyes when we cross paths as we're not to make eye contact. From dawn till night, we meditate in awareness of our bodies. Long forgotten feelings and sensations spew up like lava in me—aliveness, lust, and wild desire. My body remembers what I've been seeking in books and the mouths of teachers. I come alive, fiercely alive. So alive I can hear and feel my blood coursing through my veins. And I realize all I need to do for any decision is to ask my body. Not books. Not teachers. Not family. Not my husband. Just my body.

The last morning, I walk to the dining hall through the woods moist with dew and dawn. I stop. My breath stills. A large buck, its ears and tail quivering, locks its velvety brown eyes with mine. It waits for me get on its wavelength, as though it has something to say. Then it speaks to me of beauty, of humanity, of love, of gentleness, and of something I am to do. I don't know what, but it's something deeper than words. *Write*, it says. *Write for me, for the world, for this unutterable beauty of is-ness.*

It turns away once, twice, three times, each time stamping its hoof, then turning back to gaze at me. Time hushes still. Then after one long deep look, when it's sure I've understood, it leaps into the bushes, graceful, proud, and free.

I telephone my parents to tell them about Ashok's physical abuse, hoping to hear their outrage and protectiveness.

Naina says, "Sometimes these things happen. It's a difficult time for you both."

Amma says, "Poor man, he's going through a lot of stress."

I also decide to tell them what happened with Raghu.

"It's hard for me to tell you this, but I need to. Raghu abused me when I was a girl. For four years."

Dead silence.

"What are you saying?" Naina asks after a long pause.

"He sexually abused me as a girl."

"How can that be, Mytrae? When?" Amma whispers.

"It happened at night. In our bedroom. From when I was six to ten."

"Why didn't you tell us?" Naina asks.

"I tried," I say. "But I didn't have words for it. I didn't even know what sex was. I told you he made sounds. Those were nights he was masturbating. You said I was imagining."

More silence. Amma asks, "Are you sure?"

"Of *course* I'm sure. You don't believe me?"

Even with something as huge as this, they will always take his side.

I join a sexual abuse support group at San Jose's YWCA with Anne, a gentle and empathic counselor. I throb with guilt that I'm stepping outside my culture and telling my secret to strangers. One by one, eight women share their stories with relief, tears, horror, and shame. It's completely new for me to be in a safe space, where I'm heard with respect, and where I'm not shut down or shut up.

It's healing for all of us to speak the unspeakable. Anne's compassion makes us feel safe, as does knowing that the others have experienced some version of our own trauma. Shame does strange things. It makes us hide the darkness, and the more we hide, the more outcast and alone we feel. Shame keeps us in the dark shadows through no fault of our own. With sexual abuse, the abused person is left holding the badness.

As each woman speaks, I see how terrible things happen to little girls. When it's my turn to share, I realize, shaking with grief, that at an innocent six years old I couldn't possibly know what was happening to me, let alone how to cope with it.

Just to be able to talk about it, cry about it, and be heard with all my pain and shame is enormously healing.

Finally, I can tell.

Over eight weeks through art, poems, stories, tears, and lots of listening, we give each other strength, sisterhood, healing, and the faith that we can go on.

My hands grip the steering wheel as I drive to visit Louis, my undergraduate piano teacher in Winston-Salem. It's an hour from

Danville, Virginia, where I'm visiting my parents to take some space from my marriage.

An undergraduate music classmate emailed me a few weeks ago, encouraging me to write to Louis. I did. "I hope you are happy," he had written. Happy? When was the last time I asked myself that? We corresponded some, and he sent me two CDs. Lying on the floor of my Santa Clara apartment, I listened to his recordings of John Cage's Sonatas and Interludes and Morton Feldman's Triadic Memories again and again, letting my body and soul remember the music I've forgotten.

As I drive through Wake Forest's campus, memories rush through me. My initial years of not belonging, finding myself with music, my love of Western freedom and individualism. I park by the music building which, in my time, was the newest building on campus. It's weathered now, its brick walls wrinkled with crevices which ivy tenaciously grips. I enter the first floor feeling like a ghost come to haunt her past. The rows of practice rooms with glass doors are the same, as are the familiar odors of gray carpet, varnish, and sweat. A tenor sings scales. A pianist practices a Bach invention to the ticking of a metronome. A jazz pianist pounds rambunctiously. Someone picks a guitar haltingly. My body vibrates, remembering. I lived on this floor. I walk to my favorite practice room. The Baldwin baby grand's cream keys, once smooth and level, are now uneven.

I climb the stairs to the floor of classrooms and offices. Knock on Louis's door.

"Mytrae!" Louis exclaims when he opens the door, his voice mellower, deeper, rounder. His lean face is a little fuller, his hair has some gray. Glasses are new, behind which his eyes are gray, soft with seasoning that only age can bring and doing what one loves. We hug. He feels rich and deep, like a late Beethoven piano sonata played by a master pianist.

"You're here! You look so different!" he exclaims.

I *feel* different. And unmusical, so unlike the passionate young woman he knew.

We talk in his office lined with shelves of music books, a Baldwin grand, and an upright. Posters of his performances, paintings, and his daughters' childhood drawings brighten the walls. He's done well—teaching, performing, and recording. He talks to me like I'm an old friend, of his grown children and his worry for one of them. I vibrate to his husky timbre, his generosity as he openly shares about his life. I listen, enrapt, not only to his words, but to his being. As though our few hours together hold a key for me. Slowly, very slowly, something inside me uncurls, like a story's been asleep and forgot it began long, long ago.

"Do you remember this poem you gave me?" he asks with a smile, pulling a sheet out from a file. We shared bits and pieces of writing with each other as student and teacher. He reads it aloud.

VOCATION

Even if
my publisher calls me long distance
to tell me my books won't sell,

even if
my business colleagues consider me
a curio,

*even if
older poets
(such as I might expect to become)
are wastrels
ruin their readings
and embarrass me,*

*even if
no-one even
listens, publishes,
reads, or applauds again,*

*even so,
I am in it for good
because
the poem
the oh so lovely poem
has one arm around my waist,
the fingers of its other hand
perilously near my neck.*

*I can feel its thumb and finger
flick my earlobe.*

*It says,
"I will kill you
if I have to
and besides
I love you*

*and besides
I am the only one
who really does."*
— Rosemary Aubert

Tears well in my eyes. I gave it to him when I graduated. It was my promise to him that music would be the center of my life. Or was it my promise to myself? I feel like I've betrayed him as much as I've betrayed myself.

"Tell me about you," he asks eagerly.

I sputter out my story. "So that's why I don't play anymore. I can't play. I haven't been able to feel music like I used to."

His lips thin into a taut line. His jaw clenches. "So it was an imprisonment," he mutters protectively.

An imprisonment! I've never thought of those three years that way.

Of everyone, he most understands my loss of music. I tell him about Ashok. "I'm thinking of leaving my marriage."

"If there are no children, it's easy to leave," he offers.

My body sighs with his understanding. I haven't received anything like his gentle wisdom and sensitivity for years.

Over lunch, we talk about students and faculty we've known, music we both love. And I keep asking him, "Have I changed?"

He doesn't answer the first few times. Then he says, "There were a couple of times this morning when I remembered you the way you were."

"Only a couple of times?" I sob inside.

I don't speak much. Louis carries most of the conversation, sensing it's hard for me. And as I tune into the silver lifeline of him, his rich voice, I remember my forgotten face.

He drops me off at my car. We hug, look in each other's eyes for a long time, then hug again.

"Love," I say.

"Love," he replies, his eyes soft with gray.

I go for long walks in the North Carolina woods, turning things over in my mind. I listen to Beethoven's Archduke Piano Trio again and again, letting its sublime beauty seep into my cells and reconnect me with my truth. One night, I pace my parents' deck in the moonlight, wondering what to do next with my life. I look up at the silvery moon. Effortlessly, as the wind rustles through pines, oaks, and black walnut, swirling fragrances of hickory, dogwood, and magnolia, the answer slips into my mind.

I'll return to graduate school to become a counselor. It's something I've wanted since Ashok and I lived in India. Even if I spend the rest of my life working with the marginalized, and don't have another relationship, it will be far better than my present life. Anything else that comes my way will be a gift, beautiful and unexpected.

The next morning, my parents and I drink tea at their oval oak kitchen table. Outside their bay window a hummingbird suspended in mid-air, sips from their feeder. Amma says, "I've been crying about what you told us. I've been thinking about you as a little girl, how this happened, why it happened to you." Then, in a strange tone, "I wish he did it to me, instead."

To her? I'm shocked at her response.

Naina says, "You blocked it out once. Can't you block it out again?"

Speechless, I can't reply.

"Will you talk to Raghu about it?" I ask.

"We can't do that," Amma sets her mug down with a definite thud. "He's going through a difficult time at work and it's not compassionate to hit a man when he's down."

"Besides, what good is it going to do?" Naina draws his dressing gown tight about him. "Now, look at Oprah, she had sexual abuse and she got over it. Can't you do that?"

I look down at my tea and then up at my parents. They'll never understand.

"I've decided to leave Ashok."

Their brows furrow with anger and shock. They exchange glances.

"Marriage is your spirituality as a woman. Your dignity." Amma says.

I glare at her. "Even if he chokes me, I should stay?"

She looks down and frowns, struggling with herself. She looks up. "Well, if you think it best…" Her voice trails away. I stare at her in disbelief. Does she have room in her mind for my own happiness?

"What will you do?" she asks fearfully.

"Counseling."

"Marriage is difficult sometimes." Naina rustles his newspaper. "Amma and I have gone through very difficult times. You have to stick it out. Then it changes."

"I've made up my mind," I reply.

"How will you live?" His forehead wrinkles with worry.

"I'll be fine. Don't worry, I'll figure it out. I have savings to get started. I'll get a loan and a job for my expenses. More importantly, I'll have myself."

Naina looks anxiously at Amma. She stares out the window, her lips pursed. Fear comes and joins us at the kitchen table. They're afraid they've failed as parents. They're afraid to be shrouded with the shame of a divorced daughter. And they're afraid for me, that I'm stepping out of the world they know.

There's no map for what I'm doing. Indian women don't up and leave their husbands. And they certainly don't live their lives from their truth and heart.

I sit across from Ashok at a Starbucks in Palo Alto with my steaming chai. He's on edge, spilling demerara sugar as he sweetens his coffee.

"I want a divorce," I say.

"What?" He puts his cup down sharply.

"I want a divorce."

He stares at me. "Why don't you give us another chance, Mytrae? We've been through a difficult time. The company's dragging me down. I'm so tired. I haven't been eating or sleeping well at all." He pauses, waiting for my usual knee-jerk reaction to take care of him when he's upset.

But I don't.

He says, "I'm open to couples counseling if you want."

I haven't realized, in fifteen years, how his eyes don't look directly into mine, but dart left and right, only briefly meeting my own. "I'm sorry, Ashok, but this is what I want. We've given it our best shot. We want different things."

"Just give it more time, Mytrae. My father's not well. He's having heart problems."

It's an argument I've heard often. This time, I'm not biting.

His voice gets more desperate. "What about your parents? Your brother's off living his life. What will happen to those poor old people if we get divorced? They'll be miserable. Who will look after them? And your grandmother!"

When pulling our families into arguing for our marriage doesn't work, he asks, "What about our dreams of going back to India and doing something?"

"What *about* them, Ashok? I don't think it's what you want."

"It's this damn company. I can't wait for it to be sold. Just give me time till then."

But I look steadily into his shifting eyes. "I've decided, Ashok. I wrote to Arun to tell him I'm leaving the company, and he accepted my resignation. I'm no longer legally bound."

"You *what*?" His mouth snarls.

After forty-five minutes of going back and forth, he suddenly stands up, pushes his chair back so hard it falls to the ground. A mother sitting with her baby in a pink stroller turns to look at us. A man lowers his newspaper. "You bloody bitch. You've ruined my life. I curse the day you walked into my institute. But then what do you care, right?" He strides out of the café. I look down at the milky chai warming my hands, not wanting to meet people's inquisitive eyes. I exhale. My shoulders slump. I've done it. Finally.

I can't quite believe how simple it is. Respecting myself and finding my truth is my protection and defense. It is my power, my freedom. I gave Ashok custody of my dreams. I take them back now. *I'm* the only one responsible for my dreams. I don't need to look to someone else to have what I want.

Truth. So simple, yet so long in coming.

One September morning, I drive away from our Santa Clara apartment in my black Toyota Corolla crammed with books, clothes, a few pans and dishes. I've been accepted to the Integral Counseling Psychology Program at the California Institute of Integral Studies in San Francisco for the 2003 fall semester.

Gleaming software and technology corporations, towering icons of Ashok's dreams, whizz by as I head north on Hwy 101 towards Orinda, near Berkeley, where I've rented an in-law apartment. As I leave Silicon Valley's glittering buildings and my marriage for an unknown tomorrow, a boulder I've had in my heart for years shudders loose. I exhale deeply and shake my head. I'm finally going somewhere.

I have no idea where, but it's anywhere I want to go.

The car whines in first gear as it climbs the steep hill. The furnished in-law is the top floor of a house. After the emotional toxicity of the cookie-cutter apartment in Santa Clara, this stunning tree house breathes open and wide. Its looks out over miles of trees, chimney tops, and rolling hills. Each room has two or three windows into which nature invites herself with all her shades of green. "Sometimes you'll hear sounds at night. Not to worry, they're just deer," my landlady said. With the sunken Turkish turquoise tile tub, three-windowed bedroom alcove with a skylight, and spacious multi-level private deck, I've somehow landed in heaven.

I sprawl on the sandy carpet surrounded by boxes and gaze at the lush foliage all afternoon. Living in this natural habitat alone will be healing. After years, I have my own space. And what a beautiful space, I think, rolling over to gaze at the ceiling fan, wicker furniture with ruby and apricot flowered cushions, built-in bookshelves, tiny kitchen, and dining room with three wall-to-wall windows fitted with amber cushioned window seats.

My first taste of freedom.

"Look, Amma, look! See who we found!"

Seetha smiles to hear the excitement in her darling son, Kush's, voice from outside their hut.

"Who did you find, Kush?"

"Come see, Amma! Come!"

She puts down the wooden spoon with which she's been stirring spinach and tomato dal on her open fire. Glances at the flames to make sure it won't burn while she steps outside. Wipes her hands.

Her eyes widen in shock when she stands in the doorway of her hut. She gasps. One hand goes to her heart, the other reaches for the door jamb to steady herself. "Rama!"

It's been fifteen years and seven months since she last saw him.

She stares at him, remembering that fateful morning when he had come to her, troubled, as she was adorning herself with flowers and jewels in her chambers.

"I'm sorry, Seetha," he had said, "but a wicked rumor has surfaced amongst our people. A washerman, whose wife was found with another man, was heard saying he isn't like me who could take back an unchaste wife. So I must ask you again. Were you really chaste?"

She had put down her necklace and turned to him. "Haven't I proved it to you this past month in our marriage bed, my lord? Can you not tell that none other has touched me, known my mouth, my body, my sacred yoni? You've enjoyed me with all your long-lost desire yet you question me?"

Rama had walked away deep in thought.

The following day, he told her Lakshmana would drive her into the forest so she could bathe in its beauty and nourish herself and her unborn child.

But when she alighted from Lakshmana's chariot in the forest, he had said with a crestfallen face, "I'm very sorry to do this, sister Seetha, but Rama's ordered me to leave you here."

"What?" she had exclaimed in horror. "For how long?"

"Forever. Forgive me, sister." Lakshmana had touched her feet, jumped on his chariot, and driven back to the city.

Her blood ran cold. Her hand went to her smooth breast where she always kept a miniature painting of

her husband. Rama couldn't even tell her to her face. Her hands dropped to her womb. She was with child. Rama's child. All she had was a few clothes in a jute bag she had brought for the day.

It took her two years to make a new life in the forest, and turn to sages, deer, and rabbits as her new family. It took her five years to stop wandering through the banyan and ashoka tree groves, her face wet with tears, with the question "Why?" in her broken heart and on her lips. And it took ten years for her heart to let go of pain, expectations, disappointment, and allow Mother Earth's and the Goddess' peace and love to soothe and renew her.

But now, all those old emotions of rage, love, heartbreak, betrayal, and abandonment swarm through her like locusts on a rice field.

Rama is fifteen years older, thicker set, with gray in his hair. His face is lined with responsibility and not enough joy.

"Seetha!" Rama exclaims. "It is you!" He is awkwardly happy to see her. His body longs to embrace her but his heart pulls back.

He remembers that fateful morning too. He had thought deep and long about the washerman's words.

He had told Lakshmana, "Take Seetha into the forest tomorrow and leave her there."

"What?" Lakshmana had gasped. "Are you mad?"

"I must do it, Lakshmana. I have to be a good king in my people's eyes."

It has been an eternity since then. She has always been the only one for him.

Kush and his twin brother, Luv, look back and forth at their parents. The air is pregnant and stiff. A squirrel on a mango tree pauses from eating a cashew nut to watch. A rabbit pokes its head out from under a bush to listen, twitching its nose. Her pet deer comes and rubs against her.

Seetha finally finds words. "Where did you find him, Kush?"

"Luv and I stopped a majestic white stallion in the forest. Then some men from the palace came and took us to the king. He says he's our father, Amma. Is that true?"

"Yes, Kush. Yes, Luv, it's true. This is Rama, your father."

The boys run and hug Rama, who embraces them back, tears flowing down his cheeks.

"I've come to take you back to Ayodhya, Seetha. It's been far too long. Will you come?"

Her heart leaps. You want me back! But wait. After how you've treated me?

Rama continues, "But for the sake of my people, I have to ask you to go through another fire ritual. I cannot have them doubt my decision."

As quickly as her heart leapt, it crashes down hard onto a boulder of disappointment.

Here's how the story goes, as in the *Ramayana*, that Indian women learn when they are girls:

> Seetha takes a deep breath and raises her hands in prayer. "Mother Earth, if I am pure, please gather me into your lap."
>
> The earth trembles and shakes and heaves below them. The twins and Rama stare at her. The earth begins to part below Seetha, who stands, eyes closed, her lips moving in prayer.
>
> "Amma! Amma!" the twins cry, horrified and desperate.

"Seetha! Wait!" Rama shouts.

Mother Earth opens wide like a mouth. Seetha slides in rocks, rubble, and all. The earth closes over.

But as women, we get to weigh and question the stories we're told. And rewrite them if we choose. I would have to learn to rewrite my own.

Seetha shakes her head in astonishment. She cannot believe her ears. Rama is so not who she thought him to be.

She turns from them and walks a short distance away to her favorite banyan tree. Places her palms and forehead against it to ask for its blessing. Steps away and closes her eyes. Folds her hand in prayer.

She roots her energy deep into the earth. "Dearest Mother," she prays. "Please guide me…"

Before she completes her sentence, Mother Earth trembles and shakes and heaves below them. She booms, "Daughter mine, you are purest of the pure. You know what you must do."

Seetha turns to face Rama.

"No, Rama. It is enough. No more. No more proving myself. Luv, Kush, this is your father. It's time for to you to go and live with him. He will bring you up now. I give you my blessings." She walks to them and embraces them, rests her head on top of their black curly hair. She kisses them on both cheeks and looks deep into their eyes. "Remember, I will always love you and watch over you."

"But, Amma...?" The question trails away on their lips.

Seetha turns to Rama, her head raised high, and says, "Rama, I am pure and have always been pure. Your judgment destroyed our marriage, and nearly destroyed me. If you can't see, hear, or value me you're not worthy of me nor can you be my destiny. I belong to no man. I belong to no kingdom. I belong to no dogma. I belong to myself and follow the truth of my Sacred Heart, Mother Earth, God, and Goddess within me."

She spins on her heels, walks into the cool forest and beyond, with the squirrel, rabbit, and deer scurrying behind her, to create a life of her own.

14

finding my forgotten face

2003

I enter Namaste Hall at California Institute of Integral Studies (CIIS) in the heart of San Francisco. Ganesha and Kuan Yin art adorn the walls. Buddha and goddess statues embellish the space. The room is abuzz with thirty graduate students gathered for orientation to the counseling program this fall. I'm excited to meet my new cohort. I chose CIIS because it integrates Eastern philosophy and Western psychology. Among the faculty, I'm especially eager to meet Brant Cortright, Program Chair. Reading a couple of his papers online helped me figure out this was the right school for me. He beautifully integrates Aurobindo's—an Indian mystic—philosophy with psychology and gets India's blind spot about the human psyche and emotions.

When he walks in, slender, attractive, and purposeful, my body is electric. *I know him*! He feels so familiar. He talks about the program, leads us in some experiential exercises, then the faculty talk about the program. While Brant speaks, I have the most extraordinary experience. One part of me listens, while another part of me is lifted to a transcendent, luminous realm. A book is thrust before me, pages rapidly flipping through scenes of many, many past lives that go centuries back, even before Buddha and Christ. In each lifetime, I am shown that Brant and I were very close—as a couple and spiritual friends.

Then I'm gently lowered from the crystalline realm to the rough gray carpet of reality among my cohort who are sitting cross-legged, listening enrapt to his soothing voice as he talks about the courses.

What just happened? I don't understand, yet it strangely makes sense.

After orientation, the faculty mingle to talk with us. I walk by Brant talking to a student. He turns to look at me as I pass. I search his eyes, feeling a bit crazy. *Do you remember me the way I do you?* But he doesn't. He looks back at me with friendly hazel eyes. When he finishes his conversation I introduce myself. I tell him I want to study then take the work back to India. We're polite and friendly.

But I just can't shake that I know him.

Very, very well.

My quest to heal and find myself is like opening Pandora's box. It isn't a box of creepy-crawlies, but full of mud-encrusted jewels I pick up, look at, and scrub so the light may enter to reveal their lustrous colors. With each one, I discover a lost, buried, or forgotten fragment of myself.

With a wonderful therapist, I set out to heal. But this journey isn't for the faint of heart. I must rewind time to my dark past, learn to swim the swells and eddies of my psyche, and dive into its closed, inky caverns.

I begin to explore my raw, unfelt feelings. Especially when they bring me to my knees. If I am to retrieve my lost self and aliveness, I need to embrace everything I've shunned. Grief. Loss. Anger. Guilt. Shame. Lust. Loneliness. Betrayal. Soon, I learn to see in the land of my shadow. I smell and taste the gritty rub of my feelings. I let each one suck me into its fiery belly. After searing me with its flame, I am set free, a little more alive, on to the next. I bend over double on my therapist's couch, shaking with grief to realize I haven't lived, not just for the three years in India, but for the fifteen years of my marriage. "Keep going," she steers. "Your pain is your aliveness." I do. For, more than anything, I want to return to who I was. If I keep looking, I know I will, one day, find a mirror at the bottom of the chest and see my forgotten face.

She shepherds me into the earth of my body. I taste, then relish my sensations' slithery reptilian and luscious animality. *This is what it's like to be human. This is what it's like to be alive.* I've never felt so deliciously feminine before. "You're in between who you were and who you will be," she says. "Feel everything, so the sculpture of who you are—your true self—emerges."

I learn to face myself and my choices no matter how much I want to look away and not take responsibility. I see the ways I denied, suppressed, repressed, rationalized, and dissociated. I see how I harshly cut out joy, creativity, and pleasure just as I was harshly treated. I see how passive I've been when I could have chosen differently. And how I've lived terrified, paralyzed, and obedient for most of my life.

I face that though they are progressive in some ways and educated, my family, culture, and Chinmayananda are also abusive, patriarchal, and racist. I question the cultural edict that "elders know more" and realize that my family are ordinary people with their own limitations. I let go of my naive belief that they see me, and realize they see the version of me that they want to see. I mourn that they didn't love me in the way I needed, but acknowledge they did in the way they knew.

I let go of my need for their love and approval.

So I can begin to love myself.

I learn to set boundaries. I tell Ashok to email, not call me. Talking with him makes my head spin. I let his email sit in my inbox for a few days, then write only when I feel ready. He writes often, his sentences running into each other like desperate sheep, to say he's sorry and wants to get back together. I feel the burn of my red-hot anger. I'm learning it's okay, good even, to be angry.

My parents call every few days, urging me to get back with Ashok. I shake with rage. They prefer I return to a man who's strangled me rather than have a divorced daughter? Yet I pace, wearing guilt into the carpet, wrestling with what I've always done. And, though I feel like a bad daughter, I tell them I don't want speak to them for a few months.

When months become a year and I want to call them, my therapist leans forward in her chair, looks me in the eye, and asks with an edge in her voice, "Why?"

I buy a baby grand piano as a divorce gift to myself. It sits gleaming black, regal, and exquisite in my living room. I think I'll pick up playing where I left off eighteen years ago. Instead, week after week, I sit dissolved in tears on the piano bench, unable to lay my hand on its creamy smooth keys. Because it wasn't only music I've longed for—it was for how beautiful I felt when I played.

Louis mails me simple sheet music that isn't technically demanding. Satie's *Gymnopédies*, Schumann's *Träumerei*, and Liszt's third Consolation, among others. "It's hard to return to play after a long break," he emails. "Your ear has evolved but your body is in another timezone. It's like learning to walk after a major leg injury slow, excruciating, frustrating, and heartbreaking." He's right. Where I used to ripple, I now fumble. Where I used to fly, I can only take a step. But, I persist.

Slowly, slowly, over months, the harmonies of Bach's French suites and partitas, Beethoven and Mozart sonatas, Schubert impromptus, and Rachmaninoff preludes seep into me, transforming cells of shame into cells of beauty. And so, hour by hour, piece by piece, my closed heart cracks open to joy and beauty, weeping to remember.

Kali, nurturing, loving, and compassionate, still guides me. I've accepted her comings and goings. Huge and full like the night, she lends me strength. The great dark mother comes when I'm lonely, with the faint fragrance of sandalwood, to cradle me in her broad black arms and on her wide, folded thighs.

She says nothing but knows all—my peaks of joy and freedom, my abyss of grief, and my unspeakable shame. She holds me in a way I've never been held before. With her I can be a child, an infant, and suckle from her ebony breasts. In her obsidian arms, I let go of my past. My grief. Having to be strong. Having to know.

And fall into who I truly am.

I'm learning to be on my own. I hike on the trails of Tilden Park in Berkeley for hours. Loneliness lies thick upon my skin, and I breathe through its waves, shedding tears as I sit on a fallen trunk under the cool radiance of giant redwoods and eucalyptus as the fog creeps across the hills. Beneath them I am not alone. They are old friends. To them I take my cares and fears. My dreams of being hunted down like an animal. How I feel so open that I sometimes feel like I don't have a skin. How I freeze to do simple things like find a new address or go to a party, and sit trembling in my car for half an hour unable to open my door. How afraid I am to be on my own when I've stayed safe by taking care of others.

How ever, I wonder as I run my fingers over the crisp edges of redwood leaves, will I be a therapist when I'm so broken, so fragile, so vulnerable? If I don't make it, I'll become a cashier at Barnes and Noble where, at least, I'll be among books. That thought, and one other brave thing I know I need to do, gives me the courage to go on.

One suggestion my school readings offer survivors is to talk about incest with the perpetrator. By confronting them, we shatter the spell that shame casts over us. It's a daunting challenge, and I've been building up my courage for weeks.

One morning, I decide that today's the day.

I phone Raghu.

He answers, "Hello?"

"Hi, Raghu, it's Mytrae."

"Oh, hi, Mytrae. How are you? How is school going?" His voice is surprised. We've hardly had any contact over the years. I don't reach out. Neither does he. Though we're brother and sister we feel like we're supposed to get along, but neither one of us has ever been interested in really knowing the other. We've only made small talk and don't connect about anything real. With Raghu, I always feel like I'm with a pretense of someone, never the real person. Over the years, my parents told me he divorced his first wife and married another American woman, but that didn't work out either. Amma tried to arrange an Indian marriage, and he explored those proposals.

I felt sorry for the women.

"Raghu, I'm calling you to talk about something. It's hard for me to talk about it." I pause, trembling. Tell myself to breathe. "Do you remember when we were little you were sexual with me?" My throat clutches.

Silence, thick, murky, and dank as a swamp, swells into the telephone line.

"Hello?" I say.

"Yes, I'm here," he mutters.

"Do you remember?"

"Yes, I do. It was a long time ago."

It's the last thing he wants to talk about, but I must. "Yes, but you did those things to me. I had no idea what sex was. Why?"

"I was a child. I didn't know what I was doing." He stutters, awkwardly, like he did when he was caught doing something wrong as a boy.

"You were ten. Old enough to know. And it went on for four years."

"Some friends brought magazines to school. So I thought I would try it."

"*Try* it! On *me*?" My legs are Jell-O. I sink to the carpet. Clutch the leg of my desk.

"I stopped. I moved into the guest bedroom after I went to boarding school. Do you remember?"

"Yes, I do, but that was after four years. You were fourteen! Do you know what it's done to me? How it's affected my life? Who I *am*?" I'm sobbing.

He's silent. The golden light in the room dims as the sun retreats behind a cloud.

I wait for him to say something. Anything. Anything at all. But he has nothing to say. He won't. Is he sorry? Or stunned? Whatever it is, he has nothing to give me. My stomach hollows into a cave of disappointment. What did I expect, I ask myself for the millionth time. My family's never been there for me.

"One of the reasons I'm in therapy is because of this."

I hope he'll respond to that, at least. But he doesn't.

And he won't ever apologize.

I'm shaking with grief. "I can't talk any more, Raghu. Goodbye."

"Bye," he says. I sense his relief when I hang up.

I fling the phone at the couch. Curl up in a ball on the floor, my face pressed into the rough beige carpet, heaving with sobs, hands against my heart.

A week later, I receive a check in the mail from him. For fifteen thousand dollars. I stare at his big, child-like handwriting on the robin-egg blue and white striped paper in disbelief. I don't want to hold it. Or touch it. It feels dirty. *I* feel dirty. Is he paying me off to not tell anyone? Or is it his way to say he's sorry? I place it on a far corner of my desk. Stare at it as I walk by. What am I to do with it?

After two weeks, I deposit it to use for therapy.

15

cinnamon and ivory

2004

I curl up in my azure blue armchair, phone in hand, and look out the window. Oaks, bays, madrones with ruddy, peeling bark, and blue gum eucalyptus reach upward to stroke the cheeks of blue sky. I'm thinking about what Debira, my friend, and I just spoke about. I had said, "I think I'm ready for a relationship." For the umpteenth time she had asked, "What about Evan?" Only this time, her words rung me like a gong.

Evan! Funny how the universe bangs on our doors and windows but unless we're ready, we don't hear. I shake my head and smile. I dial Evan's friend, Anna, whose number I found online.

"Hello!" she answers in her breathy voice.

"Hi Anna, this is Mytrae, Evan's friend from Chapel Hill."

"Mytrae! Hi! Great to hear from you!"

We briefly fill each other in on our lives. She lives in Virginia and is a single mom. I tell her about my marriage, divorce, and return to school.

"Anna, I'm trying to reach Evan. Are you still in touch with him?"

"We talk sometimes and I visited him last year. Yeah, I have his number."

"Where is he?" I hold my breath. Probably in some foreign country.

"He's in San Francisco."

"What?" I squeal. "That's where *I* am!"

"Oh my *God*! Can you imagine if you saw each other on the street?"

"I can't believe it!"

"He's a doctor now. He went to medical school in Charleston and moved to San Francisco about ten years ago for his internship."

So he *did* become a doctor! "Is he married?"

"No, but he's been with someone for about four years. When I visited them last year, they were talking about marriage and children." She gives me his number and address.

"Thank you so much! I really appreciate it."

"You're welcome. Good luck with school and everything else."

"Thanks, Anna. Good luck to you too. Take care."

We hang up. I stare at his phone number and address incredulously. Noe Street. Evan Johnson could have been in any part of the world but he's right here in San Francisco!

But will he want to see me? I put the kettle on for a cup of ginger-lemon tea to digest the news. I go to my desk and pull out my favorite handmade Indian stationery. It's soft and pliable, the color of sandstone with bits of rouge and mahogany straw.

Dear Evan,

I spoke with Anna and got your address from her. I'm so surprised you're in San Francisco, because I live in Orinda and go to school in the city. I don't know if you want to see me again, but I'd love to meet if you want to.

Love, Mytrae

The phone rings a couple of nights later as I lie in bed reading. I let it go to the answering machine. "Hi Mytrae, this is Evan…"

I leap out of bed and grab the phone. "Evan! Hi! How are you?"

"Hey, Nitro. Great to hear your voice!"

"And yours!" My body's quivering.

"When did you get out of India?"

"Sixteen years ago."

"That long! I'm so happy for you. I knew you would. I wasn't surprised when I got your letter. I've been thinking about you."

"You have?"

"Yeah, I'll tell you all about it. Orinda's so close. We can meet!"

"You want to?"

"Of course I do!"

We make plans to meet Sunday afternoon.

We talk about safe things, like what we've done. "I went to medical school in Charleston where David lived. You remember David? Med school was really hard. I'm not a good learner like you. I had to work my butt off. Then I came to San Francisco for an internship with UCSF and worked for a few years. Now, I work at the Haight-Ashbury clinic. It's a non-profit for the homeless."

"You *did* become a doctor after all! That's awesome! I know you wanted to work with the marginalized." I tell him about my life, ending with, "Last fall, I went back to school to become a therapist. I'm divorced now."

"I'm sorry. Do you have children?"

"No."

"It's probably easier, isn't it? I ended a relationship last fall, too. We were together for four years, but it didn't work out. I broke it off. I thought about you a lot last year."

After we hang up I lie on my back on my bed, smiling as I look out over the Orinda hills awash with night's soft mystery, the crescent moon, and twinkling stars. Everything looks magical. I'm going to see Evan again. How amazing he's been thinking about me just as I have. And how amazing that he wants to see me. And he's not in a relationship. Whatever is going to happen? Sunday can't come soon enough.

On a bright spring afternoon, excited and nervous, I drive through Duboce Triangle, a calm neighborhood with sunlit, tree-lined streets. Painted Ladies are one of the things I most love about San Francisco—Victorian and Edwardian homes in a rainbow of colors such as cornflower blue, plum, lilac, primrose, and saffron. I park my car on Noe Street. Remind myself to breathe. I walk down the sidewalk uneven from thrusting tree roots, climb the steps to the porch of Evan's teal and white Victorian, and ring the bell.

Footsteps come down the stairs. My heart pounds like I've run five miles. Evan, in a chunky cream sweater and black jeans, opens the door. He looks the same: youthful though more serious, thicker set, his facial lines furrowed. He smiles groggily at me, as though he just woke up. His energy is haggard, jagged, and spent, not like the fresh, vibrant young man I remember.

"No!" erupts from deep inside my heart. I'm shocked by my own response.

"Hi, Mytrae! Come in." He looks at me with his chestnut eyes, then quickly glances away as though he has something to hide.

Surprised by my intense initial reaction, I step into the doorway and reach up to hug the tall leanness of him. He pulls back quickly, turns, and hurries up the flight of wooden stairs. I follow, a small hole growing in my stomach. Is he upset, or feeling obliged to see me for old times' sake? We enter his light-filled Victorian flat with amber hardwood floors, high ceilings, beautiful moldings, and large bay windows overlooking Mongolian oaks, weeping elms, and the California Pacific Medical complex. The living room has a tired dark brown couch and armchair, an oak coffee table, a tall fuchsia plant by the window with mustard drapes and ivory sheers, a television, music system and desk cluttered with papers, as if piled in haste for months. Something other than its dank mustiness makes me cringe. "It's beautiful," I exclaim, remembering his sparse yet wholesome two rooms in Chapel Hill. He gestures to the couch. I sit at one end, he sits at the other, leaning away from me. His eyes are small, watchful, and wary.

There's an ocean between us.

Eighteen years of water.

We look at each other in a mild state of shock. As I try to get over how different his energy is, all I want to do is throw myself into his arms. "You look just the same, Evan!"

"And you haven't changed. You look great! You still look twenty-two."

"No, I don't."

"Yes, you do. Only a little older, and your eyes are sad, but the rest of you is the same."

"You look just the same, too. No, you have a few more laugh lines."

"I've thought about you so much. You're an amazing being and I knew you'd find your way back to who you are, however long it took. I wasn't surprised to get your letter."

"Why not?"

"I kept thinking about you last summer. A lot. You know how connected we used to be."

I nod.

"My relationship wasn't going so great. I started to go to the beach on my own to think, and sometimes I'd look at the ocean and think of you, our times together, and our horrible separation. I missed you and wondered where you were. And in my heart, I'd send you love. Then I looked you up online and saw an excerpt of an article you wrote. 'Lotus Eyes' or something? The writing was so you."

"With Eyes of Lotus." It was an article I wrote for a book.

He nods. "I found one of your posts in a Vedanta newsgroup. You're probably the only person in the world who spells your name the way you do, otherwise you'd be impossible to find. I found the number of the company in the South Bay where you worked. I called."

"You called?"

"I got your extension. It was so great to hear your voice. I didn't leave a message because I wasn't sure if anyone screened your messages. I didn't want to get you in trouble. I'd call at night and listen to your recording a few times just to hear your voice."

I melt. "When was this?"

"Last summer."

"I wasn't working then. But my voicemail was still there."

"It was so great to hear your voice."

"I was so nervous to write you. I thought you might be married, maybe even had children. I didn't know if you'd want to hear from me."

He said, "Your handwriting was unmistakable. I called you right away. Tell me about you."

I tell him about my marriage and my divorce. "My friends wouldn't stop asking about you. One offered to look for you online. I kept thinking of you every time I walked on Church Street." Church Street is a few blocks from Noe.

"That's incredible," he says, and pauses. "Hungry?"

I nod. He stands up and I follow him into his long, narrow kitchen bright with afternoon sun. On his white vinyl counter is an espresso machine, blender and toaster. He slices a loaf of whole grain bread, and opens the fridge for Gruyère, brie, Dijon mustard, and green olives, which he arranges on a tray. His fridge is sparse with a few deli containers, cheese, bottles of German ale, Orangina, and a couple of wizened apples.

"What would you like to drink?" he asks, brushing his arm against mine.

I gasp at his touch. Lean against the counter to steady myself. "I'd love some tea. Do you have any?" I try to sound as normal as I possibly can. All I want is to throw myself into his arms.

He nods and puts a brass kettle on the stove, pouring a Heineken for himself. My heart tugs to watch him getting food ready as he used to. I look around in surprise at a glass cabinet filled with wine, vodka, and gin, an assortment of liquor glasses, and the big garbage can overflowing with empty beer and alcohol bottles.

"Tell me about you," I ask when we return to the couch, sitting gingerly at one end. I slice some Gruyère, place it on a slice of bread, and take a small bite.

"Well, the first three years after they took you back were the most difficult years of my life." He digs a knife into the brie and slathers it on bread. "I couldn't get over you. I didn't date for three years."

"Really? For three years?"

"I just couldn't bring myself to. There was the odd encounter every now and then, but when it got to making love, I wanted them to be like you," he says, his hands gesture helplessly. "I kept getting frustrated when we didn't go to the places you and I went. So I didn't date. I kept hoping you'd somehow find your way back to me. I wanted to come and get you but I knew it was something you had to work out with your parents." He pauses and says in a sharp, accusing tone, "I thought you chose them over me."

My eyes fill with tears. "I didn't choose them. I was choosing you and that's why they took me away. I've been through so much because of that, Evan. All these years, even through my marriage, I've loved only you."

He stares at me, his jaw clenched taut. His eyes soften. "Come 'ere," he says huskily, stretching out his arm.

I thought he'd never ask. I slide across the couch and lay my head upon his chest, feel the scratchy weave of his wool sweater against my cheek. I breathe him in. He smells of ale, brie, and Neutrogena shampoo. Listen to the strong thud-thud thud-thud of his heart. He strokes my hair. Rests his head upon mine. My whole body sighs, letting go of something I've hauled around for so long I can't remember when it wasn't there.

I am home again.

We hold each other, barely breathing, as our bodies remember. I feel the long leanness of him, quiet and resounding. And our bodies loud with desperate, untold stories only we can tell each other.

"You've been through so much. You're so thin," he says.

"I can't believe we're holding each other again!"

"I can't, either."

"We've both been through a lot," he says.

"Yes," I say. But none of that seems to matter now.

He pulls me closer, his hand tightens around my waist. I bury my face in his chest the way I used to and sink into his embrace. I lift my face to kiss his neck, his cheek. He lowers his head and, light as gossamer, brushes his lips against mine. My spine chills upward, electric. After eighteen years, our lips meet, soft, hesitant, familiar. His tongue parts my lips like a delicate flower. My arms curl around his neck. His fingers whisper to my neck and earlobe. And we remember each other, as we surrender slowly at first, then thirstily, like parched desert travelers fall upon the shores of an oasis lake. The hands of time whirr, blurring past into present. Our mouths and tongues travel deliciously, consumingly, to when we were twenty-two and twenty-five in Chapel Hill and no one had the right to separate us.

The couch grows cramped. We move to his his snug bedroom with hardwood floors the color of a cello. There is a beautiful French armoire and chest cluttered with dusty knick-knacks. We fall on his high queen bed with forest-green sheets and make love. A lovemaking full of anguish to have lost each other, delight to have found each other, and the ecstasy we only knew with each other.

I open, arch, and ride with desire. My body blooms like a parched, withered plant after the rain. Evan, it seems, is the only one in the world who could bring me back to life. Our eyes lock, full with tears at the beauty of our love. Our bodies once again sing the exquisite song we sang together.

But I'm not accustomed to so much love or so much pleasure. I'm Rip Van Winkle awakening after a long, long sleep. I get off him, sobbing and shuddering, and lie in his arms. Grief for how much I've missed him. Grief that I was born to feel love and ecstasy, and haven't for so long. Joy that we've reunited so unexpectedly, so magically, in his San Francisco bedroom smelling faintly of laundry detergent, shoe polish, and acrid sweat. Evan holds me tenderly and cries. For me, and for himself, his pain, his worried waiting, and helplessness. We hold each other close that night, waking every few hours to look and stroke each other and make sure we're not dreaming. Then make eager, exquisite love and cry all over again. And so, we spend the next two days entwined in each others' arms.

"Tell me everything." I ask, hungry for his story. We lie facing each other, legs entwined, hands clasped.

"When you called from Charleston before you left for India, I went into my closet, shut the door, and sobbed like a child. I've never cried that way before. I knew I'd lost you. I knew they'd keep you there, that you'd never come back. I couldn't convince you not to get on that plane. Of course I knew three months was nothing. You thought I couldn't wait that long. But I knew they were taking you away from me."

"Why didn't you tell me?"

"I did, sweetie. I tried so hard but you wouldn't listen. You believed them. You wanted to believe them. You trusted them. But I didn't. Not after what you told me about them."

"I didn't believe they'd do such a thing."

"You'd joke about it, though. You always said if they knew about us they'd take you back. I called so many times. First, I had to get your phone number. Once I got through, your family wouldn't let me speak to you. I tried several times, posing as different friends. I asked David to try. Then I called your friend, Jeannette, on a three-way conference call hoping they'd let a female friend through. They wouldn't.

"I was so frustrated. We all were. David was so mad at your parents, he was ready to drive down to Charleston to talk with your father, threaten him. But I knew that wasn't how your father would listen to us."

He shifts on the sheets. "I simply couldn't live at my place anymore. Everywhere I looked, I saw you, felt you, smelled you. I had to get out. I stayed with David for a few days. Then a woman at work had a house in Pittsboro in the woods. Do you remember Pittsboro, some miles out from Chapel Hill?"

I nod, smiling. I remember this part from his letters sixteen years ago, but I let him go on anyway.

"She wanted to convert it into a retreat center and needed someone to caretake it. It was perfect for me. I didn't even have to pay rent. It was a huge house in the woods, and came with a gorgeous German shepherd. Initially, some people came to stay a few days at a time, but after a few months I was alone. There was no heat, so I chopped wood. It was great therapy. I'd hack away at the logs, getting my anger out, then start up the two wood stoves that heated the house. I grew my own vegetables, cooked my own food, and tinkered on my bug."

"Your bug!" I stroke his cheek. His beige VW bug was one of his most precious possessions.

"And at night, I sat under the stars sending you love and protection. I held us in a golden bubble, just you and me, safe from those who were hurting you, keeping you from me."

I sigh. "I didn't feel you, Evan. I was in such shock." In Chapel Hill, we often telepathically felt each other even when we were apart.

"I wrote to you, love. Letters and letters but when I didn't hear from you, I knew you weren't getting them. At first, I hoped one of them would somehow reach you. Then I stopped writing, thinking I'd get you into more trouble. If I let them think I'd forgotten about you, maybe they'd let up."

"The mail was always intercepted. And there was a guard outside."

He shakes his head. "Remember George from the Siddha Yoga meditation group?"

I nod, kissing his long, expressive fingers.

"He was awesome. He told me about Indians, how they think. 'They're tough, man,' he said, 'and really tight. They seem open but once they gang together, they won't let any Westerner in. And when it comes to family, you simply can't get in. Education, degrees, and a professional career is important. Otherwise, you're nothing.' I asked him if he'd help me get a job in a lab. I had to develop credibility if I was to speak with your parents."

"Speak to my parents?"

"George helped me find a job as a research lab assistant in Research Triangle Park. I worked there for a few months." Evan pauses and smiles at me. "Then, I went to see your father."

"My *father*?" My jaw drops.

"Yes. Your mother was with you in India at the time. I called your father, telling him I wanted to talk with him. He said he didn't want to see me. But I didn't take no for an answer, instead told him I was coming at 11 the next day. And I went."

"You went to see my father!" I put my hand to my cheek.

"I walked up to the front door and rang the bell. He opened the door. 'We have nothing to talk about,' he began, nervously.

"'Yes, we do,' I said and stepped in, without giving him a chance to shut the door. He was nervous, but let me in. We walked into the living room and sat down. I told him I was working at a biology lab in the Research Triangle Park. I said, 'My father's a doctor, and I always planned to go to medical school. I took a year off after Wake Forest to travel, then spent some time at Chapel Hill. But now, I'm on track with my goal. In a year or two, I'm going to medical school.' Then I told him I wanted to marry you."

"*What!?*"

"I loved you, my sweet. I've never loved anyone the way I love you. I would do anything. I couldn't bear you being imprisoned."

"Marry me! Evan, we never even talked about it. What did he say?"

"He said, 'No, there's no way that will happen. I won't agree to that.'"

"I confronted him, 'What are you doing to her by keeping her there?'"

"He exploded. 'What are *we* doing to her? What have *you* done to her? Do you know you've ruined her life?'"

"'You're ruining hers in ways you don't know. Do you even know how she is? You're keeping her from her music which she loves?'

"'That's none of your business. You've spoiled her. You've ruined her.' He started to wail loudly."

"I was pretty alarmed by his wailing, so I tried to deescalate him. I said, 'I know you didn't expect this to happen. It's such a shock.' I waited till he calmed down, then said, 'Don't you understand you can't just keep someone against their will? It's a human rights violation. It's illegal. She's an adult and you can't do this.'"

"He was silent for a while. Then he said, 'I think you'd better leave.'"

My heart's pounding to hear all this. "I can't believe you did that. You're so brave."

"Man, he's tough. I got a real sense of what you'd had to go through for what you wanted—your music, your life. I really got what George said about Indians, that I couldn't get through to him, I couldn't do anything to get you out. I felt terrible," he sighed, shaking his head. "I gave him a letter and asked, 'Will you give this to her?' He said he would. I didn't believe him, but it was my one last attempt to reach you."

I curl into his arms. "After that, you stopped writing?"

"I did, sweetie. I thought the more I wrote, the more they'd think I was still in love with you and keep you there longer. The most important thing was your freedom. Somehow I had to have them believe I was no longer interested, so they'd let you go. That even if you stayed in India, you'd have some freedom." He sighed. "I was so worried. I had no idea what they were doing to you. I even thought of coming there but I was afraid. I didn't know India. I knew your family was powerful. I was afraid they'd throw me in jail without my passport. The more I thought about it, I felt like you chose to go back to your family over me. You had things to work out with them and needed to be strong enough to leave them. So I decided I'd be here for you only if you chose to be with me. If you took that step towards me."

I feel a spark of anger. "How did *I* choose, Evan?" I sputter. "They said three months, but they never intended me to return. And how could I possibly leave once I was locked up?"

"Yes, sweetie. But some part of you chose to get on that plane. You believed them." He shakes his head, exhales in exasperation, and looks away. His lips twist with doubt.

I simply can't understand him. On the one hand, his incredible love for me, on the other his thinking I could leave my family while imprisoned. I can't see what he sees—the part of me that needed my parents' approval. And he can't see that leaving the tribe to forge an independent life is a Western way and utterly foreign to me. But I feel his hopelessness. And I'm moved to my core with his brave, dogged love for me and everything that he tried. I stroke his back and say, tenderly, "The last thing I wanted to do was leave you, Evan. There wasn't anything I could do. It all happened so quickly and once I was in India it was impossible to leave."

He looks at me, tears welling in his eyes.

"Did you feel like I abandoned you?" I ask.

He nods.

I reach for him and take him in my arms. He buries his head in my chest, puts his arms around me, and heaves with sobs.

"I lost you," he sputters. "And I couldn't do anything to bring you back. I was devastated and so guilty that I'd caused you so much pain."

I hold him, stroking his hair, his face.

His tears subside. We look at each other, filled with long years of heartbreak and wonder that we've found each other again. We make love, which dissolves our differences, and fall asleep in each others' arms.

"Why did you stop writing?" I ask Evan.

"I didn't. You did."

"I didn't stop. Not right away. When I didn't hear from you, I wrote four or five more times. I thought I wrote something that upset you, or that my asking for help was too much. Maybe you didn't want to be bothered with me or were in a relationship."

"You're kidding. When I didn't hear from you, I thought you'd been found out so I stopped because I didn't want to get you in trouble."

"So what happened to our letters? Where did they go?"

"I have no idea."

We look at each other, puzzled.

Evan asks, "Did anything change?"

"Nothing that I can think of. I was getting your letters at Nupur's house, then when I started working I asked my office boy to mail them."

"Do you think he did?" Evan asks.

"Yes, because you replied to several letters when I mailed them from there."

"Would anyone intercept them?"

"No, who would?"

"Who else was at your office?"

"Just a few students and another teacher. What would they possibly get from intercepting my letters?

"Ashok?"

"No way." I pause. "You don't think he'd...?"

"I don't know. You should know. Would he?"

"Oh my god. I can't imagine. I told him all about you and my plans to escape. But we also started becoming lovers."

Could he have...?

One morning, we're lying between rumpled lavender sheets in my bedroom alcove overlooking the Berkeley hills. Evan's head rests on his elbow. He strokes the bend of my neck down to my shoulders, a contented smile on his lips.

"I'm coming alive!" I say. "Only you could unlock my body."

"Your face looks so much softer after one week. Your body really hasn't changed at all. Your breasts are incredible. I feel eighteen again. I can't get enough of you." He stretches his arms in a yawn, then nuzzles my neck. He sits up. "We have to commit."

"What do you mean, commit?"

"You know, that we won't see other people."

"You know I'm not going to see anyone else."

"Yes, but we need a ritual or something."

I think for a moment then hold out my hand. I lead him to the living room picture windows where the hill slips sharply away and the landscape stretches like a green scarf for miles into the pastel blue horizon. We sit in our favorite position, *yab-yum*, look deeply into each other's eyes and wordlessly commit.

"Maybe after all that we've been through, we're finally meant to be together," he says after our communion.

"It does feel like that, doesn't it? It's so unbelievably karmic."

I go into the kitchen to warm up a cauliflower, zucchini, and chickpea curry, tomato dal, and jasmine rice with caramelized onions, raisins, and toasted almonds. Evan pokes around in my cabinets in long green shorts, nibbling cashew nuts and humming tunes I don't know. We eat on amber cushioned window seats in my dining room nestled in the woods, the hillside so close that deer scramble by, ears quivering, to stare. We stare right back into their limpid eyes. All afternoon, we share portions of our stories over mango and vanilla ice cream and cups of chai, until the two stories begin weaving into one.

"C'mere." He stretches out his hand. I walk toward him and he leads me to my piano. "Play for me."

"Now?"

"Yes. Now." He lies underneath the piano, the way he used to when he listened to me practice in Chapel Hill.

My breath catches. I'm squeamish. My playing isn't fit for others' ears. I struggle enough listening to myself. But, for him, I pull out the music for Schumann's *Träumerei* and play. *Träumerei* means dreams. It's a simple, haunting piece evoking innocence, childhood, and that everything is possible. When the last chord fades I bend to look at him under the piano. He looks back at me, hands on his heart, tears in his eyes.

"I kept this tape of your recital." Evan hands me an audiotape as he drives us in his red Porsche to Vik's Chaat Corner in Berkeley. The label read "Mytrae's recital, May 27, 1985." Less than a month before I was taken back.

"Oh my God! I can't believe you kept this!"

"I listened to it so often to feel you. Whenever I wanted to remember you. Not only is it you, but it's also great music."

I stare at the cassette, afraid to open the door to my musical past. I'm not sure I want to hear it. He gently tugs it from my hands and slides it into the cassette deck. It's Haydn's Sonata in C Major Hob. XVI/50. I've forgotten how I sounded. This performance was utterly alive, free, and bewitching. Was it really me? It sounds as though someone else is playing—a distant, estranged part of me in some other place, in some other time. Yet, it *is* me.

I lean against the car door, sobbing, Evan's hand on my thigh. Parked on Channing Way, we listen for an hour to Haydn, Mozart, Skryabin, and Debussy, to my past life.

That we aren't who we were eighteen years ago shocks us. For we're both more and less than who we were.

I'm surprised about his substance use. It's not just alcohol he leans into. He comes home wasted, cancels our dates at the last minute to do "E" or coke with friends at raves and parties. In Chapel Hill he drank beer and bragged about his Irish tolerance, but never indulged in hard liquor or drugs. Now, a murky energy surrounds him and his home, which is hard to be with. Most painful of all is his shifting and sliding of the truth about his use. I reluctantly tiptoe to the question: Should we be together? An endless wail arises from me: How can we not?

I share with my friends. "There are times he's present, but so often, he's not."

"He went into the darkness and you into the light. Don't you see?" Debira says, her dark loamy voice full of care and protectiveness. "When you were separated both of you split. He took one route and you the other. You became spiritual and he went this way. You'll have to take some of the darkness and he some of the light."

Brandee, another dear friend, says, "Both of you were ripped apart. You kept a piece of him, and he a piece of you. You'll have to give it back to each other. It'll be a weaving and stitching back and forth. Go with whatever speaks to you without judging yourself or him."

I'm different too. Evan can't bear to see me hesitant and scared, so unlike the free spirit he knew. He reads about trauma and consults with friends. I'm relieved when he agrees to my suggestion that we both need help with our issues after experiencing so much pain.

We meet each other's friends. I meet his twenty-something friends in a bar. They party a lot and I don't, so we don't connect beyond polite pleasantries. He meets Debira and Brandee, friends my age who are into deep conversations and connection. Beyond telling our story, he doesn't relate with them either.

We keep running into the brick wall of reality that we've changed despite our sizzling chemistry, beautiful love, and tortured past. We break up three times that summer, each time after his substance use. "I can't believe I'm saying this, Evan, but it doesn't feel right."

"What d'you mean? After all these years of being apart? We have such a karmic connection. How can we *not* be together?"

"I know, I love you so much, but when you drink or use drugs it's really hard for me."

He stares at me. "Is that why you didn't want to make love last night?"

"I can't make love when you have alcohol on your breath."

"There's nothing wrong with a couple of drinks."

"I get that that's what you're choosing, Evan. But I want to deepen our relationship and I'm not sure you really want to be together. You work all week, then you mostly spend weekends with your friends."

"You don't even try to get to know them."

"It's not that I don't want to know them. I'm not interested in going to clubs or drinking. I don't do that with anybody."

"Yes, but that's how the world *is*. It's not like your school where everyone processes all the time. You're just like your family."

A chill runs through me. "What do you mean?"

"You're not how you were in Chapel Hill. You're so afraid. You live here in Orinda, hiding away from the world, away from life.

I'm in the world. I meet people, I go out, I do things. And you're afraid of me because I threaten your lifestyle."

I don't feel at all understood by him. "You've no idea what I've been through. This place feels safe. And the nature here feels healing to me. I know I'm not out in the world like you. I need time." It's true I'm cautious, even scared, of new experiences. It's true I don't like crowds, raucous bars, and parties, and instead prefer intimate groups and one-on-one conversations.

We go round and round in an endless loop. And break up, devastated and confused. Each time I face letting him go. And letting go of the dream that we were. We talk for hours on the phone. It's easier that way, rather than in person. We can be in the fairy tale of who we were.

Always, after a few days, Evan asks, "Can I come over?"

"Sure," I say.

We talk, sprawled on the sandy carpet by my piano, interlocking our cinnamon and ivory fingers. And we cry. Me, because of my trauma and long, dark years. Him, because of his pain, loss, and helplessness. We both cry at the thought of losing each other. We hold each other, trying to restrain ourselves, then hurtle into each others' arms and hearts with the inevitable kismet and intensity of a comet.

"I can't not be with you," I say, as we lie entwined after.

"Neither can I. We can work things out. Just give us time."

And so, we make up.

I move to San Francisco to be closer to school. I find a sweet Victorian studio with walls the color of mango lassi at Haight and

Divisadero. It has high ceilings, hardwood floors, built in bookshelves, a gas stove, and a tiny heater that struggles to heat the space. My baby grand piano nestles in the bay window where I teach piano lessons. From my window I watch outpatients stroll into a drug rehabilitation center across the street and a group of ragtag men puff cigarettes outside a halfway house. I've fallen in love with the city where not being okay is okay, where races and genders commingle, where so many people misunderstood and unseen by their families find home. I'm like them, I think, between imprisonment and freedom, struggling to cope.

San Francisco feels like home.

I sigh. Evan's late. We're meeting after a break of three weeks without phone contact to decide whether we want to be together.

I've been in a fever for most of the time. The more I stay with him, the more I realize I can't be with him. But letting him go is to let go of a lifeline. I've clung to the idea of him, of us, for so long. Yet, if I want to fully live, I must unclasp my fist. Let go. I've come this far. What's letting go one more time?

There, lying on my futon, I decide to release him. I expected to fall into a dreadful depression but, to my surprise, I'm not heartbroken.

Instead, I feel free.

I put the kettle on the stove for a cup of tea. The doorbell rings. Evan strides in wearing navy blue pants, a gray silk shirt soft as moths' wings, and black pointed-toe shoes. Our eyes lock. We know we've both arrived at the same decision.

"It's not working, is it?" we say to each other with relief.

We tell our stories again, this time without blame, mourning what cannot and will not be. We are naked with each other in ways we haven't been before. We hold each other close and cry.

We let our love breathe and move and flow. We make love with nothing to lose and nothing to gain. Connected, passionate, tender, and expansive, we are beautiful, bright, and luminous as two full moons. We have no future but we have this now, the pearls of our wide open arms, bodies, and hearts. And the treasure of our sweet, deep, remarkable love, which we can let fly into the sky, now, setting it and ourselves free.

The next morning, I walk him to his car. We stand on the curb of Broderick Street as traffic whizzes by, holding each other.

"I will always love you," I say, feeling the strength of his back and the thud-thud of his heart. Inhale his sweet muskiness one last time.

"And I you," he says, his arm tight about my waist.

We gaze into each other's eyes. He gets into his car, rolls down the window, and raises his hand in one final wave. I watch him drive away, as the October morning sun warms my cheeks and arms. I cross Haight Street, pass the Muni at the bus stop, professionals beginning their day, a couple of homeless people lying swaddled like long bundles on the sidewalk.

I climb the steps, smiling, to my bright studio. I feel light, deliciously light. I am no longer a prisoner of my past. Even if I never love again, at least I've loved with all my heart.

I look into my mirror and see myself, eyes shining in the way they only can be from love.

For I am a child of the sun, once again.

16
love, again

2005

Brant and I sit across from each other in Ananda Fuara, a bustling Indian-fusion vegetarian restaurant on Market Street in San Francisco. The noon sun streams in through large windows on our beige and cream vinyl table with simple tableware. A single pink rose in a brass vase. Pictures of Sri Chinmoy from the walls smile down at us. Our laminated menus lie open and unread. We look at each other. The air between us is electric. Something profound between us always rings me like a tuning fork right down to my toes. Words are unnecessary.

He's close enough to desire, yet too far to touch.

I was attracted to him my two years in graduate school, but he's married with children. I took a couple of his classes, and we had a few teacher-student meetings in his hushed office. Witnessed by a beautiful, golden, reclining five-foot Buddha, resplendent with jewels and elongated earlobes, we were very boundaried and professional. We shared a love of Shri Aurobindo's philosophy and a fervent hope that India will evolve beyond its spiritual superiority to acknowledge and embrace psychology. Each time we said hello or goodbye, I looked in his eyes and silently asked, "Don't you remember?" or "What *is* this?" I didn't dare speak it out loud, but always left our meetings reeling from our powerful soul connection and intense chemistry. I processed my feelings for him with my close friends and in therapy, as my unavailable father. Any illusions I might have had got a cold shower of reality when my therapist exclaimed, "Brant? You'll never be with him!"

Since Evan and I ended several months ago, I've graduated and begun my three-year-long internship. I don't know if I'll ever love again. But after Evan, a prayer from my heart floated out again and again to the Universe. It started as, "I've been through so much, you owe me. Give me a man like Brant," but changed to, "Give me Brant." I was shocked because it was audacious, absolutely absurd, and I feel ashamed of my desire because of his wife and children.

A couple of weeks ago Brant emailed me asking me to review his book manuscript and meet for lunch to discuss it. I did, bringing my notes. After the waitress floats twice by with an enquiring glance, we open our menus. Between reading about soy meatloaf and el salada mexicana I look up. His menu's closed with decision, his eyes are on my cleavage. My body surges as I look at his chiseled features and feel his deep presence.

We discuss his manuscript in detail over our meal. When we end, he pauses like he has something important to say. "Are you in a relationship?" he asks.

"No."

"I separated a few months ago from my wife. We'd been struggling for some years."

"Oh!" I'm taken aback, as I often am by the ease with which authority figures in the U.S. share their personal lives.

Without missing a beat, he asks, "What do you think about us getting together?"

Him? With me? The air catches in my throat. The blood rushes to my face. I stare at him, my mouth open. Really? I've felt so crazy asking the Universe for the impossible. I didn't believe it could happen. I sputter, "I didn't think… I didn't know… really? You aren't married?"

He smiles at me. "No, we separated in the spring and I moved out. I live close by so the kids can come and go easily as they get used to the transition."

I look at him, still stunned.

He says, "I haven't met anyone who gets the spiritual like you. When I was questioning my marriage, I sat in meditation and asked for a relationship with someone spiritual. I haven't had anyone like you in my class before. I was really wowed by how you got Aurobindo. I even prepared a lecture for you. And," he grins, "I'm attracted to you."

I can't speak. I'm flying among stars and floating on clouds, but still sit shell-shocked, smiling.

"Is that a yes?" he laughs. "Can I take you out for dinner?"

I nod. "Yes… yes… of course! I'd love that. It's just hard for me to believe. I felt like I knew you from the moment I saw you, and couldn't understand it."

He reaches across the table and takes my hand. "Well, we'll get to find out, won't we?"

We make plans to meet. When we hug after our meal, crackling streams of light flow between our chakras. I haven't experienced that with anyone, not even Evan.

That night I toss and turn, wondering how my absurd prayer has come true. So it *is* possible to ask the Universe for something impossible and get it?

But my questions and doubts seethe like unruly waves. Why would he, such an authority in his field, want to be with a novice like me? And why would he want to be with me when he's so emotionally mature and I have so much trauma left to heal?

I don't deserve someone like him.

I don't deserve his love.

I don't deserve love!

The retreat center in Brazil is set amidst gently rolling green hills. The landscape, dotted with grazing cows, is a lush palette of greens with tropical plants, mango and avocado trees. Cuckoos coo, macaws and parrots screech their delight about this beautiful summer day.

I came to this simple village with humble, colorful homes on a retreat to try and heal. Everything.

Brant and I have been together for a few months and are discovering, to our amazement and delight, that we're soul mates. We're simpatico on every level—physical, emotional, mental, and spiritual. But I feel unequal to him and unworthy of his love. We won't stay together long if I continue to feel this way. I came on retreat to heal my unworthiness, feeling less than, and trauma so I can receive his love and be in my power in our relationship.

The keepers of the center say it is a place where spirits can heal. Though I'm a little skeptical, I also believe them, for the energies here are unlike any I've ever experienced. My intuition burst open like a dandelion pod after arriving. I was shown visions about my past lives and future, and hear messages about my family and the work I am to do. Some terrifying, some daunting.

I walk towards the broad arbor of a mango tree to sit beneath its shade. I sit on a bench, its back carved with a big heart and the word *Amor*. A loving feminine presence envelopes me. The wind gently rustles the leaves, cools my warm cheeks, and the feminine presence surrounds me with a loving force. I hear the word *Fatima* a few times. Who is Fatima? My eyes close with the exalted sweetness of her presence. I see and feel brilliant beams of light from higher realms, three feet wide, stream into my body. I hear: *Hold onto the light. Receive it.*

I do. I'm not afraid. She is peaceful, loving, and full of grace.
You are loved.

Along with the light, a sublime love cascades into me. It enters my body, cracks my heart open, and penetrates every broken, wounded, closed cranny. It permeates parts of myself I haven't shown to others. Parts I haven't known existed. It's a love I've yearned for yet didn't know was possible. The waterfall of Divine Love bathes my body, my heart, my soul, suffusing my deepest wounds with exquisite, sweet tenderness.

It's a Love I have never experienced before. It's a Love I didn't imagine existed.

Unconditional. Extraordinary. Otherworldly.
I don't have to do anything or be anything to be loved.

I sob uncontrollably, drenching tissue after tissue. A lifetime of feeling different, unworthy, bad, an outcast, and that something's wrong with me, washes away.

I am loved. I am loved. I am loved.
I am worthy. I am beautiful. I am sacred.

Then, words, like blue ink on white waters, drop into my right ear.

What if everything that happened to you was love?

My mind explodes into a million pieces. Everything? Love? I thought it was anything but that. My mind blurs, trying to grasp the thought.

My crazy, broken life? Love?

I wait for more, but there isn't any. Has she left? Or is she still here, watching me detonate. I want to pluck her by the sleeve and ask, "Wait, can you say more? Who *are* you?"

But there's only silence. The rustling of the mango tree leaves. My body humming like a tuning fork. And the air throbbing with love.

I don't understand what just happened. But what I do know is my deepest wounds just received a healing from spiritual realms.

Weeks later, I learn that Fatima is another name for Mother Mary.

I ask in meditation, please give me healing with my mother. Instantly, I hear the words, *That woman is not your mother. You come from a different place.* What? Somehow, the words untwist a part of me that's tried to make sense of what hasn't made sense. That feeling I had as a girl of not really belonging to my family. That we can have human families, but our souls belong elsewhere.

Mother Mary appears to me holding a baby girl. The infant is me! She cradles me close and looks at me with infinite love. The cells in my body relax and let go of something so deep it feels like it began before time.

I hear, *I held you in my arms as an infant. I was always with you.*

I see myself as a toddler playing peekaboo in her long, sky-blue skirt. I crawl inside the refuge of her gown to hide and be close to her and safe from the world, then peek out. I do that many times. She allows me to play with her body and her dress as long as I want.

I see myself as a young teenager bringing her what I'm learning in school. Her face lights up. She bends and throws her arms around me in a long, warm hug. Tilts my chin and tells me how talented I am and how proud she is of me. The pleasure and pride in her eyes and voice make me glow on the inside.

I tell her I want to major in music and her eyes are stars of joy. She wants it for me just as much as I do.

I see myself introducing Evan to her. She lights up right away, embracing him like a son. She is delighted for us both and talks to us for a long time about our relationship. He is now part of our family, her family. She puts her arm around my waist, happy that I'm a young woman opening to the delights of my body and sexuality. She takes me aside and teaches me about the beauty of sexuality, and the ancient secrets she knows.

I emerge from my meditation, dazed. I've just been re-mothered. By Mother Mary! I have no idea why she's coming to me as a brown Hindu Indian woman, but all my dark fissures are now filled with peace and knowing that I am loved.

The sun warms my skin as I walk with other visitors down a dusty red road headed towards the sacred waterfall at the retreat center. I am told that when we stand under it even for a minute, we receive a torrent of Light, Love, and healing. The mud road narrows to a paved path and we hear the crash and flow of the water. A toucan with startling orange and red colors and a long, hooked bill streaks across the robin-egg-blue sky. The air is effervescent with healing, moist energy, and I inhale big lungfuls of it. We're surrounded by emerald forest, where hummingbirds dart about, and large blue and primrose-yellow butterflies alight on hibiscus and orchids. This is a sacred place. A healing place. I can feel nature *devas*, spirits, here. My heart effortlessly lifts to joy and delight.

Magic is possible here.

A cobalt-blue butterfly the size of my palm alights on my bare shoulder. I stop in my tracks, looking down at it with delight as its wings open and close, its feelers tickling my brown skin. It is said the butterflies here are Spirits in form, healing us. My eyes close. I want to believe. Anything is possible. *This* is why I'm here. The butterfly rests on me for a full minute or more, then flutters away into the dark depths of the forest.

I gasp out loud as the icy water shocks my body. The waterfall pounds my scalp then splays like wet wildfire around me. My soles and toes grip black rocks. My hands clutch a wooden safety beam. The water is crystalline and my body fills with brilliant white light. Prayers spring from my heart: *Please wash away everything that keeps me from being in my power. Please heal me so I can love and receive love. Please heal my trauma so I can be and live true, radiant, and big.*

Instantly, I have a vision. My negative emotions fly out of me like black rocks and explode into multi-colored flowers. I am shown visions of past lives where I was persecuted and tortured, my whole body screaming with agony. The black energy of those lifetimes spews out of me and washes away.

I gasp again, not from cold this time. A slag of black rock in my heart shifts open to reveal an underground spring. The slag is my anger, my bitterness, my judgment, and my blame. The spring is love. The spring is my heart flowing with forgiveness.

I hear, *Peace, sister. You can't judge them from where you are, from what you know. They did not know what it was for you.*

In my mind's eye my parents, brother, family, and Swami Chinmayananda stand before me. I put down the axe I've been carrying for over thirty years.

It is over. My war is over.

Relief floods into and through my heart.

Please help me let it all go. The gushing waterfall pounds on my head, washes around my face, my shoulders, my chest, my abdomen, down my legs and feet, and flows down and away into the cascading stream below.

I am washed. Cleansed. Purified.

I never thought I could feel this. Forgiveness. Never thought I could let go. Never thought it possible.

I step out from under the waterfall pulsating with light and energy. I wind up the path to a bench in the sun where I left my clothes. I put on my clothes without drying off, for we're told the water on our skin continues to heal. Silently, I walk up the path, past others waiting in shorts and tank tops, on to the dusty trail up towards the blue and white buildings of the retreat center.

My heart is a song set free.

A river of love and forgiveness flows through my heart. Soft, wet, and true. Like a newborn babe it slips its hand into mine. *Everything is about love. Everything is love.* I can't open my heart to the Divine, love Mother Earth as much as I do, while I stay closed and shut out my parents, family, and everyone else I've been angry with.

I sit on a bench overlooking the mounds of hills. Beside me, the red flowers and yellow stamens on a hibiscus bush open their hearts wide to the golden sunshine. My clothes, still damp, cling to my skin. I shiver a little. I've been afraid to forgive. I thought if I forgave it meant everything that happened was all right. That the violence and brutality would be overlooked and forgotten. That my family would be let off the hook. I don't agree with what they did. But I don't have to keep carrying hate, blame, and anger. I can protect myself now and speak out, not retaliate or hurt them to avenge myself. It's their work to realize what they did, not mine to hold against them for eternity. Forgiveness is letting go of the hate and anger I've carried. It sets *me* free. And, I don't need to have a relationship with anyone if I don't want to.

I gaze beyond two giant mango trees, their boughs gently bending with their green fruits, to the valley below undulating with shades of green and yellow, and an endless peace descends upon me. I sigh and settle back into the bench. My heart is soft, open, and ethereal as a butterfly.

Today is the beginning of everything.

I have a vision:

> *I am dancing with my mother and grandmother. First with halting steps, then quicker and quicker until our feet are alight with rhythm, our smiles wide, our bodies laughing, our heads flung back in joyful abandon as they, too, realize that they* **can** *have what they want. And we dance the sweet deliriousness of that knowing. We dance, three women of three generations, joined not solely by blood but by the sweet music and magic of freedom, all that we are, and all that we*

can have. We are surrounded by a multitude of women and men, Indian and from every corner of our planet. Each one slowly realizes they, too, can have what they have. One by one, with lilting steps and joyful bodies, they join us in dance.

A globe of brilliant light, no bigger than my thumb, forms in my heart. It is Divine light. It is my heart, my soul.

I am astonished by its beauty. *My* beauty.

For inside, a tiny, exquisite, radiant goddess dances.

17

forgiveness

2014

Good God! It's been a decade and a half since I've heard country music. My feet pad the Roanoke airport carpet. I take in the cowboy hats and boots and soft twangy drawls. The South is such a different world from California. But ooh, here's a restaurant serving buffet-style breakfast. Biscuits! I haven't had them in a couple of decades. Oh, I can break my gluten-free diet once in a while. So I get a plate of scrambled eggs and a hot soft mound of white flour goodness on which I slather butter. Mmmm. Perfection. After, I sign for my rental car and head north on I-581.

It takes me an hour and a half to drive to Lexington, Virginia, where my parents now live. They moved here after Naina retired, to be closer to Roopa Aunty. It's where we landed when we first immigrated. I haven't visited my parents *anywhere* for ten years.

I drive through the gates of their community with stately brick homes, some of them mansions, and into their driveway. It's a beautiful and immaculate pink brick home, with big windows, and a large yard. Pink is Amma's signature color. The garden is a floral delight, revealing Naina's long and patient labor. Orange and yellow pansies, white and fuchsia impatiens, burnished Japanese maple, and pink and white dogwood trees adorn the neatly trimmed emerald lawn.

I jump out of the car and bound up the front steps. I ring the bell. Naina was expecting me. He opens the front door in his navy blue paisley dressing gown. His eyes are warm, his smile questioning.

"Hello, Mytrae. Come in, come in. How was your drive?"

"Hi, Naina."

I step inside bursting to tell him, yet unsure how he'll receive me.

His eyes are warm. I reach to hug him. His arms fold me into his chest.

I look over his shoulder. Amma, in a rose pink kaftan, walks cautiously from the kitchen. Her short hair, almost fully gray, is curled in a perm. Her eyes are guarded.

"Hi, Amma," I say and stretch out my arms towards her.

"Hello, Mytrae," she says, smiling cautiously.

Her embrace, as always, feels a country away. But I reach through the space between us to draw her close. We stand in a circle by the front door still ajar, my left hand around Naina's waist, my right around Amma's.

"I've come because I've forgiven you," the words burst in a sob from me. "I forgive you for everything. For taking me back to India. For keeping me there all those years. It's all over now." I tremble like a quivering pine.

We stand, a trio, looking at and holding each other as we never have. We can't speak, for the space between us whirls, then reaches up to the sky like a chapel. And in the center of us, something old and anguished cracks, breaks, and drops to the cherry floorboards. It washes out into the ground.

Tears stream down Naina's cheeks.

Amma's eyes question, "Can it be true?"

"Yes, yes!" I say, "Yes! Believe me. It's true."

"That's very good news, Mytrae." Naina's voice is a warm bath. "We've been waiting for this."

"What happened?" Amma asks hesitantly.

"Let's sit and I'll tell you."

We sit in their den. I tell them about the retreat and what happened under the waterfall.

"Hmmh!" Naina shakes his head, his cheeks wet with tears. "We've waited so long for this."

"It's a miracle. Wonderful," Amma says, and pauses. "But what if it doesn't stick?"

She *would* say that. "It *is* a miracle. I can't guarantee anything. I'm sure it's a process. But I'm here now."

"We didn't know if you'd ever come back to us," Naina says.

More than what they say, I see in the lines of their faces and their sad eyes the desperate pain they've felt over the years I haven't spoken to them. They didn't know how to reach me. Let me know they loved me. They were brought to their knees with regret and sorrow that I'd shut them out.

Perhaps for the first time, I see them for who they are. And that their taking me back to India, however misguided, was an act of love.

"When you took me back to India, I was a tree happily and freely growing in the sun and rain. And you hacked me down to a stump," I tell Naina the next morning as we sit in his garden looking at maples, the sun dappling light and shadow on their leaves. I hope he'll understand as a gardener. "I felt like you cut the life out of me. I wasn't alive anymore. I had lost all my branches. It took years for new shoots to grow. But for so many years I never felt like the original tree, always like a few struggling branches from a sawn trunk, trying to return to who I really am. Therapy has really helped me. It's not something Indians know about or do. And spiritual healing. I've healed so much."

"I'm so sorry, Mytrae," he says. His eyes are pained. The corners of his mouth turned down with years of sadness. "I see that now, we shouldn't have kept you in India for so long. How much pain you have carried in your heart because of it and for so long. I should have done something. I shouldn't have listened to Amma. I should have stepped in and brought you back to America after a year. But I went along with her. And I accept responsibility for that. I accept full responsibility. I've always let her handle the parenting. I focused on providing. But we made a mistake. It was a big mistake. I've told some people in the family that we were too hard on you in taking you back. That was why you didn't speak to us all these years." His eyes, filled with sorrow and apology, reach across the table to me. "You've been unhappy for so long. It's good therapy and spiritual healing have helped you."

His words land like soft raindrops in my heart. And I let them seep into my cells. I've waited for decades for this. He's heard me. He understands now. I feel a little uncomfortable, guilty even, to hear his apology as my old film of "parents are always right" whirrs through me. But I make myself stay open to receive it. As we sit across from each other in the morning light, I feel our past gently shift its weight.

"We want you to be happy, Mytrae," Naina continues. "That's more important than anything. We're happy you're in a relationship where you're happy. That's what's important. We want you to be at peace, *bidda*."

It's the first time he's called me "daughter" in Telugu. I squirm a little to hear his unfamiliar endearment and love it at the same time. Our family doesn't speak or show affection out loud. His words gather me to him and wing me back in time to where we've travelled from, to when I felt like his daughter. To India, to Banswada, his village that we visited a few times a year where I ran among fields of sugarcane as a girl, among pale pink and white stalks as thick as my wrist and double my height while he talked irrigation and rains and harvest times with the farmers. After, he, Raghu, and I sat on grassy mounds among fields to chew and suck sweet liquid from a plateful of sugarcane pieces like cows chew cud, then drink a glass of its nectar with a squeeze of lime. He must have been in his thirties then.

How much he didn't know what lay ahead.

For him. For us.

How much he's opened and changed in the last ten years. How far he's come to just want me to be happy, whatever that looks like. I've kept him at an arm's distance for most of my life, not trusting him because of his allegiance to Amma. But now, his words reach out to me to connect heart to heart. I see his pain, his regret. He wants a relationship with me, now, independent of her. It's what I've always yearned for. I reach past my discomfort and any remaining mistrust, smile at him, and grab on to the green shoot of peace and love he extends.

"Thank you for understanding," I say. "It means a lot to me that you apologized."

I smile at him. We hold each other's gaze as the past melts away. Something tender and true and sweet, like a newborn lamb, opens between us.

It is love.

Amma and I sit opposite each other at my parents' kitchen table. The wood is a light honey color. Made by Mormons, she said, proudly stroking it when I first admired it. A glass covers it to protect the wood. Refined rustic spindle chairs. Pink paisley placemats. Silver salt and pepper shakers. To my right, in a bay window, orchids bloom their pink and white pleasures. A fern spouts green into its corner. Beyond, their manicured lawn glistens in the sunlight without a single weed as far as I can see. Then the land dips away into an unruly forest with oak, hickory, dogwood, and sycamore.

"Every morning you've been in my prayers," Amma says. "We had *pujas* done for you in India. I asked for you to be returned to us, to our family. Everyone loves you, Mytrae. Everyone in the family asks after you. What a sweet child she was, they say. What happened? What could we say?"

I'm surprised she prayed for me. And I quell my indignation. What happened, indeed.

"When you first stopped talking to us, Daadi said such cruel things to me."

"What did she say?"

She shudders. Her head shakes no, I can't tell. "Some things about me as a mother," she says, her voice like a closed shell. "She died in 2008, you know. I wrote to you."

She had. I was still angry and hadn't written back.

"For three years she was bedridden with diabetes, the last two years with a tube down her throat. And I couldn't be there. Not with my health. I had so much guilt. As her daughter, I couldn't be there. And you weren't talking to us…" Her voice fades to a whisper.

She looks at me from across the table. Her black eyes anguished, her mouth scrunched in a plea. No tears, but her vulnerability wobbles like a delicate, fragile dewdrop for a teetering instant in her eyes. My heart softens. I drink it in. Hold her gaze. Of everyone in the world, she most loves and was afraid of Daadi. And, for the first time, I see past my own hurt and rage and blame. For the first time I see her long, slow years of trying and failing as a mother. I see how much my years of not speaking to them have hurt her.

Her eyes tell me everything. How she's tried to reach me despite doing to me what her mother did to her. I haven't wanted to see it. Because I couldn't forgive. Didn't want to forgive. I had to hold fast to the memory of it or it would be forgotten. I didn't want the waves to wash my sandcastle of pain away.

She's tried all this time to reach me. In her own way.

For years. In ways she knows. Through her Vedanta, listening to audiotapes of her new favorite teacher, reading philosophy and spiritual books that fill and overflow her bookshelves. Watching Oprah's Super Soul Sunday. Her meditation practice for which she wakes at 3 a.m. In her birthday cards written in careful, upright handwriting, every vowel and consonant a carved Victorian woman on a high-backed chair, punctuating every March 12th for ten years though we hadn't spoken, always signed with love. I never acknowledged them, anger flaring through me as I opened them and threw them in the trash.

She tried.

That's everything. That she tried and is trying, I will receive with both hands now. For Lord knows I understand what it's like to try and fail a million times, creeping forward like a snail, then sliding backwards like a koala bear down a tree trunk. Coming into my power, not abandoning myself and giving myself away have been the hardest lessons of my life.

Besides, I've failed her just as she failed me.

I am not the daughter she wanted.

But here we are. Woven together like a figure eight holding opposite gifts for each other. She holds Power and I hold Love. It's the easiest and most effortless thing for me to love. Even foolishly, at great cost to myself. And it's the easiest thing for her to be powerful. So overpoweringly that she bludgeons love out. She's here on earth learning to love, just as I'm here learning to be powerful.

We are each other's rub, and so, each other's teacher.

Perhaps that's what our souls signed up for.

The hard coconut of our past together splits open.

As I look at her from across the honey-colored table I want to reach out, touch her arm and say, I love you. I am a fool for love. You can feel it if you allow the bud of your heart to open just a sliver. I promise it won't hurt. I promise you will feel like a thousand stars. And the dead weight of all that you carry will drop, perhaps even your asthma, as you fall into love's ocean for the very first time. That's what you're searching for in all the books you read and all the hours you sit in meditation.

But I don't. And won't. For she doesn't like to talk about such things.

"Next life I don't want to be a mother," she says with a shudder. A curtain slides shut over the dewdrop of vulnerability in her eyes.

The moment's passed. I smile at her.

But it was there. A teetering mother-of-pearl, a glimmer of the truth of her I will always treasure.

"You never left India," I tell Amma. "You live here, but your heart is there. You didn't open to America."

"Yes," she says. "Our family is there. The fun, the people. Here there's no one. No one to look after you. No one." Her loneliness and loss wrap around her like a Saharan desert.

I feel for her.

"I want to go back one last time," she says. "I don't know if I will, what's destined. Must be happy here."

"How different your life would have been had you been allowed to go to Oxford," I say. "What you would have done… who you would have been would have been so different."

She inhales sharply. Looks up and away, out the window, into the woods like she's wrestling a whale. The room fills with something huge and heavy and painful. A giant nerve ending.

"Yes," she says softly, with a longing that calls from the back of the sky. "Yes. So different."

We sit together in the pale yellow of late afternoon, she and I, in quivering moments of what might have been but didn't get to be. I can imagine her proud and tall and free. Brilliant. A professor perhaps. I would have been proud of her. But she didn't get a chance to discover all that. Everything for her, who she might have been, stayed locked up in England, in that one lost opportunity. Nothing else ever quite measured up. Nothing possibly could. I, of everyone, can understand the cavernous loss of one lost chance, a road you cannot travel because your parent prevents you.

"But that's how it was in those days," she says in a plaintive tone, her eyes scanning the maples.

"Thatha wanted you to go."

"Thatha, yes. But Daadi, no."

"Couldn't he have overruled her?"

"No, he listened to her. She made the decisions. She wanted me to get married. I was twenty-four, which was late. But that was her way of thinking. That's how she was brought up. That's how things were those days. Women had to get married. Nobody sent their daughters abroad then…"

"Who you might have been…" I interrupt, fierce for her.

"Yes… yes…". Her body softens. "Who I might have been," she whispers. She turns to look at me for a few long moments with her dark black eyes. Her hand lets go of her mug to rest, open, slack, on the table.

I've touched that giant nerve. I've learned to do that as a therapist. For something sacred happens when you touch long-lost wounds, ancient banshees that howl and stomp with rage and loss and hate. They drop to their knees like whimpering children and nestle into a parent's chest.

Outside, evening falls silent. A wilted orchid, once pink now beige with age, drops from its plant in the bay window beside us.

"Thank you for understanding," she says, out of nowhere.

"These are for you," Amma says as she puts a plastic shopping bag on the dining table. She takes out blue and red velvet jewelry cases. "I've kept these for you, hoping you'd return to us some day."

"What are all these?" I feel touched and guilty at the same time.

"I had these made for you when you were young. Others are from the family. I know you won't wear many of them in this country, but they're yours."

She takes out the cases and sets them before me. I open them one by one. Gold chains and strands of pearls. Diamond, ruby, and emerald earrings shaped like flowers. Pearl bangles with a lion's head at each end. A beautiful thick bracelet handed down through generations with uncut diamonds, rubies, and emeralds. And her favorite piece from her aunt, a ruby and pearl pendant on a thick gold chain.

"So many!" I exclaim. "Why are you giving me all these? Why don't you wear them?"

"My days of wearing them are over."

"They're beautiful," I say. She's giving me what she loves. What she believes makes an Indian woman. I see her love for me in them. Her hopes and dreams for me. "Thank you," I say, overwhelmed. I hug her.

"And these," she takes out two more boxes, "Daadi wanted you to have."

I open them. One is a ring with a large coral at the center and pearls encircling it. The other is a necklace, a diamond mangalsutra pendant hung on three strands of tiny black beads. It's a piece Daadi often wore herself. I would tell her how beautiful she looked in it.

"She wanted me to have these?" I'm surprised and moved. I feel her love across the miles, beyond life and death. Guilt stings me. She wanted me to have these even though I didn't talk to her for years before she passed.

I lift the diamond mangalsutra out of the box and hold it in my palm. It's stunning. It doesn't need a second pendant as a traditional mangalsutra does, to show a woman's dignity and power is her husband. This pendant, so unique, is resplendent on its own.

In fact, that's why it's magnificent.

Daadi and I had untraditional marriages. And I'm living an untraditional life. Of all the jewelry here, this is a piece I will wear. Because I feel connected to her and all the women before her.

And to the Goddess within me.

18

a circle of love

2014

What will they think of me? How will they receive me? Divorced. Living with Brant, a white man. A therapist. It's been more than a decade since I've visited Bangalore, India, and my family there. Certainly, all hell will break loose when I tell them. Maybe they'll get it. Most likely they won't. But I have to tell them. It's another thing I realized on my retreat in Brazil. That I must speak my truth to everyone in my family who doesn't love me or might be ashamed of me. It's the only way for me to fully claim my dignity, my worth, my power.

I emailed my aunt, Jayapinni, who lives in Bangalore to tell her I'm visiting. She replied, "Come for lunch. I'll invite everyone so you don't have to visit them separately."

"I'd love that. And thanks for inviting everyone!" I replied.

At Jayapinni's spacious penthouse apartment with carved mahogany furniture and colorful Indian art, fifteen aunts, uncles, cousins, and their husbands gather to visit with me one beautiful December mid-morning. Three from Amma's generation. The others, about ten years younger or older than me, are my cousins. We greet each other, catch up on our lives, and eat a delicious lunch. After dessert, I ask my cousin, "Meera, please can you ask everyone to gather? I want to say something."

We sit in a circle in Jayapinni's beautiful living room with large windows. Orange blossoms the size of my hand from a flame of the forest tree sweep the outside indoors. All I want to do is speak my truth. Tell them my side of what happened. Not abandon but honor myself despite what they think or say.

As everyone gathers, I look around at my hardy old aunts and uncles, beautiful and handsome cousins. At lunch, they've been too polite to discuss anything beyond pleasantries.

I sip some water to moisten my dry mouth. "It's been really good to see you all after so long. I'm sure you're curious why I've stayed away from the family these past ten years. I want to tell you why. I want to clear my name because things have been said about me which aren't true. For that, I must tell you what happened when I was twenty-two.

"I was brought back because I was in love with an American man. All I wanted then was to be free to live my life. To do what I love. To be with whom I love. You were told I was on drugs and in a cult. I wasn't. I didn't do drugs. I was high on music and on love. I just wanted to be free. I couldn't imagine a family like ours would lock up a woman. I might have expected this had I grown up in a village but we're supposedly a Westernized, progressive family."

They all look increasingly uncomfortable. An uncle pulls out a handkerchief and wipes the sweat from his forehead.

"What I want to say to you is that no one here came to check on me when I was locked up. You all visited Daadi's house many times the three years I was there. Yet none of you knocked on my door or took me aside to ask, 'How are you doing? Are you okay?' This family talks and gossips about everyone. I know you did about me, but no one *did* anything. I *wasn't* okay," I choke back my tears. "I almost committed suicide. What if I had? What if it was too late? Is that what family is? If we're not there for each other, if we don't care but only talk about each other, how can we call that family?

"And… women are beautiful. We are sacred beings. We have every right that men have. Our bodies are ours. No one has a right to say who we can love, or what we can do. We must be free to choose how to live our lives. Choose our men. I say this not just for myself but for every Indian woman. There's so much oppression, abuse."

Now my younger women cousins are fully crying.

"And," I pause, my body trembling, to gather my courage to say the final terrible thing that must be said. "You also need to know I was sexually abused. By Raghu. From when I was six to ten."

Everyone gasps. Shame darkens the room.

Dead silence.

There.

I've broken the taboo. I've spoken not just about sex, which no one does, but incest. I've broken the spell that we're a perfect, progressive family who educates and advances their women. I've broken my allegiance with Raghu, my loyalty to protect my parents and family at the cost of myself. I've spoken as a woman. Not as an Indian, and not as a member of my family. I feel so good to be naked, to have spoken my long-held secret.

Everyone knows everything now. What they do with it is theirs. I've said what I needed to.

After I finish, my cousins gather around me.

"We had no idea about all this," Anupama says, sniffing and wiping away her tears. "We were told you were a bad girl when you ran away and not to have anything to do with you."

"Of course what I said wasn't meant for you," I said. "It was meant for the older generation."

"Nothing will surprise me about this family anymore," Anupama says.

"I can't believe you went through all that," Meera says, her arm around me.

"The next time you visit you must come and stay with us," Rohit says.

"So our family's failed you," says Rita, a counselor, but her eyes are cold.

"We didn't know," Jayapinni says. "And we believed your mother. We thought what she said was true, that you were brought back to dry out. We were also afraid of her and your Daadi. And we didn't want to interfere. It wasn't our business."

Gowripinni, my aunt, says with distaste, "It's not good to talk about such things. What's the point of talking about them? Some things you need to just let go of. Your mother loves you. You must learn to forgive, Mytrae."

Sundar Uncle comes toward me, his mouth tight with anger. "Have you no consideration for your parents? They're getting old. Why are you bringing up these things now?"

No one will speak about the incest. I didn't expect they would. It's too painful. And shameful.

Gowripinni and Sundar Uncle are tough barnacles and I feel a pang from their disapproval, loyalty to Amma, and unwillingness to hear my side. But I've reached my younger cousins, the future generation. That's something.

My dear friend Mithoo comes to pick me up after lunch. I'm still shaking when I get into her car. "I did it," I tell her. "I feel like I've just climbed Mount Everest."

"We release so much every time we take a step forward, don't we?" she says. "What do you need now?"

"Let's get coffee."

As we drink cups of strong, delicious south Indian coffee and I tell her about it, my body stops trembling and feels more restored.

"I didn't know," she says. "I didn't know we could talk about such things to our families."

I smile at her. "Yes. We can."

And I have one more place to go.

I'm glad to visit Hyderabad in December when it's cool. Sweat doesn't stream down my neck and back. It's grown into a sleek town I can hardly recognize. Once sleepy and casual, where no one was in much of a rush to do anything, the city now bustles with purpose and energy. People are going somewhere, with things to do. Chaos has been transformed into neat, broad roads and highways with painted lanes, pedestrian crossings, and lined with trees. I smile to see drivers actually obey traffic laws, not dart everywhere as they please. I grip the auto-rickshaw's leather handle, drinking in the city I grew up in, with its *mitthai* sweet shops, *chaat* street-food pushcarts, and fruit stands selling *seethaphal* custard apples, guavas, and *sapotas* sapodillas.

I'm going to visit Roshan Uncle and Leela Aunty, and the place where I was imprisoned.

As I alight from the yellow and black three-wheeler at the white wooden gate in front of Roshan Uncle and Leela Aunty's house, I remember my guides' message in my meditation that morning. *It's not what they wanted for you. They didn't want you to be imprisoned.*

Really? That's not what I thought. Leela Aunty, maybe. She was kind to me those three years, checking in on me now and then. She tried. But not Roshan Uncle. He refused to even speak to me about it.

I walk into their compound and up the driveway to their large white home with a brick tiled roof. Their lovely garden is lush and well-tended. The teal iron benches send shivers through me. I sat there most evenings with Thatha those three years. He in his white billowing pajamas, occasionally getting up to pace on the lawn, bend over a bush to smell a flower, or tap his hearing aid. My eyes scanning the sky streaming orange and pink against white-blue as it turned to indigo. Waiting. Waiting for whatever this was to end. For life to begin. Each evening an eternity in the cup of a day.

I ring the door bell. A servant in white uniform opens the door and gestures for me to enter, pointing to Roshan Uncle's study up the stairs. I walk up the nine carpeted stairs that curve onto the landing. Nothing's changed. The semi-circular telephone table and oval backed chair in the corner. A miniature brass cannon on the marble floor. I peek into the study. Roshan Uncle, smaller, his hair completely white, bends over his iPad. He's in a white T-shirt and shorts so he's probably just come home from playing tennis.

"Helloooo," I say with a smile.

"Oh hello, Meetross," he says nonchalantly. He looks up then returns to his iPad like I'm not there. I never liked that he called me that and I don't like it now. I smart a little at his rudeness but walk in. Years ago, I'd have slunk away, not wanting to disturb him.

I sit down on the brown upholstered sofa opposite him. He reads his iPad like I saw him an hour, not twelve years, ago. I look around. Everything's the same. I know this house well. It was the house next door, the only other place I was allowed to go to for a year. I take in the bookshelves lining the wall behind him. The record and CD player with piles of Western classical records and CDs. Sepia prints of battle from the time of the British Raj. The ornate mahogany table decorated with a silver peacock and booklets from his trips to England. Those are different. His desk to the left neatly organized. His love of all things British irritates me. I decide to interrupt his reading.

"*So*, how are you doing?"

"I'm well." He finally looks up, his eyes smoldering, and switches off his iPad. "So, you've talked about all kinds of things in Bangalore, have you?"

"Yes, I have," I'm surprised, and also not. "Word travels fast here."

"It does." His voice is cold. "Why did you?"

"I needed to say my side of things. People need to know, especially if they call themselves family."

"I've heard a little about it from Leena. She said a few words. Actually, she could hardly get the words out. She mostly told me with long silences. Your parents don't know I know." He pauses. His eyes narrow as he looks at me closely. "How do you know it happened?"

My stomach jolts. *He doesn't believe me!* "What do you mean, how do I know it happened? It happened."

"How can a nine-year-old boy know to do such things?"

"You'll have to ask him that."

"But how could he know anything about that?"

"About sex?" Weird how no one wants to say the word. "I've asked him."

His eyes bulge in surprise. "You *have*?"

"Yes, we talked about it. I called him when I was in school. He said other kids brought magazines to school so he wanted to try it out."

"On his *sister*!" He stiffens with surprise and pauses. "Was it fondling?"

"No, it was intercourse. For four years. It stopped when he went to boarding school."

His thick eyebrows shoot up. "So it wasn't a one-time thing?"

"No. It wasn't."

"Why didn't you tell your parents?"

"I didn't even know what sex was. I was six when it started. He was a bully…"

He nods like he knows what I'm talking about.

"…and I thought it was another way he bullied me."

His eyes bore into mine.

"I didn't even know the word for sex, just that he did things to me. I tried to tell my parents in my childish way, but they didn't understand. I don't know what you know about incest, but it's rampant."

"Is it?" His eyebrows shoot up again.

"Yes. More than 30 percent of women are victims of incest, regardless of culture, education, or social class."

He listens intently now. No one else in my family has even wanted to listen.

"And 75 percent of people in therapy have been sexually abused."

He shakes his head. He's clearly disturbed. "You've had a bad start in life, Meetross. You may know more about the psyche but my advice is to erase your memories. Just make a decision and erase them."

"That's the most ridiculous thing I've ever heard. You're right, you *don't* know anything about the psyche."

"You need to make a choice and get over the angst. Life is about joy. Have you thought about forgiveness?"

"Of course I have, but it's not a switch you can turn on."

"You should definitely try.

I decide to let it alone. Leela Aunty walks in looking beautiful in a lavender starched sari. "Hi, Meetross!" she says, her voice warm and loving.

I stand up. We hug and smile at each other. "Hi, Leela Aunty, it's good to see you. You look beautiful."

"Getting older, you know, getting older."

"How are Aditi and Kalpana?"

"Very well. You know Kalpana's in Paris now and has two daughters. And Aditi's married again and very happy."

"Oh, I'm so happy to hear that. I want to hear all about them."

"Yes, of course, after you finish talking here I'll show you pictures." She sits down.

I have to finish my conversation with Roshan Uncle. "I also wanted people to know about my imprisonment, and that I wasn't on drugs or in a cult."

Roshan Uncle says, "I talked with Daadi when you were brought back. I told her your mother needed to take you back to the U.S., not leave you here."

"You did?" I'm touched. "I didn't know."

He nods. "I did. And I was horrified that your mother wanted you to marry a Tamilian Brahmin. Can you imagine? A Tamilian Brahmin!" he says in a shocked voice, his eyes huge.

So he too thought it was nuts. I wish he'd said something then.

Leela Aunty says, "I didn't at all agree with your staying here.

How much I talked to your mother but she wouldn't hear a word of it. You know how she is. That's why I tried to connect with you."

I nod. "Thank you so much for that. That was so kind of you."

They didn't agree with my mother. But couldn't get through. I assumed that, like my parents and grandparents, they thought I was bad and shameful.

I've judged them all these years. I thought they were preoccupied with their lives and didn't care. I thought that they preferred to stay out of the fray and not stand up to Amma or Daadi. But they *did* care.

They loved me, then, as they do now. And they tried.

It's my turn to face how I judged my family.

A cement step has replaced the pile of loose bricks that wobbled up to Daadi's bedroom. I step on it and pull the screen door open. It squeals as it always did. Twelve years since I've been here and it still hasn't been oiled. The air in the house sucks me into the past like a mausoleum. I've moved on, yet time's stopped here.

I step into her bedroom and halt. My breath stills to a hush. This house was my prison. Every inch of it shrieks of my confinement. I am back in time, at twenty-two.

Thatha's and Daadi's twin beds are still here by the windows overlooking Roshan Uncle's front lawn with yellow and pink crotons. Her divan with a low wooden back, emerald-green bedspread, green and red and gold silk cushions that face her lawn and Roshan Uncle's rock garden beyond. She would sit on it late mornings after the maid had left, reading the *Deccan Chronicle* or *The Hindu*, mending a blouse or petticoat, or gazing out the window nodding to herself as she agreed with her own thoughts. The oval black and white picture of her father still hangs on the wall beside their beds. White wall-to-wall cupboards with her steel *almirahs* inside. Her dressing table used to be in the alcove leading to the bathroom, at which she sat to comb her thin gray hair, weave in her long darker hairpiece, wind a bun at the nape of her neck, and push in hairpins to keep in place. Pat it then turn around to look at it this way and that with a hand mirror. Dab a circle of Vaseline on her forehead, press red *kumkum* powder and shape it into a quarter-size circle. Sometimes she'd stand by the window and pluck out her chin hairs and I thought how ancient she was. Her ironing table against the wall with small piles of clothes and English Philips iron with its ratty cord. She wouldn't buy a new one because it still worked, and I was always afraid I might be electrocuted when I used it.

She is here. Her presence is unmistakable. Daadi fills the house, even now as she did when she was alive. Even though she passed away seven years ago. Even though Roshan Uncle and Leela Aunty have transformed it into a guest cottage for when their friends and daughters, my cousins, visit. Even though Roshan Uncle uses Thatha's office for his own. Does she stay to watch over her granddaughters and their families? Does she stay as protectress for her son and daughter-in-law?

I am struck by her powerful, unmistakable presence. Thatha's long gone, and feels like a wisp of memory, but she's definitely here. I tune into her energy. The family also wants her here, and she wants to stay for them. Occupying, blessing, watching over them. Ruling or blessing, I wonder wryly, with a stab of anger. Blessing, I hope, for their sake.

I feel her eyes on me, watching.

Since I arrived she's been telling me to walk through the house alone. There's something here for me. For us. *Find a way to be here alone for fifteen or twenty minutes,* she said.

I am, and am not, surprised to hear her. "I'm here," I say out loud. "I'm ready." Whatever happens, I promise myself, I won't abandon who I am.

As I say the words, a light in the shape of an upright palm, a Buddha hand *mudra* of blessing, flares in my heart like a star just born. It blesses me first. All my inner work has led to this, whatever's pulling me to walk through this house of my tormented past. A mirror image, a twin flame flares outward, in front of my heart, to bless the house.

Both must happen.

I need to bless myself, and my past in this house, for me to fully let go.

I walk into the living room. It's dim, as always, but there's no need for light. I'd know my next step on every marble tile of this room even without her standing lamp, with its square teak post and its round wheat linen lampshade crooked with dust.

Daadi's here, sitting in one of the two leather chairs from *Laughing Waters,* reading. She's standing by her writing table with its glass top, on which she had her black dial telephone, tattered yellow telephone directory, pen stand, and black leather address book, its cover curled with use. An old, crooked picture of a vase of roses on the wall above. My childhood bookcase now painted white and filled with books about cricket, Oxford, and cooking.

The light in my heart flares brighter as I walk into the center of the room. The ground yawns open. Suddenly, like water breaks for a woman about to birth, the river of loss and pain and rage and hate pent up in me for almost three decades gushes down my thighs, down into the marble floor, and flows into the earth. *Bless this house and all who pass through it and live here.* The words spring forth from deep within me, despite myself. I stand for a few minutes, astonished at my release.

I've needed to clear my karma with this place.

It is done.

Go into the bedroom, she tells me. The bedroom, my prison for three years. My body clenches tight and hard, expecting pain and grief, but as I enter, the room is only a ghostly husk of my past. The air is light and loose here now, cleared of stashed furniture that used to be here, the twin beds refreshed with lime green–colored paisley bed covers and pink wall lampshades. My spirit isn't locked here anymore. Really? I check again to be sure. No, I've left. Completely. I exhale. In my mind, I've returned to this room hundreds of times to rescue and resuscitate my twenty-two-year-old self. I step into the bathroom with its marble tiles and faint Phenyl smell. Switch on the dim 30-watt bulb. Look at the bathing area where I once contemplated suicide.

Nothing here either. It is done.

I walk back into the living room. Is it over? I ask. *Not yet*, she says. *Go to the kitchen*. It's the last quadrant of the house. I walk inside. Turn on the ceiling light that spills gold into the room. The small gray granite floor tiles have been replaced with large ones the color of cornfields. She's here, too, sitting on a smart Parisian-style cafe chair at its round table where her three white wicker stools used to be. What does she want me to see? I look around.

She tugs at me. *Go into the puja room*. Why? I wonder. What could be there? But she's drawing me into the small four-by-six-foot room that served as her pantry and altar space. Her meat-safe greets me, a tired dark teak cupboard with grimy blackened mesh doors, its legs on round concrete bowls like moats that used to be filled with water to keep insects out. Instead of sugar, biscuits, *murukkus*, and snacks, Roshan Uncle keeps his old books in it now.

One wall from floor to ceiling has white concrete wall shelves on which she stored rows of aluminum bins with dals, rice, and provisions. Now, they hold her large tarnished brass cookware, the kind they used in villages decades ago to feed lavish wedding and *puja* crowds, the kind that would sell as antiques for hundreds of dollars in the U.S.

What does she want me to see? I look around. My eyes land on top of the meat-safe. Her pink and lime-green checkered tablecloth wraps around a bulky figure. Instantly, I know what it is. It's her beloved Krishna. The one she had in her bedroom. She bought the three-foot-high clay statue as a young mother for a handful of rupees from a street vendor who hollered at her gate one day. It was painted custard, then. Every time she moved, she carefully wrapped it in a thick bedspread to travel with her. She had it painted white when she moved into this house since the custard paint had chipped and faded over decades. I reach around the veiled statue to tug the pink and green tablecloth out from under its base.

It falls away.

Her bare-chested Krishna stands playing his flute, one leg crossed over the other, his lower body draped with soft folds of a cotton *dhoti*. A peacock feather sprouts from the turban wrapped around his head. A long necklace dangles from his neck, and bangles and anklets encircle his wrists and ankles. His bow-like lips curve upwards in a smile. Behind him, a cow grazes, listening to his music. His eyes, pools of infinite peace and play, look into mine.

My arms encircle the white Krishna. I feel a rush of descending light, and a waterfall of energy waves like I'm standing in a *sangam*, the confluence of two rivers. *This* is what she wants me to see! *This* is why she's led me here!

She loved him. He was her god, her confidant, her guide. Every day she tucked her garden's best bloom behind his ear—a jasmine, a frangipani, or a hibiscus. A leaf when her garden was flowerless. Every morning he greeted her when she woke. Every night he was the last one to whom she said good night before her eyelids softened and lowered to close. Some afternoons, I'd seen her rounded form in a blue, yellow, or pink cotton block-printed sari, lying on her bed, wordlessly looking to him. Those were times she was sad or weary. The rare times she was stuck, devastated, and brought to her knees. When she didn't know her way, or didn't have answers for life. Proud and self-reliant, she wouldn't ask anyone for help. But him. With him she could bare her heart. Fall to her knees. Pray. With him, in silent communion, she could be vulnerable as she never could with another. He was her rock. He nourished her soul. Her father's picture beside Thatha's bed reminded her who she was as a woman—of her family's high birth, her place in society, and who she had to be to uphold her family dignity and integrity.

But Krishna was the lighthouse for her soul.

My tears flow. I look up at his angelic face, his enchanting smile, his playful loving eyes, the blue ribbon dangling from his flute, the seductive crossing of his thighs. And in an instant, the movie of her life flashes through me. Her family was the lifeblood throbbing through her veins. They were her fiercest love, for whom she went to battle. Rooted as a tree trunk, she believed in herself and found her truth within. She didn't bow before anyone even if the world clamored at their feet, even Swami Chinmayananda, to whom I and so many had prostrated to as a guru. Like a tigress she faced her unknowns, wrestled with her struggles, dropped to the earth with her losses only to rise and blaze again. The human ways she loved, both successful and failed.

Her love for me was mixed. She loved me as her granddaughter. Her blood. But she also hated and was angry with me for hurting her daughter, my mother; for bringing shame and disappointment instead of dignity to our family.

For being a bad girl.

But now, from beyond the veil, in the clearer, lighter realm of her soul, she's led me here to this four-by-six room, to her Krishna, to her softly beating heart. She couldn't unveil it to me then. *My imperfect human love cost you*, she says. *Yet however mixed and true, cruel and protective, inadequate and complete I was, I always loved you. I still do. I struggled to understand you, protect you, give you what I thought you needed. But I failed to give you what you truly needed, and loved. We've had to love across the chasm of generations and opposite cultures, you and I.* I see her as an innocent Indian girl playing in pigtails and a frock, at sixteen in a half-sari on the banks of the River Krishna, then as a new, young, blushing wife. How could she, coming from there and in that time, possibly understand me, and how the West tugged me towards freedom and romantic love? Only days before I turned sixteen, I had flown from the arms of our family to the distant shores of the Atlantic Ocean.

Despite our oceans of difference, I want you to know I love you. And I want you to be happy.

I shake with sobs to hear her. I sink to the floor, Krishna on my lap, clutching him like he's her, my head upon his peacock crown. I remember the ivory Krishna locket she asked Amma to give me before she died. She'd been dead a few years when Amma gave it to me. I shoved it in its blue velvet box to the back of a drawer, still angry with her and my family then. And I remember when I was here, locked up, when my future seemed bleak and unclear as fog, I lay on her divan looking out past Krishna to her lawn as she lay in her bed. She had said to me about him, "You're the only one who knows the value of this. The others don't." What had she seen in me? Did she feel connected to me in spirit even then, but I couldn't feel it? Or didn't want to?

Now, here, at the *sangam*, confluence of two rivers—her love for Krishna and my love for the Divine—we meet and unite. Who we are as blood and who we are beyond blood. My heart surges with love. The painful padlock of our past snaps open to release our three years together. It was all love. Everything she did for me was her love.

We just looked at it differently.

Words arise in me like blossoms. *Be at peace. Blessings. Rest in peace. Fly where you need to go to next. Godspeed.*

My heart blooms open and wide, a yellow and white frangipani of forgiveness.

Blessings to you. And to this house and all who pass through it.

Often, I go for long walks in the San Francisco Bay Area where I live. I hike on undulating hill slopes and Mt. Tamalpais. I walk barefoot on the dancing line where the Pacific's blue-green waves swell and surge against the shore, leaving white foam in their wake.

Today, I'm meandering through a lush grove of towering California redwoods listening to their *ooooo-eeeeemmm* songs, as a gentle breeze rustles their leaves. A hummingbird hovers close, its turquoise wings an iridescent blur. A squirrel leaps from one branch of a redwood to another, its bushy tail flicking rows of green needles in its wake. Deep in the cool, dark forest an owl hoots *tu-whooo tu-whooo*. And the late afternoon fog whispers misty secrets from the ocean to the breasts of hills in the distance.

I fill with wonder and awe as I often do on my walks. How did I get here from there? How do I get to work from my heart and soul? How do I get to be with a wonderful man I love and who loves me so? How ever did I find all this beauty and magic? *How?*

Brant and I have been together for six years and counting. We have a beautiful, soulful love. Our relationship has been extraordinary and healing. Romantic love is an essential freedom of the heart that no one, even family or culture, has a right to take away. It's truly incredible for me, after being imprisoned for love, to have found it in such a profound way.

And my music flows now, not from other composers, but from my soul. It descends from realms above, like a waterfall of light and love, that my heart cups to receive and my hands effortlessly play. It shimmers like patchwork colors of a stained glass window I couldn't compose if I tried. My guides tell me it is part of my Divine Purpose.

I watch the whirring hummingbird, tears of gratitude filling my eyes. "I have such incredible guides. And so many wonderful people helped me."

For I am grateful to be free. I am grateful to live from joy instead of fear. I am grateful to have music in my life again, and to create. And I am deeply, deeply grateful after my lifelong quest, to live freely and fully from love.

I step off the trail and walk towards a redwood. Caress its craggy ebony bark. Put my arms around it and embrace it. Press my body and cheek against its broad ridged chest. And listen.

We love you, it says. *And we love your music. Play. Play for us.*

I look up at it and its circle, its fairy ring, who soar like great cathedrals to the sky. Nestled among their branches, a Swainson's thrush sings her heart out to the sun.

THE END

also by
Mytrae Meliana

How I Healed From Lyme Disease: My Story, Lessons, and Steps to a Miracle

available on Amazon

Serenity: Piano Healings and Meditations

available on Apple

available on Amazon

Chakra Sonata: Piano Healings in 432Hz

available on Apple

available on Amazon

Please Leave a Review

If you enjoyed *Brown Skin Girl*, I'd appreciate an honest review at the retailer where you purchased it. Your support in spreading the word and message makes a huge difference in helping new readers find the book, and really does matter.

Thank you!

Need Support?

If you'd like support on your journey to heal, free yourself, and create your true, bold, inspired life, join my reader list and you'll get the free eBook, ***7 Steps To Speak Your Truth Even Though You Feel Afraid, Guilty, or Ashamed***. You'll also receive my blog posts and be the first to know about upcoming programs and workshops. Sign up at:

www.mytraemeliana.com/SpeakYourTruthEbook

Invite Mytrae

Would you like Mytrae to speak at your event or teach a workshop/ program/ retreat?

Drop her a line at:
www.mytraemeliana.com

Acknowledgments

I am grateful to so many people and beings who have helped bring this book into the world. Books, like all creations, are midwifed and birthed. For *Brown Skin Girl* to be born, I needed to heal and be re-birthed. My deepest love and gratitude to you all.

First, to Great Goddess and God. Without You, I wouldn't exist. Because of You I have wings with which to fly and songs to sing.

To Mother Earth, for your beauty and bounty. I am grateful to walk, be nourished by, and dance upon your exquisite body.

To the deer who asked me to write. And to all the animals, trees, and waterfalls who nurtured and communicated with me. Your energy and messages pulse in my heart as I do my part for a better world.

To Mother Mary, dearest Divine Mother, for your healing and mentorship. I do not know why you have come to me—I receive your Presence in my life as a holy Mystery.

To Kali, thank you for showing up when everything needed to break, for cradling me, and for teaching me fierce love.

To my extraordinary Spirit guides for your ever-present guidance, magical healing, and ushering me to miracles. I would not be who I am without you.

To Music, beautiful One, who hums and pulses through everyone and everything. May I always listen for and sing the Song I am here to sing.

To my grandparents, Ammamma ("Daadi") and Thatha, for your love, nurturing, and ancestral guidance both in this world and from beyond the veil. You taught me kindness, integrity, and service, and I hope to pass on some of what you have shown me.

To my mother, Amma, for bearing and giving me life, care, delicious food, the best education, and encouraging my love of words and music. Thank you for your love.

To my father, Naina, for giving me life and providing, for teaching me humility, patience, and that renewal is a certainty in the garden of life. Thank you for your love.

To the rest of my family for your kindness, generosity, and love.

To Louis, no words can ever convey my gratitude to you for opening the portal to great, great Beauty and Music. Your sensitive teaching and musicianship allowed me to dream new dreams, because of which nothing could ever be the same again. You are a paramount teacher.

To "Evan," this book would not have been possible without you. Thank you for taking me to the stars. Your love, tenderness, and wisdom at a young twenty-four were incredible. I still shake my head that you loved me as much as you did. You always have a place in my heart.

To Brant, thank you for your love, wisdom, and emotional maturity on our soulmate journey. Thank you for showing me what a conscious relationship can be and for loving me, warts and all. Your love healed and transformed me, and made me (almost) whole.

I couldn't have done this without my family of friends, old and new. It would be impossible to list everyone here, but know that your sisterhood, support, and love mean the world to me. I adore and treasure you. Thank you for lifting me up, believing in me, and giving me the gifts of you again and again. Special thanks to: Kerry Cadambi, Charlene Nevill, Pam Alexander, Debra Wagner, Catherine Tucker, Kay McNamara, Mithoo Wadia, Jeannette Sorrell, Brandee Prugh, "Nupur," "Nina," and "Caroline."

I am who I am today because of my therapists and healers. Lauri Neidell, Staci Haines, Leah Lazar, and Laurel Parnell, I am beyond grateful for your empathy, heart, professional skill, and sacred spaces in which to fall apart and come undone so I could piece myself together. Thank you for seeing me and letting me voice the unspoken.

This book was revised over years in a writing group. Thank you, David Fredrickson, Gabriella West, and Gina Genovese for holding a newborn lamb with so much compassion and grace, and for believing in my story. David, thank you for your dear friendship, welcoming home, delicious food, and the unforgettable gift of Rufus. Thank you, Karen Pierce Gonzalez, for your wise, enthusiastic writing friendship.

To my wonderful editors Jen Pooley, Pat Verducci, Chandika Devi, Kelly Notaras, and Adair Lara for helping sculpt, shine, and believe in *Brown Skin Girl*.

Finally, thank you, Kat Lynch and Domini Dragoone, for your beautiful cover and interior designs. Many thanks to Gabriella West for your careful proofreading. Thank you, Carole Hénaff, for permission to use your lovely art, and to Rosemary Aubert for your poem.

Thank you all from the bottom of my heart.

About the Author

Mytrae Meliana (pronounced "my-thray-yee") is an award-winning writer, spiritual teacher, speaker, and holistic psychotherapist. She leads workshops for women who desire to heal from trauma, liberate themselves from patriarchy, connect with the Divine Feminine, and create true, bold, inspired lives.

Her own life experience and 15-year career as a holisitc psychotherapist shaped Mytrae's professional approach. She increasingly sought ways her clients with trauma could heal quickly so they could live their dreams. When she had a miracle healing from Lyme disease, she was ushered into a paradigm of Spirit and vibration where change can happen at the speed of light.

Mytrae is Founder of Temple of Sound Healing and teaches individuals and organizations the practice of sound, story, and Spirit medicine for trauma. She channels healing music transmissions on the piano and has recorded two CDs. She is also a channel for Mother Mary. When she isn't working, you might find Mytrae hiking by the ocean and on hillside trails, traveling, or discovering restaurants with friends in the San Francisco Bay Area.

Connect with Mytrae:

www.mytraemeliana.com

www.Facebook.com/mytraemeliana

www.twitter.com/mytraemeliana

www.Instagram.com/mytraemeliana

www.templeofsoundhealing.com

www.Facebook.com/templeofsoundhealing

www.Instagram.com/templeofsoundhealing

Made in the USA
San Bernardino, CA
16 February 2020